On the Learning of Chinese

On the Learning of Chinese

Edited By

Ference Marton
University of Gothenburg, Sweden

Shek Kam Tse
Wai Ming Cheung

The University of Hong Kong, China

SENSE PUBLISHERS
ROTTERDAM/BOSTON/TAIPEI

A C.I.P. record for this book is available from the Library of Congress.

ISBN: 978-94-6091-267-2 (paperback)
ISBN: 978-94-6091-268-9 (hardback)
ISBN: 978-94-6091-269-6 (e-book)

Published by: Sense Publishers,
P.O. Box 21858,
3001 AW Rotterdam,
The Netherlands
http://www.sensepublishers.com

Printed on acid-free paper

Cover description: The small boy is playing a game of word acquisition. The cards on the table are Chinese words but they are also components that can combine to form many more Chinese characters.

TABLE OF CONTENTS

LIST OF FIGURES

SHEK KAM TSE

PREFACE

Increased interest in China from those outside has led to a corresponding interest in the study of Chinese. Spoken by one-fifth of the world's population, Chinese is one of the official languages of the United Nations and the most widely used language in the world.

Notwithstanding its popularity, Chinese is often considered as one of the most difficult languages to learn by many language learners. Two major difficulties often perplex learners: (1) the basic writing units of Chinese are semantic-phonetic compounds called characters, and each of them has its own meaning and pronunciation; and (2) word meanings of homophones in Chinese are distinguished specifically by lexical tones. Due to the very large number of Chinese characters and words, it seems impossible for learners, regardless of their native languages, to master the language by rote memorization. The acquisition and processing of the Chinese language, thus, have provided interesting fields of study in psycholinguistic research.

Although originally developed by Swedish scholar Ference Marton, the Theory of Variation has been shown to be particularly useful in understanding and promoting learning and teaching in Chinese by a large body of research. Essentially, the theory describes learning and teaching from the perspectives of learners: to learn about something implies that learners must discern that something from its background. If there is no variation, then there is no discernment. The goal of teaching and learning of Chinese, therefore, is to help learners identify and contrast patterns of variation and invariance of different aspects of the Chinese language, from components of individual characters, to daily communication and even comprehension of literature.

Using the Theory of Variation as the primary framework-or at least relating to it- the authors of this book have conducted a number of rigorously-designed studies to investigate the relationship between learning and teaching of Chinese, starting from understanding the phonological and orthographical acquisition of characters, to developing a comprehensive curriculum. Each of the study presented in this book represents long-term sedulous efforts of all the contributors.

Our thanks go to all authors for their excellent contributions, and for their willingness and efforts to revise, adapt, and improve their chapters to make this book a comprehensive, consistent, and significant work. We would like to extend our gratitude to Ference Marton especially, for his development of the Theory of Variation, its application in the Chinese context, and his ardent participation in promoting Chinese language education in Hong Kong. Indeed, many of the authors in this book were his former Ph.D. students. We are also indebted to the schools, teachers, and students who have participated in the studies, and our colleagues for their encouragement and support of the project. In addition, the Hong Kong SAR Government and the University of Hong Kong provided generous support for some of these projects, for which we are grateful.

We sincerely hope that this book will provide empirical reference for educators, parents, policymakers, and readers who are interested in Chinese language education, as well as illuminate the path for Chinese language pedagogy and curriculum development.

Shek Kam Tse
Director
Center of Advancement of Chinese Language Education and Research (CACLER)
Associate Dean & Professor, Faculty of Education
The University of Hong Kong

SHEK KAM TSE AND WAI MING CHEUNG

1. CHINESE AND THE LEARNING OF CHINESE

INTRODUCTION

Chinese is spoken by one-fifth of the world's population (Li, Tan, Bates, & Tzeng, 2006) and is one of the official languages of the United Nations. Today, Chinese is the most widely used language in the world and has become an increasingly popular second language amongst the people in the Western world (Weber, 1997). From 2000 to 2004, the number of students in England, Wales and Northern Ireland taking Advanced Level exams in Chinese increased by 57% (Ramzy, 2006). About 117,660 non-native speakers took the Chinese Proficiency Test in 2005 alone, an increase of 26.52% from 2004 (Xinhua News Agency, 2006). Currently, over 3,000,000 people are studying the Chinese language, and Chinese language courses can be found in more than 2000 universities around the globe.

Despite its popularity, many language learners, particularly those whose native language is an Indo-European language, often consider Chinese as a very difficult language to learn as it differs significantly from most Indo-European languages and offers unusual features in its orthographic, phonological, lexical, and syntactic structures. The traditional approach to teaching and learning Chinese of repeatedly copying words and dictation seems to be less than helpful in addressing these differences. Nevertheless, by understanding the specific properties of the Chinese language, as will be demonstrated in this chapter, innovative pedagogy can be developed and effective teaching and learning can be made possible.

OVERVIEW OF THE PROPERTIES OF THE CHINESE LANGUAGE

Unlike English and many Indo-European languages, Chinese is a tonal and logographic language. Instead of using alphabetic letters as the basic writing unit, Chinese uses logograms, more conventionally referred to as characters, which are written within imaginary rectangular blocks. These characters are morphemes independent of phonetic change. For example, both *yi1* in Mandarin and *jat1* in Cantonese[1] share an identical character "一" and mean the number "one". Therefore, compared with a written word in English, a Chinese character has a stronger association with its meaning. Phonologically, tones are used to distinguish meanings of characters. Orthographically, characters are often composed of both phonetic and semantic components. Morphologically, words are formed by agglutination of these characters and have only one grammatical form. It is indecipherable about the total number of

F. Marton, S.K. Tse and W.M. Cheung (eds.), On the Learning of Chinese, 1–7.

Chinese characters from past to present, as new ones continue to be developed. The latest *Zhonghua Zihai* (Dictionary of Chinese Characters), published in 1994, records a staggering 85,568 single characters (Leng & Wei, 1994). However, generally, knowledge of about 2,500 characters is needed for basic literacy in Chinese (National Education Commission & National Language Construction Committee, 1993; Ministry of Education, PRC, 2001).

Phonology

A distinctive characteristic of Chinese characters is that each of them corresponds to one syllable that carries a particular tone. All varieties of spoken Chinese use tones, but the number may vary from dialect to dialect. For example, Mandarin has four main tones, with the first tone having flat or high level pitch; the second tone having rising or high-rising pitch; the third tone having low-dipping pitch; and the fourth tone having high-falling pitch (Chao, 1948). In contrast, Cantonese has six contour tones: (1) high level; (2) high rising; (3) mid level (4) low level; (5) low rising; and (6) low falling, although it is often said to have nine as people usually treat the three tones used for characters that end in a stop consonant — upper entering one (which is similar to upper level tone); upper entering two (which is similar to upper departing tone); and lower entering (which is similar to lower departing tone) — as separate tones.

Unlike most Western languages, in which tones are only used to express emphasis or emotion, lexical tones in Chinese serve to provide contrast in word meanings. In fact, Chinese has a large number of homophones, which are only distinguishable by tones (Institute of Linguistics, The Academy of Social Sciences, 1985). For instance, even though all of them correspond to the syllable "*wan*", the meanings of the characters "溫" (sound: *wan1*, upper level tone); "穩" (sound: *wan2*, upper rising tone); "搵" (sound: *wan3*, upper departing tone); "雲" (sound: *wan4*, lower level tone); "允" (sound: *wan5*, lower rising tone); and "暈" (sound: *wan6*, lower departing tone) in Cantonese are "warm", "stable", "find", "cloud", "allow", and "dizzy", respectively. Therefore, for speakers of non-tonal or intonation languages, in which the meanings of words do not change with tone, tone has presented great difficulty as well as ambiguity in learning the language. Processing of Chinese characters, therefore, may require a cognitive system that differs in essential ways from that of English and other intonation languages.

Indeed, as pointed out by Ki, Marton, and Pang in Chapter 3 of this book, speakers of intonation languages, although equally well-equipped to sense tone patterns in speech sounds, often view these patterns as if they belong to the sentence rather than to the syllables. They also tend to see the tone and semantic features of characters as two separate units instead of one integral part. Drawing on Phenomenography and the Theory of Variation, the authors discuss some possible strategies to help speakers of intonation languages restructure the way they attend to meanings in speech sounds and achieve more effective learning experiences of Cantonese.

Orthography

The majority of Chinese characters are composite characters assembled from more than one multi-stroke component fit into the square space. Xu Shen identified 540 components in his *Shuo Wen Jie Zi* (Explaining simple and analyzing compound Chinese characters, as cited in Honorof & Feldman, 2006), a classic work on Chinese characters. Sometimes characters can differ by as few as one stroke, and non-Chinese readers may find two characters with roughly the same number of strokes. Even so, the arrangement of internal components within a character can be rather obvious to fluent readers of Chinese, as individual components are written in a highly constrained order. Generally speaking, four rules guide the writing of Chinese characters: (1) components are written top-left to bottom-right, (2) horizontal strokes are written before vertical strokes, (3) center components are written before their embellishments, and (4) small strokes are often written last (Honorof & Feldman, 2006).

Some components of more complex characters can indeed stand on their own as characters and function to provide information about the meanings and pronunciations of the larger characters in which they appear (Honorof & Feldman, 2006; Ki et al., 2003). According to Lee (1989), approximately 90% of modern Chinese characters are made up of a combination of at least two components: semantic radicals, which carry important clues about the meaning indicated by the full character; and phonetic radicals, which contribute to the general sound of the larger character as a whole. For instance, the characters "嬡" (daughter); "娘" (mother); "姑" (sister of father); and "姥" (maternal grandmother); all share the same invariant semantic radical "女" (female) and represent different kinds of females. Meanwhile, the variants "愛" (sound: *oi3*); "良" (sound: *loeng4*); "古" (sound: *gu2*); and "老" (sound: *lou5*) on the right are phonetic radicals that contribute to the sounds of "嬡" (sound: *oi3*); "娘" (sound: *noeng4*); "姑" (sound: *gu1*); and "姥" (sound: *lou5*), respectively. "女", "愛", "良", "古" each can stand of their own but taking different function in indicating the meaning and sound of a character. Because of these part-whole properties of many Chinese characters, learners with substantial knowledge of Chinese characters are sometimes able to guess the meaning and pronunciation of an unfamiliar character from its components (Zhang, 1987). However, many of these radicals are themselves compound characters, which consist of two or even more components (a part-part relation). Moreover, these individual components of radicals often have nothing to do with the whole character and may be confusing for beginning learners trying to understand Chinese characters.

To facilitate the learning of Chinese, it is essential to develop a pedagogy and curriculum which are based on the needs of learners and subsequently increase their orthographic awareness to distinguish the similarities and differences among different characters. In Chapter 4, Lam investigates the progressive development of children's orthographic knowledge of the part-whole and part-part relations of Chinese characters, as well as suggesting some effective ways to enhance their orthographic awareness. Armed with this knowledge, in Chapter 5, Tse, Marton, Ki, and Loh introduce a perceptual approach to the learning and teaching of

Chinese characters by utilizing a learner's own language. In this approach, characters are taught in contexts which are meaningful to learners and in relational clusters. Special attention is paid to their structural features, written forms and pronunciations. Similarities and variations among related characters in these clusters are highlighted, and crucial aspects of Chinese characters and words are emphasized. The approach was shown to be effective in an investigation in three primary schools in Hong Kong.

Morphology and Vocabulary

While many Chinese characters are single-syllable morphemes and can stand alone as individual words, in modern Chinese, they more often agglutinate with one another to form multi-syllabic words. Chinese words can thus consist of more than one character-morpheme, usually two, but words with three or more characters are also not rare. Words such as "筆" (pen, sound: *bat1*), "蛋糕" (cake, sound: *daan6 gou1*), and "東張西望" (look around, sound: *dung1 zoeng1 sai1 mong6*) are examples of words formed by one, two, and multiple characters, respectively. Studies on the teaching and learning of Chinese words often focus on foreign language learners and word identification, due to the fact that in written Chinese text words are not separated by spaces as in English and in many other languages (e.g. Chen & Liu, 1992; Ge, Pratt, & Smyth, 1999, Lin, 2000).

In order to explore the relationship between the teaching and learning of words in native speakers of Chinese, in Chapter 6, Chik, Leung, and Marton report the results of the different word teaching strategies used by two different Primary Two Chinese language teachers in Hong Kong in teaching their classes. The findings reveal that the students' perception of what they had learnt was closely related to what was made possible for them to discern by the pattern of variation and invariance of words and their context of usage enacted in lessons. Students who were able to discern different aspects of words were also found to have outperformed their counterparts in the written task. These findings indeed have very important implications for developing reading and writing skills in Chinese learners and improving existing language pedagogy.

TEACHING AND LEARNING CHINESE IN CLASSROOMS

Reading and writing, unlike spoken language, almost never develop without formal teaching (Adams, 1990; Stanovich, 2000). This is especially true in the case of Chinese (Li & Rao, 2000). Enhancing students' ability to read and write Chinese has thus been one of the key objectives in the Curriculum Reform in Hong Kong (Curriculum Development Council, 2001). Traditionally, practices in the classroom are heavily dictated by commercially produced textbooks and teaching guides which contain a great number of independent short passages or simplified Chinese literature. The lack of cohesion in the themes and writing styles of these passages have imposed obstacles for both teachers and students as it often leads to difficulty in perceiving the focus of lessons.

Aware of the deficiencies of existing practices in schools in Hong Kong, in Chapter 7, Tse, Marton, Loh, and Chik developed an innovative one-year curriculum which focused on novels, both fiction and non-fiction, for Secondary One students in three schools. The use of novels instead of a number of independent short passages allowed students to engage in studying the materials over a longer period of time and to receive a degree of continuity over lesson content. Fiction and non-fiction novels were contrasted to illustrate various language applications and the uses of different reading and learning strategies. Sharing of opinions and interpretations of particular episodes in the novels were encouraged among students through an on-line discussion forum. Compared with their peers who were taught in similar fashion, but received the conventional input of Chinese passages to study, students who experienced the new curriculum scored significantly higher on tests of reading comprehension and expressive writing. These findings support the conclusion that Chinese literacy can be fostered by a more coherent curriculum and guided discernment of the variation among different texts and interpretations.

However, merely enhancing the literacy of Chinese language learners is not enough. It is also essential to enhance the creativity of students and teachers. All scholars of creativity seem to agree that creativity has to do with opening up, providing space for the individual to move around freely. We look at creativity as a certain way of handling Chinese writing and teaching. Chapter 8 and Chapter 9 illustrate how creativity can possibly be enhanced in the classroom through the systematic use of variations and invariance in the teaching of Chinese writing.

In Chapter 8, Cheung, Marton, and Tse look at creativity from a pedagogical point of view and try to enhance creativity in Chinese writing by applying the Theory of Variation. They carried out a quasi experimental trial within the framework of Learning Study in Primary Three classes for one year. Teacher participants discerned the capability of writing creatively in lesson planning and then used the creative writing strategies developed to teach writing skills to the student participants. It was found that students in the target group significantly outperformed those in the comparison group in the creativity score. The enhancement of creativity in Chinese writing was to a significant extent associated with the teachers' awareness of the role of variation and invariance for learning as demonstrated in their method of conducting the lessons.

Teachers also play an important role in boosting creativity in Chinese teaching. In Chapter 9, Lee, Marton, and Tse show how creative teaching was implemented in a Chinese Language lesson of a pre-service teacher after having attended Creative Teaching Training. The theoretical framework of the Theory of Variation was employed to analyse one of her lessons, discerning key characteristics of her teaching in order to demonstrate possible qualitative differences in teaching of potential relevance for the fostering of creativity in students.

CONCLUSIONS

While it is impossible to represent all the exciting research in the field of Chinese language education in one book, this book provides a serviceable view of the application of the Theory of Variation in the teaching and learning of the Chinese language. From the learning of tones, shapes, and semantics of Chinese characters, to fostering creativity in both Chinese learners and teachers, the topics of the chapters are diverse as well as comprehensive. It is our genuine hope that this book provides a valuable reference for educators and policymakers, as well as serving as a catalyst for further research in the field.

NOTES

[1] Mandarin examples are given in the Romanization scheme, known as Hanyu Pinyin, introduced in 1956 by the People's Republic of China, in which tones are numbered from 0 to 4. Cantonese examples are given in the Romanization scheme developed by Wong Shik Ling (also known as S. L. Wong), in which tones are numbered from 1 (high level) to 6 (low level). The online edition of S. L. Wong's Chinese Syllabary is available at http://humanum.arts.cuhk.edu.hk/Lexis/Canton/.

REFERENCES

Adams, M. J. (1990). *Beginning to read: Thinking and learning about print*. Cambridge, MA: MIT Press.

Chao, Y. R. (1948). *Mandarin primer*. Cambridge, MA: Harvard University Press.

Chen, K. J., & Liu, S. H. (1992). Word identification for Mandarin Chinese sentences. In *Proceedings of the 14th conference on computational linguistics. Morphology, phonology, syntax* (Vol. 1, pp. 101–107). Morristown, NJ: Association for Computational Linguistics.

Curriculum Development Council. (2001). *Learning to learn: Life-long learning and whole-person development*. Hong Kong: Curriculum Development Council.

Ge, X., Pratt, W., & Smyth, P. (1999). Discovering Chinese words from unsegmented text [Poster Abstract]. In *Proceedings of the 22nd annual international ACM SIGIR conference on research and development in information retrieval* (pp. 271–272). New York: ACM.

Honorof, D. N., & Feldman, L. (2006). The Chinese character in psycholinguistic research: Form, structure, and the reader. In P. Li, L. H. Tan, E. Bates, & O. J. L. Tzeng (Eds.), *The handbook of East Asian psycholinguistics* (pp. 195–208). New York: Cambridge University Press.

Institute of Linguistics, The Academy of Social Sciences. (1985). *Xiandai hanyu cidian* [Modern Chinese dictionary]. Beijing: Commercial Press.

Ki, W. W., Lam, H. C., Chung, A. L. S., Tse, S. K., Ko, P. Y., Lau, C. C., et al. (2003). Structural awareness, variation theory and ICT support. *L1 – Educational Studies in Language and Literature, 3*, 53–78.

Lee, C. M. (Ed.). (1989). *Lee's Zhongwen Zidian* [Lee's Chinese dictionary]. Hong Kong: Hong Kong Chinese University Press.

Leng, Y., & Wei, Y. (1994). *Zhonghua zi hai* [Dictionary of Chinese Characters]. Beijing: Zhonghua shu ju ; Zhongguo you yi chu ban gong si.

Li, H., & Rao, N. (2000). Parental influences on Chinese literacy development: A comparison of preschoolers in Beijing, Hong Kong, and Singapore. *International Journal of Behavioral Development, 24*, 82–90.

Li, P., Tan, L. H., Bates, E., & Tzeng, O. J. L. (2006). Introduction: New frontiers in Chinese psycholinguistics. In P. Li, L. H. Tan, E. Bates, & O. J. L. Tzeng (Eds.), *The handbook of East Asian psycholinguistics* (pp. 1–9). New York: Cambridge University Press.

Lin, Y. (2000). Vocabulary acquisition and learning Chinese as a foreign language (CFL). *Journal of the Chinese Language Teachers Association, 35*, 85–108.

Ministry of Education, People's Republic of China. (2001). *Yuwen Kecheng Biaozhun* [Standards of Chinese language curriculum]. Beijing: Beijing Normal University Publisher.

National Education Commission and National Language Construction Committee. (1993). *Xiandai hanyu changyong zibiao* [A list of commonly used modern Chinese characters]. In Yuyan Wenzi Guifan Shouce. Beijing: Yuwen Chubanshe.

Ramzy, A. (2006, June). Get ahead, learn Mandarin. *Time Asia, 167*(26). Retrieved October 23, 2008, from http://www.time.com/time/asia/covers/501060626/story.html

Stanovich, K. (2000). *Progress in understanding reading: scientific foundations and new frontier.* New York: Guilford Press.

Weber, G. (1997). Top languages: The world's 10 most influential languages. *Language Today, 2*(3), 12–18.

Xinhua News Agency. (2006, January 16). *HSK Center: Almost 120,000 foreign examinees in 2005.* Retrieved October 23, 2008, from http://www.gov.cn/jrzg/2006-01/16/content_160707.htm

Zhang, Z. G. (1987). Chinese characters and reading. *Reading News, 8*, 7–8.

Shek Kam Tse and Wai Ming Cheung
Faculty of Education
The University of Hong Kong

PAKEY PUI MAN CHIK AND FERENCE MARTON

2. CHINESE PEDAGOGY AND A PEDAGOGY FOR LEARNING CHINESE

INTRODUCTION

Two things the chapters in this book have in common are that (i) they are concerned with the learning and teaching of Chinese, as a first or second language, and (ii) they are underpinned by the same theory of European origin.

Stigler and his research colleagues (Stigler et al., 1999; Stigler & Hiebert, 1999) argue that teaching may be regarded as a cultural activity. In particular, they point out that there are noticeably similar patterns of educational beliefs and practice among schools in the same country, and that these often differ markedly from educational practice in other countries. If their reasoning is correct, it may be possible to discern a distinctive pattern of pedagogy in Chinese schools, which leads Chinese students to perform so well in international comparisons of performance on attainment tests of literacy and numeracy. The pedagogy Chinese students typically encounter in their schooling might indeed in large part help explain why they perform so well. In this chapter we outline a Western theory of learning that identifies some necessary conditions of learning; then refer to a number of international comparison surveys of attainment in which Chinese learners excel. If Chinese students are so good at learning, it seems reasonable to presume that the prevailing Chinese pedagogy they have experienced has been able to supply the necessary conditions specified by the theory. We go on to argue that this is actually the case and point out how elements of a Western theory are remarkably congruent with a Chinese pedagogy and cultural philosophy rooted in ancient times. From our studies of the learning of Chinese, we show how a theory of learning operates that is conceptually and, in practice, harmonious with the Chinese pedagogy observed in Chinese classrooms.

THE THEORY OF VARIATION

The "Theory of Variation" casts light on how teachers can help students learn. Learning is an experience known to everyone, so we first turn to what the "person in the street" takes learning to be. A very widely shared belief about learning is captured in the ancient proverb: "*repetitio est mater studiorum*" (repetition is the mother of learning). Equally well known is the proposition that "practice makes perfect". In Chinese, "practice" is a component of the word "learning [學習]": the first character "學" having the meaning of "learn" and the second "習" meaning "practice" in the sense of "doing something again and again" - a synonym for "repetition".

F. Marton, S.K. Tse and W.M. Cheung (eds.), On the Learning of Chinese, 9–29.

When learning and teaching are discussed in educational circles today, there seems to be less emphasis on the amount of practice and more on the purpose and meaningfulness of the practice. Relevance, motivation, participation, interaction and so on are stressed, but so too is the notion that a certain element of repetition is usually essential. We are not suggesting that learning will inevitably ensue and endure simply from the mechanical repetition or recitation of unconnected items of information; nor will it ensue if everything varies simultaneously so that an abundance of information is presented and learners are confused. Learning endures when there is carefully planned repetition and systematic variation of information input.

The basic idea of the "Theory of Variation" is that in order to grasp the meaning of something you must notice how it differs from other things. Also, in order to notice the ways in which the target phenomenon differs from other things, there must be a difference in that respect, a difference which the learner can discern against the background of invariance in all other respects.

Learning, Discernment, Variation and Simultaneity

Learning is in general a process in which people become capable of doing things in new ways. When people engage in learning, they act in ways in accordance with the given situation and what is to be achieved in that situation. To be able to act in a certain way, in turn, calls for the learner to experience things in a certain way. When we come across an object in the real world, we are frequently exposed to many aspects of that object at the same time. However, as suggested by Miller (1956), our capacity for holding information in mind in the short-term is limited, meaning that it is impossible for us to be focally aware of and retain all aspects of the object simultaneously. Rather, we pay attention to, and thereby discern, aspects of the object in the forefront of our awareness, and take less notice of other aspects in the background. Often the background is ignored, skimmed over or taken for granted. In other words, the discerned aspects and aspects which are taken for granted constitute a sort of figure-ground relationship. Such relationship helps define the structure of the object and allow the learner to attach meaning to it.

Learning to experience a phenomenon in a certain way is governed by the dynamics of discernment and those aspects that come to the fore of the learner's awareness at the time. Research studies into the phenomenographic approach to learning since the 1970s consistently show that people understand the same thing (phenomenon) in the same situation in qualitatively different ways; and that such differences reflect different aspects of the phenomenon that different learners are aware of at the time (Marton & Booth, 1997). Bowden and Marton (1998) further point out that discernment presupposes variation in the aspects that are held in the learner's focal awareness and are experienced as varying by the learner.

> When some aspect of a phenomenon or an event varies while another aspect or other aspects remain invariant, the varying aspect will be discerned. In order for this to happen, variation must be experienced by the learner as variation (p. 35).

For example, in order to discern the taste of sweetness, one must have experienced tastes which are not sweet, such as bitterness or saltiness. If everything in the world tasted sweet in the same way, people may not have the concept of taste. On the other hand, when people have experienced different tastes and are aware of such difference at the same time, they are able to discern the concept of "taste". Here, "taste" constitutes "a dimension of variation", and sweetness, bitterness, saltiness and so on are "values" along that dimension.

Discernment may occur in two different ways. As noted above, an attribute may be discerned (sweetness) and at the same time a dimension of variation (taste) in which the attribute is a value may also be discerned. In the other case, a phenomenon (a whole) may be discerned from a context and parts of the phenomenon may be discerned from each other and from the whole as well. Taking the example of a deer in a wood given by Marton and Booth (1997), in order to see a deer in a wood, we need to have discerned its contour among the trees. In so doing, we may also have seen its parts, such as eyes and nose, and how these relate to the body. Once the whole (contour of the deer) is discerned from the background context (the woods), the meaning of the parts (e.g., eyes and nose) and their relationships with each other and to the whole may become clear. Once a part (e.g., eyes) is discerned, its relationships with other parts (e.g., nose, body) and with the whole may also become clear. The whole contour of the deer may hence stand out.

However, having learners face the same situation does not imply that the relationship between parts and wholes will be discerned in the same way by all. Säljö (1982) carried out a study of how people came to understand a text about learning and found that Swedish adults tended to comprehend it in two distinct ways. One way was to see the text as being about forms of learning (main theme) with the different forms illustrated by different examples (sub-themes). From this perspective, the text was conceptualised in terms of a hierarchical structure. The structure perceived by the other group was linear in the sense that it was thought to be about different things: first about learning followed by different events and discrete cases. It was not seen as consisting of subordinate examples supporting a superordinate theme or concept (in this case, forms of learning). Those adults who understood the text in the hierarchical way were able to grasp the gist of the text more in line with its author's intentions than those who understood the text as being linear in structure. Although the same elements in the text were identically present, members of the two sub-groups had structurally different perspectives reflecting the differences in the positions and functions of those elements, and hence, the meaning they thought the text presented (Marton & Booth, 1997).

Inspired by Säljö's study, Chik (2006) used the Theory of Variation to analyse the outcomes of Chinese language lessons taught in contrasting ways. Three pairs of Chinese language lessons were studied, with teachers presenting the same subject matter to students at the same level of studying. In each pair of lessons, structural differences comparable to the hierarchical and sequential ways of responding to the text in Säljö's study were observed. For example, in two Grade 2 Chinese language lessons, the teachers used the same text, the objective in each lesson being to help the students learn a number of new words in the text.

However, they organised the lesson differently so that the new words in the text were focused on in different ways during the lesson. In one lesson the teacher focused on the overall construction of the whole text, particularly the gist of the passage, the paragraphs and sentences, the words and their characters. Throughout the lesson, she drew the students' attention to part-whole relationships between the linguistic elements, housing them in a hierarchical structure: characters are made up of components and radicals; characters are the component parts making up words; words are component parts of sentences; and sentences are component parts of paragraphs which, in turn, contribute to the central theme of the text. In contrast, her colleague organised the teaching of the new words stressing three attributes of the words, form, pronunciation and meaning, dealing with each attribute separately. Post-lesson individual interviews with students uncovered different understanding gained by the students in the two classes and how these had affected learning of the target words. The patterns of the students' understanding of the target words clearly reflected what the teacher had brought to their attention in the lesson. Chik (2006) attributed differences in students' understanding to the different learning possibilities opened up for students and the differing opportunities for the simultaneous discernment of different aspects of the target words focused upon in each type of lesson (see also Chapter 6).

Similar observations have been presented in a study reported in Chapter 8. Here, two groups of teachers teaching at the same level, worked together to plan the teaching of creative narrative writing in Chinese language lessons in a primary school. Stress was deliberately placed on using the Theory of Variation in the lesson planning stage, with a researcher guiding the target group; the other group, the comparison group, worked alone. It was found that even within the two classes in the target group, remarkable differences were observed in the students' creativity in Chinese writing, in terms of fluency of expression and number of original ideas shown in their writings collected throughout the year. Further investigation revealed differences in the organisation of teaching content of the lessons experienced by the two classes. In one class, teaching content had been hierarchically structured highlighting part-whole relationships in various aspects critical to narrative writing; in the other, teaching content was sequentially organised with lessons consisting of isolated and discrete items covered by the teacher one after another. Students' creativity in Chinese writing was found to have developed impressively during the year in the former class, but not noticeably so in the other class.

The meaning learners acquire about a certain object in a particular situation depends very much on their way of experiencing it, and their way of experiencing the object is in part governed by which aspects they see as relevant or available for them to see and keep in focus when encountering the situation. It also pertains to how the aspects are related or structured for their discernment. In other words, there is a "relevance structure" in each learning situation that draws the learner's attention to particular aspects and the relationships between those aspects considered critical, in consequence bringing about certain qualities in the learning (Marton & Booth, 1997: p. 143). More powerful ways of experiencing are then pertinent to the simultaneity of critical aspects; that is, the number and relationships of aspects critical to achieving a certain aim, which are in focus and also discerned at the same time (Chik & Lo, 2004).

Bransford, Brown and Cocking (2000), discussing studies about the nature of expertise in specific domains (chess, for instance), conclude that the difference between experts and novices rests with the higher sensitivity of the former to the relevance of information available (such as interpretation of configurations on the chessboard) when they are dealing with situations or problems. To put it in a slightly different way, experts and good learners are capable of grasping simult-aneously critical aspects and their interrelationship and, unlike novice learners, are able to capitalise on this ability to achieve objectives in given situations. Chase and Simon (1973) report that chess masters can simultaneously keep in mind seven or eight pieces in every configuration or move on the board and interpret a great number of possible lines of attack or defence and their consequences; and such ability is critical for mastering chess at an advanced level. This is similar to an extent to the situation in classrooms where students show different levels of understanding of the same lesson taught by a teacher. Students who can see clear relationships between critical aspects (of what is being taught), and between these aspects and the whole presentation of the lesson, are more capable of comprehending the lesson than fellow students who cannot. Thus, it is important to plan lessons in such a way that the discernment of critical aspects of the lesson, their relationship to each other and to the lesson as a whole are made possible through highlighting pertinent patterns of variation and invariance (Marton, Runesson, & Tsui, 2004). This also calls for teachers to consider the content and constitution of specific topics so that they can be presented in such a way that learning is facilitated for the student.

The Object of Learning

"The object of learning" refers not simply to "content" in the Theory of Variation, but also to capability to do something with that content. Capabilities as such, accor-ding to Marton et al., (2004), consist of two aspects: the "general" aspect, referring to what the learner is capable of doing with the content, "the act-side of learning", such as remembering, interpreting, grasping or viewing something in certain ways; and the "specific" aspect, the content of learning, which refers to what is acted upon, such as formulae, engineering problems, simultaneous equations, World War II and Kafka's literary heritage. Whereas the specific aspect concerns what the learner is supposed to become able to handle (the direct object of learning), the general aspect concerns how the learner is supposed to become capable of handling the "what" (the indirect object of learning) (Marton & Booth, 1997). In the case of learning to comprehend text through interpreting the meaning embedded in the text, the meaning of the text is the direct object of learning, and making use of that meaning (for retelling the text, using it for making sense of every-day situations and so on) is the indirect object of learning.

The "object of learning" often has different meanings and importance in the eyes of the teacher and the eyes of the students. Teachers usually have clear ideas about the subject matter they hope students will learn, be it appreciation of modern poetry, how to calculate the area of a triangle or the concept of the water cycle. They will also have considered what they hope students will be able to do with such knowledge, for example how to analyse aspects of modern poetry such as rhythm and syllabic arrangement. All these make up what Runesson and Marton (2002) refer to as the "intended object of learning", which "may sometimes be used synonymously with others such as learning objectives, learning goals or targets" (Pong & Morris, 2002: p. 16).

Teachers frequently have to make instant adjustments during the course of lessons in response to real and dynamic classroom situations, which may end up in a deviation from, or enrichment of, what they had originally intended. Hence, while the intended object of learning specifies what the lesson is supposed to be about and how it will come to the fore of students' awareness, the possibility for learning is also shaped by what aspects of a particular object of learning are highlighted, how they are related and made available for the students' discernment in the classroom setting. This possibility for learning is referred to as "the enacted object of learning" (Runesson & Marton, 2002) and is often described from the researcher perspective, especially in terms of what patterns of variation and invariance are present in the object of learning; in other words what might vary, what might be invariant and how these might interact to generate learning.

The subject matter the teacher presents for learning may in many instances differ from what the students actually end up learning. Students may have focused on and discerned aspects of subject matter the teacher had not thought students would pay attention to and learn. With this in mind, Marton et al., (2004) introduce the concept of "the lived object of learning" to describe what the students might actually focus on and discern.

The distinction between the intended, enacted and lived objects of learning may be regarded as representing three different perspectives on a specific object of learning. The intended object of learning is very much taken from the teacher's perspective and reflects his or her understanding of the subject matter and what they plan students will focus on and manipulate in the lesson. The enacted object of learning describes the researcher's perspective of what constitutes the actual conditions for the learning and how the object of learning may have brought to the students' awareness. The lived object of learning is derived from the students' perspective of what they actually focused on and discerned, and how they made sense of what was being taught in the lesson. In short, by focusing on the object of learning intended and enacted by the teacher and lived by the students, we are actually looking at the process by which the intended object of learning is actualized into the enacted object of learning and reflected in the lived object of learning.

This model has been used as the launch-pad for a number of research studies linking learning and teaching in the classroom. For instance, Lo and Ko (2002) studied two Grade 1 English language lessons in Hong Kong, the intended object of learning for the two lessons being the same - to be able to relate ones' daily activities. One of the teachers kept using the pronoun "I" as the subject throughout the lesson. The other teacher varied the pronoun between "I", "he", "she" and "it".

This variation in pronoun thus allowed the learners to see how the form of the verb in third person singular contrasted against the form in first person singular. Lo and Ko found that the students who had experienced the variation in pronoun performed better than their counterparts in terms of their use of proper verb forms in relation to subject-verb agreement. In a study reported in Chapter 6 and mentioned earlier, a close relationship was also revealed between the different patterns of variation and invariance constituted in the focused aspects in the two Chinese language lessons about learning new words in a text and the corresponding students' learning outcomes. For instance, in one of the lessons, the words were kept invariant while the three attributes and the usage of each word varied in terms of linguistic context (e.g., the meaning of a word as it appeared in a sentence). This pattern of variation and invariance provided students with the simultaneous experience of the word attributes and usage, and this contributed to the superior achievement of this class in using the words actually taught in both classes to complete a short passage.

It is, however, not our intention to suggest here that there can be a one-to-one correspondence between teaching and learning detected by merely focusing on how objects of learning are experienced by students in the classroom. Other aspects such as the forms and approaches to teaching are also important. Nor do we want to give the impression that introducing variations in lessons and teacher presentations necessarily implies higher achievement by students or good quality of learning. What we want to point out is, as Marton and Morris argue, that among proximal factors (i.e., factors that operate in the very classroom), how the objects of learning are dealt with is "the most potent source for accounting for differences in learning achievement between classrooms" (2002, p. 133).

In fact, what students are supposed to learn is not always synonymous with the actual learning outcomes. As Nuthall (2004) noted, while differences in the outcome of learning are frequently seen in the professional culture of teachers as something hard to explain, they can actually be traced back to what happens during the lesson and how students experienced those events. We believe that the nature of the relationship between teaching and learning can be characterized in terms of the object of learning as it is enacted, on the one hand, and as it is lived, or experienced, on the other hand.

The Enacted Object of Learning and Patterns of Variation and Invariance

As illustrated earlier, the kind of learning focused on here is taken as a function of discernment of the critical aspects of the direct object of learning. It presupposes certain experienced patterns of variation and invariance in these critical aspects. Thus, in the classroom situation, when the teacher and the students, or the students among themselves, interact around a specific object of learning, patterns of variation and invariance are constituted, or enacted. In such enactment, some aspects of the object of learning remain invariant while other aspects vary. The resulting enacted patterns of variation and invariance in the object of learning afford different possibilities for learning. Depending on how the patterns of variation and invariance are enacted, i.e., depending on what "the enacted object of learning" is like, certain aspects are brought to the students' focal awareness and hence, discernment of those aspects and their relationship is on offer to the students.

Marton (Marton & Runesson, 2003; Marton et al., 2004; Lo & Pong, 2005) identifies four types of pattern of variation and invariance, each carrying particular functions in the light of what is being focused on in relation to a specific object of learning. He refers to four types of function that a pattern of variation and invariance may serve: contrast, generalisation, separation and fusion.

Contrast comes into play when variation is introduced between different values or features in a dimension of an object, concept, or phenomenon. It helps to facilitate the discernment of what makes the feature in focus distinct, e.g., the colour of red as distinct from the colours of yellow, brown and so on. Here the focus is on a particular "value" (red) in a "dimension of variation" (colour). In addition to the focused value, there is at least one other value in the same dimension (blue), while other potential dimensions of variation (e.g., shape) between the two (or more) objects are invariant.

Separation occurs when the learner's attention is focused on the dimension of variation between objects, concepts, or phenomena. As such, it is the dimension that is discerned by the learner. For instance, the concept of "colour" can be separated from other aspects (which are kept invariant) by focusing attention on the variation between colours. Juxtaposing two or more objects that vary in a certain dimension affords both contrast (e.g., red versus blue) and separation (e.g., the dimension of variation in colour), depending on the learner's focus (on the colour of "red" or the concept of "colour").

If one wants to separate a particular value (e.g., red) from the object (or objects), one has to keep that value invariant (i.e., one has to compare red objects), while there is variation between the objects juxtaposed in other dimensions (e.g., shape, size). This is called *generalization* by Marton and is the most frequently used pattern of variation and invariance in educational contexts.

Fusion takes place when the learner's attention is focused on several aspects of an object, a concept, or a phenomenon which vary at the same time. *Fusion* may bring out the relationship between the varying aspects and the object of learning as a whole. For example, exposing students to simultaneous variation in demand and supply helps them to consider both at the same time. This helps cement the relationship between the two concepts (Marton & Pang, 2006).

The pedagogy developed based on the Theory of Variation can be characterized by a focus on the object of learning and the use of patterns of variation and invariance to maximize the opportunity for students to discern part-part and part-whole relationships within the object of learning, on the one hand, and critical differences between instances of the object of learning, on the other. Since 2000, this pedagogy has been used to improve teaching and learning in the context of single lessons through "Learning Study" (Holmqvist et al., 2009; Lo, 2006; Lo et al., 2004; Lo et al., 2005; Marton, 2006; Marton & Pang, 2006). It has also been used to design sequences of lessons which aim to enhance students' general capability in learning, for example the attempt by Marton and the Chinese Language Research Team in the government (2009) to enhance Grade 9 students' capability to learn how to learn through reading expository passages.

"Learning study" takes its inspiration from collaborative and interactive procedures in studies of teachers in China (Ma, 1999) and the Japanese Lesson Study (Stigler & Hiebert, 1999), and is grounded on a conceptual framework based on the learning Theory of Variation. In each learning study, teachers form subject-based groups and meet regularly among themselves and with university researchers to develop a number of "research lessons". For each research lesson, they carefully study the object of learning and its critical aspects, taking into account the students' varying understanding of the subject matter, ascertained in pre-test and/or pre-lesson interviews with the students. Together they then develop ways to structure the lesson using patterns of variation and invariance in the identified object of learning. Next, teacher members take turns to teach the lesson while the whole team observes. Evaluation of each lesson and modifications to the use of patterns of variation and invariance are made in a post-lesson conference with reference to the lesson observations and student learning outcomes ascertained in post-test and/or post-lesson interviews with students.

ON THE APPARENTLY PARADOXICAL EXCELLENCE OF LEARNERS FROM CONFUCIAN HERITAGE CULTURES

The stereotypical view held by some educators in the West of pedagogical practices in Confucian heritage cultures and of ways of teaching and learning in China is that they focus on repetitive drill and rote learning. Such practices do not seem conducive to learning, especially in creating the necessary conditions for learning as set out in the theory presented in the previous section. As is obvious in what is reported below, learners from the Confucian heritage cultures excel when compared to learners from other cultures. Thus there is a paradox indicated by Marton, Dall' Alba & Tse (1996) and Marton, Wen and Wong (2005): how can seemingly adverse pedagogy yield such good learning? This paradox is addressed in the section that follows and an attempt is made to show that Chinese pedagogical practice is grossly misrepresented. Repetition is frequently the reiteration of certain elements and the variation of others. Hence variation is just as much a cornerstone of Chinese pedagogy as is repetition. But let us first look at some international comparisons of educational attainment.

From the 1990s, international school attainment comparison studies have attracted considerable scholarly discussion. These include TIMSS 1995, involving third to eighth grades and TIMSS, 1999 and 2003 involving fourth and eighth grades' mathematics and science prowess; PISA, 2003 involving 15-year-old students' reading, mathematical and scientific literacy; and PIRLS, 2006 dealing with fourth graders' reading comprehension. In these studies, attainment data of students from a number of countries have been collected, analysed and compared. The results consistently show the superior performance of students from Confucian Heritage countries such as China/Hong Kong, Singapore, Japan and South Korea in the subject areas concerned when compared with their Western counterparts. The findings of such international comparisons not only pose a serious challenge to the stereotype that students in Asian countries learn in harsh and inflexible educational settings, with large class size, lengthy periods of direct teaching and limited resources other than chalkboards and textbooks. They also provoke the curiosity of some researchers to examine the cultural differences in respect of classroom teaching and learning, with the aim of revealing what underlines the excellent performance of learners from Confucian Heritage countries in international comparisons.

Stigler and his research colleagues carried out a follow-up video study of TIMSS 1995 on eighth-grade mathematics classrooms sampled from the USA, Germany and Japan (Stigler et al., 1999; Stigler & Hiebert, 1999). They noted a remarkable difference in the way the teachers habitually focus on and handle the content of teaching: USA teachers, for example, tended to focus on teaching procedures and skills via the learning of terminology and practising of procedures, whereas the Japanese teachers focused on teaching conceptual understanding by means of structured problem solving. Similar observations were also made in other studies, for example by Rohlen and Le Tendre (1996) who compared Japanese and USA mathematics teaching in Grades 1 and 5; and by Ma (1999) who compared mathematical understanding among the USA and Chinese elementary school teachers in relation to their classroom practice. In these studies, lessons taught by Japanese/ Chinese teachers were found to have transcended seemingly undesirable whole-class teaching to achieve many of the educational ideals voiced by the USA educators, and their students did so better than students in the USA in terms of their grasp of conceptual and procedural understanding.

Research in Chinese classrooms suggests that, despite the large class size and the predominance of whole-class direct teaching, Chinese students are regularly and purposely subjected to thought-provoking tasks and questioning (Bruce & Bruce, 1997; Cortazzi, 1998; Cortazzi & Jin, 2001). This is believed to enhance students' conceptual understanding and to contribute to their excellent performance in inter-national comparison studies (Stevenson & Lee, 1997). Other researchers characterize the Chinese style of teaching by its emphasis on the knowledge and personal qualities of the Chinese teachers themselves, the teacher as a "virtuoso" (Paine, 1990) and by the teachers' assiduous attitude to meticulous lesson planning (Cheng, 1992). Stigler and his colleagues note that Japanese teaching is characterised by a conscious and continuous attention to careful and systematic analysis of practice, and a deter-mination to reflect on and improve practice in every lesson (Hiebert et al., 2002; Stigler & Hiebert, 1999). This kind of intense and thorough lesson planning and evaluation is less common in some Western countries.

Other studies have found that the seemingly non-conducive pedagogical approaches favouring the use of memorization among students in Confucian-heritage cultures do not necessarily imply that the students engage exclusively in rote learning, recitation and repetition; there is a good measure of reflection, understan-ding and conceptualization of what has been covered in their learning by memorization (Biggs, 1996; Lee, 1996; Marton et al., 1996). In other words, repetition and understanding are regarded as two intertwining processes in learning by learners in Confucian-heritage cultures (Marton et al., 2005). This view is not shared by most learners in Western classrooms. Dalhlin and Walkins (2000, cited in Watkins & Biggs, 2001) compared the views of Chinese and Western secondary school students about repetition and understanding and found that, unlike Chinese students who considered repetition as a means of developing full understanding of a certain problem through revisiting it piece by piece in repetition, Western students regarded repetition simply as a tool for them to reinforce memory, understanding being more of "a process of sudden insights" (Watkins & Biggs, 2001: p. 6).

The above discussion indicates significant cultural differences between the East and the West in terms of beliefs about pedagogy and the nature of lasting learning. Two major features characterize Asian classrooms: the focus on the subject content during lesson planning and delivery, and the emphasis on the teachers' directive role in engaging students in learning tasks in lessons. It is suggested that these two features contribute in large part to the different achievement levels of students from the East and the West in international comparison studies. This is in line with a range of academic publications that suggests that the teachers' subject knowledge, perceived role in teaching and the way they engage students in learning are crucial to how students encounter and experience their learning; in turn, this influences what they learn in lessons (Fishman & Davis, 2006; Kilpatrick et al., 2001; Muijs & Reynolds, 2000; Nuthall, 2004, 2005; Wenglinsky, 2000).

Chinese Pedagogy and the Theory of Variation

In the previous section we looked at an apparent paradox: according to the stereotypical view of Chinese pedagogical practice, lessons are characterized by adverse conditions of learning and the over-incidence of repetition and rote learning. Despite this, Chinese learners do very well indeed when compared with learners from other countries. We attempt to resolve this paradox in this section by arguing that Chinese pedagogical practices are misrepresented, and that they actually highlight strong features related to systematic variation rather than concentrating on monotonous repetition.

In the second part of this chapter, we elaborated on key notions of the Theory of Variation, referred to so often in this book. Unlike theories of learning that focus on learning in a broad sense, the Theory of Variation deals with how the learner comes to experience what to learn (the object of learning) in order to achieve certain aims in given situations. Acquiring knowledge, according to this theory, is not a progression from basics (or parts) to more complex and advanced forms (or wholes). Rather, it moves "from an undifferentiated and poorly integrated understanding of the whole to an increased differentiation and integration of the whole and its parts..." (Marton & Booth, 1997, p. viii). Learners need to discern the component parts and relate these to the greater whole if they are to arrive at an understanding of a given situation where the parts and the whole blend with each other.

A focus on the object of learning and how it is experienced by the learner in a given situation or context in part-whole relationships is a distinctive feature of Chinese pedagogy. Phillipson (2007) reviewed the literature on the learning approaches of students in Confucius Heritage cultures and concluded that Chinese students and teachers tend to pay attention to "the field (whole) within which an object is found", whereas Western students and teachers tend to focus more on the properties (parts) of the object (p. 10).

Besides an emphasis on the object of learning, the pedagogy informed by the Theory of Variation focuses on the use of patterns of variation and invariance as a guiding principle of lesson design. This theory-driven pedagogy concurs with Gu's (1991, 1994) conceptualization of a long prevailing feature of mathematics teaching in the Mainland into a theory of mathematics teaching in China - Bianshi [變式], which literally means "pattern or form of variation". According to Gu, good mathematics teaching involves two forms of "variation", namely "conceptual variation" and "procedural variation". Gu et al.,'s (2004) concept of "conceptual variation" resembles the kinds of variation that function to generalize the invariant concept in focus (e.g., "non-coplanar line"), by varying concrete examples (e.g., students' daily sensory experience of visual models), and contrasting the invariant concept or figure with counter-examples (of what it is not) (e.g., non-standard versus standard geometrical figures). Below we show that a close resemblance can also be delineated between good teaching practice in Chinese language lessons and the use of variation and invariance in the Theory of Variation.

Teaching and learning of Chinese language

Ko (2002) studied what constitutes exemplary pedagogical practice in China by focusing on Special Rank Teachers in Chinese language (winners of a state conferred teaching award). Ko and Marton (2004) employed the Theory of Variation to examine in depth a sample Chinese reading lesson on semantics by a Special Rank Teacher. The teacher was seen to be constructing the lesson in a highly systematic and sophisticated manner, emphasizing the use of context and the students' own experience. For example, one of the objectives of the lesson was to help students establish different semantic relations between words: (a) homonyms, the same words with different meanings; (b) synonyms, different words expressing the same meaning; and (c) antonyms, words of opposite meanings. Instead of presenting linguistic knowledge directly, the teacher made use of a story to illustrate that the meaning of the same word can vary according to the context. This helped students grasp the semantic relation between words that are homonymous.

The story:

Afanti was a hairdresser. There was one customer, Ahung, who always went to Afanti's place to have his hair cut but never paid for the service. This made Afanti very angry. He wanted to play a trick on Ahung. One day Ahung came to Afanti's again. Afanti first cut Ahung's hair. Then, he began to shave Ahung's face, and asked, "Do you want your eyebrows?" Ahung replied, "Of course! Why ask!" Then, quick as a flash, Afanti shaved off Ahung's eyebrows and said, "You wanted your eyebrows, so I will give them to you!" Ahung was too mad to say anything, because he had indeed said he "wanted" his eyebrows. Meanwhile Afanti asked, "Do you want your beard?" Ahung had a beautiful beard, and he immediately said, "My beard? No, no! I don't want my beard!" But again Afanti proceeded to shave off his beard. Ahung stood up and saw an egg-like head in the mirror. Furiously, Ahung reproved Afanti, "Why did you shave off my eyebrows and beard?" "I was only following your orders, sir!" Afanti answered calmly. There was nothing Ahung could say to that! (translation adapted from Ko & Marton, 2004, pp: 46–47)

After telling the story, the teacher asked the students how Afanti had played a trick on Ahung. In response, the students pointed out that Afanti played a trick by exploiting the ambiguity of the meaning of the word "want" [要, yao], which can mean "give [給, gei]" or "keep [留, liu]". Intentionally, Afanti first used the word "want" to mean "give" when Ahung meant to "keep" his eyebrows. He then used the word "want" to mean "keep" when Ahung interpreted it as to "give" his beard. As a result, Ahung lost both his eyebrows and beard. In the teacher-led discussion, the students, without knowing the technical terminology, became aware of the semantic concept of homonyms, words that can vary in meaning according to the context.

Later in the lesson, the teacher introduced another kind of semantic relationship between words that express the same meaning: synonyms. He did so by first making a contrast with the concept of homonyms that had been developed using the story about Afanti and Ahung. She then asked the students for examples of this from their daily experience. Using the examples provided by the students, she went on to discuss with the students that synonymous words, though expressing the same meaning, are often used in different contexts. For example, "father" is used in a formal situation, whereas "pa" and "daddy" are used in informal situations; "sodium chloride" is a chemical term whereas "salt" is usually a non-technical word; and "wrinkly old fellow" is an impolite form of addressing an elderly male person compared with the label "Grandpa". The teacher then drew on the students' own experience and solicited words that have contrastive meanings, thus bringing out the semantic relation between words that have opposite meanings, antonyms.

Ko and Marton analyzed the patterns of variation and invariance used in this lesson. They noted that the teacher was actually making a purposeful, systematic and sophisticated use of variation and invariance, while highlighting the importance of context and students' experience in the complexity of the meaning of words. For example, when she introduced the concept of homonyms, she purposefully made use of the story of Afanti and Ahung and kept the word "want" invariant while having the students focus on its varying meanings of "give" and "keep" in the given context. This then made it possible for the students to see a separation between word and meaning, with the latter being reliant on the context. The subsequent contrast between the concepts of homonyms and synonyms enabled students to discern the complexity of the meaning of words by varying the semantic relations between them. By having the students offer examples of synonymous words (what varies) but express the same meaning (what remains invariant), the teacher helped the students discern the concept of synonyms by the generalization of what was invariant. Thus, she brought to the students' awareness the notion of synonyms by commenting on the appropriateness of the synonymous words that varied with the context. The simultaneous variation of both the synonymous words and the context in which each should be used then led to fusion, contributing to students' deeper understanding about the relationship between the meaning and the usage context of those words.

The above study and the large-scale research over a long period on mathematics education in China described earlier add weight to the proposal that the systematic use of variation and invariance is a distinctive feature underlying effective Chinese pedagogy.

THE ROLE OF VARIATION AND INVARIANCE IN THE CHINESE CULTURE

As proposed above, the systematic use of variation and invariance is a characteristic of good practice in teaching mathematics and Chinese language in China. Interestingly, this kind of systematic use of variation and invariance is central to the ancient ways of learning and teaching the subjects in the country. For instance, about 2000 years ago, *Jiu Zhang San Shu* (九章算書, Nine Chapters on Mathematics) was one of the leading and most influential mathematics classic. It was formally included in the official curriculum of mathematics for preparing students for the state examination in the Tang Dynasty, considered the most established system at the time and serving as a model for later dynasties to comply with or improve on (Siu, 2004). Each chapter of this classic began with the introduction of a topic focusing on a particular concept or phenomenon (for example, excess and deficit), then followed this by a set of problems which were structured in such a way that, within the same context (for example, joint purchase), each problem was drawn upon to contribute to a new aspect of the topic dealt with (for example, one of the four possible cases of excess and deficit) (Ma, 2000). This way of teaching mathematics is still common in Chinese mathematics classrooms today and is noticeably different from the Western approach in which, according to Hägglund (2008), problems following the introduction of a new topic simply form a set of unrelated problems of the same kind.

Another historical example of the use of variation and invariance can be seen in the ancient Chinese way of learning and teaching children basic reading literacy. One of the most widespread and influential ancient texts to-date has been *Qian Zhi Wen* (千字文, Thousand Character Text) by Zhou Xin Si in the Liang dynasty (A.D. 502–557) (Pan, 2007). It was composed of 1000 different characters (in traditional form) showing clear part-whole relationships in the Chinese language, with every four characters forming a sentence, two sentences forming a pair, and four sentences forming a cluster focusing on particular themes. With such a rigid construction, the text affords highly sophisticated patterns of variation and invariance in different aspects of Chinese language and encompasses a wide range of lexical items, structures and phonology. This helps make the learning of key language aspects available. To illustrate this, we focus on how a pair of sentences in the text reproduced and translated in Table 2.1 below can enhance the learning of Chinese word semantics by means of systematic variation.

Table 2.1. Example of a Chinese word semantics

Original:	性	靜	情	逸
Direct translation:	nature	calm	feelings	relaxed
Interpretation:	With a calm nature, people are relaxed in their feelings.			
Original:	心	動	神	疲
Direct translation:	temper	restless	spirit	weary
Interpretation:	With a restless temper, people are weary in spirit.			

The above two sentences, typical for the construction of text, are identical in structure, both being composed of words, in this case, four single-character words that are syntactically and semantically comparable across sentences. For example, the first two characters in the two sentences "性 nature" and "心 temper" form a pair of nouns and represent different aspects of people qualities; the next two characters "靜 calm" and "動 restless" are two adjectives depicting opposite states that something or someone is in; "情 feelings" and "神 spirit" are two noun words, referring to different aspects of people's internal states; and "逸 relaxed" and "疲 weary" constitute another pair of adjectives that indicate differing people conditions. Each pair of characters thus constitutes a dimension of variation in which each character is a value and *contrasts* with another to show its own specific meaning in that dimension or semantic category. It also facilitates *separation* of the semantic category, i.e., the dimension of variation (e.g., "people qualities") from its values (e.g., "nature" and "temper") when the learner focuses on the dimension in which the values appears. When looking at the two sentences at phrase level, it can be seen that the paired phrases, each consisting of two single characters, actually carry *contrasting* meanings in the same category: "性靜 calm nature" and "心動 restless temper" denote opposite qualities of people; and "情逸 relaxed in the feelings" and "神疲 weary in the spirit" show distinctive states people are in. In turn, these phrases jointly give meaning to the sentences: With a calm character, people are relaxed in their feelings; with a restless temper, people are weary in spirit.

The construction of the Thousand Character Text (and probably, texts of similar kind, such as *San Zi Jing* 三字經, Three Character Classics written later in the Song dynasty, A.D. 420–479) provide a rich opportunity for the ancient Chinese to teach children vocabulary. Central to such a construction has been the systematic use of "pairs" between characters of opposite meanings (e.g., "靜 calm" and "動 restless", "逸 relaxed" and "疲 weary") or similar meanings (e.g., "性 nature" and "心 temper", "情 feelings" and "神 spirit") in the same category. Put in a slightly different way, the construction of Chinese classical texts can be characterised by the systematic use of variation and invariance that helps *contrast* the meanings of specific characters/ words (variant) and *separate* these characters/words from the semantic category (invariant) in which they appear.

The use of "pairs", more commonly referred to as *dui ou* (對偶, antithesis), has also been a longstanding feature of ancient Chinese poetry and rhapsodies, the most prevalent types of text in ancient China. Usually, there are one to two antitheses in each Chinese ancient poem or rhapsody. In terms of content and structure, an antithesis consists of two consecutive lines which are parallel in structure, use comparable characters in the same category, and together contribute to a central idea, image or message. Table 2.2 below shows an antithesis used in a poem by Wang Wei, a famous poet in the Tang dynasty.

Table 2.2. English translation of the poem adapted from Yang (2009)

Original:	明	月	松	間	照
Direct translation:	bright	moon	pines	through	shining
Interpretation:	The bright moon is shining through the pines.				
Original:	清	泉	石	上	流
Direct translation:	limpid	stream	stones	over	gurgling
Interpretation:	The limpid stream is gurgling over the stones.				

As with the example quoted from the Thousand Character Text, the two lines of the antithesis show a neat arrangement of characters/words and phrases that are comparable in syntactic functions and semantic category. At the character/word level, characters/words in pairs are *contrasted* in the same category, contributing to the differentiation of the specific meanings of the paired characters. For example: "明 bright" and "清 limpid" are adjectives describing "clarity" in different senses; "月 moon" and "泉 stream" are different nouns representing varied scenery in nature; "松 pines" and "石 stones" are different noun objects in nature; "間 through" and "上 over" are different prepositions denoting different "positions"; and "照 shining" and "流 gurgling" are verbs portraying "movement" in different forms. Similar *contrasts* can also be noted when the same set of characters/words are coupled in various phrases: "明月 bright moon" and "清泉 limpid stream" are two noun phrases denoting the scenery in in nature at night, whereas "松間照 shining through the pines" and "石上流 gurgling over the stones" are verb phrases depicting certain movement that can be noticed in a peaceful surrounding. Together, these phrases contribute to the main theme of the antithesis: the scenery in nature on a peaceful night.

Seen in this light, reading to understand antitheses in an ancient Chinese poem or rhapsody necessitates a simultaneous awareness of, at least, semantic and syntactic aspects of the language. This may relate to the characteristics of the Chinese language that is monosyllabic and has flexible word compounding and order that are semantically driven. How well these aspects specific to the Chinese language have been dealt with in forming an antithesis in a poem or rhapsody represents a good indicator of the literacy prowess of the author. This may be one of the many reasons why writing poetry and rhapsodies has been a component in state examinations in ancient China, legendarily believed to have started in the Sui dynasty (A.D. 581–618) and historically afforded great importance from time to time since the reign of Emperor *Gao Zong* (高宗, A.D. 628–683) in the Tang dynasty.

The above examples support the use of variation and invariance to facilitate the learning and teaching of basic literacy in ancient China. Specifically, the use of "pairs" or antitheses in ancient texts, poetry and rhapsodies embraces a simultaneous variation implicit in the dimensions (or aspects critical to learning the language) in which different linguistic parts are paired. Interestingly, a similar way of dealing with literacy learning and teaching has been shown by Xia Mian Zun and Ye Sheng Tao, two great language educators in the early 19th century, who provided a lively discussion of various topics they had learnt and used to teach Chinese in the form of a story book in 1935. Learning vocabulary is one such discussion. Through reflections of one of the main characters, Xia and Ye pointed out that the essence of learning vocabulary and being able to use it precisely in writing is systematically to compare words that can be associated with one another in the same semantic category (e.g., "怒 angry", "憤 resent", "動氣 irritated", "火冒 rage", "不高興 unhappy" in the category of negative emotion) in terms of ways that they differ (e.g., tone, scope of meaning, and context of usage). Thus, what seems to have characterised the way Xia and Ye learnt and taught Chinese words and their usage in writing is the drawing attention to differences between specific words based on sameness in the semantic category. This follows the same line by which ancient texts were constructed for learning words and, as pointed out earlier, the antithesis was used in ancient poetry and rhapsodies. This, in turn, supports our speculation that a systematic use of variation and invariance is inherent in Chinese pedagogy.

On Some Features of Ancient Chinese Thought

As suggested above, the idea of variation and invariance as depicted in the Theory of Variation is not only largely shared by the characterization of what constitutes good contemporary teaching in mathematics and Chinese language in the Mainland. There also seems to be a tendency to focus on how things differ and not only on how they are alike, even when they are alike, in traditional Chinese learning and teaching. This tendency is consistent with Hansen's distinction between how European and Chinese classics see meaning in language. According to Hansen (1989), language plays a descriptive role in representing absolute reality in classical European thought, whereas it is primarily functional in classical Chinese thinking so as to guide behaviour that is believed to be morally good and worth pursuing. Hansen claims that Chinese thinkers do not worry so much about what is the true state of affairs, e.g., "What is X?", "What is Y really?", "What is the essence of Z?". What they care about is "Is it better to do X, Y or Z?" In order to answer such questions, they do not so much worry about what X, Y or Z are, but about how we can tell X, Y and Z apart. Following this line of reasoning, language is about making distinctions in Chinese, rather than about producing propositions as in European languages. The lines below are quoted from the Book of *Lao Zi* (老子), or *Tao Te*

Ching (道德經), one of the earliest Chinese classics, seemingly lending support to this claim.

> The whole world recognizes the beautiful as the beautiful, yet this is only the ugly; the whole world recognizes the good as the good, yet this is only the bad.

> Thus, Something and Nothing produce each other; the Difficult and the Easy complement each other; the Long and Short offset each other; the High and the Low incline towards each other; Note and Sound harmonize with each other; Before and After follow each other.

(Tao Te Ching, Chapter 2)

The lines quoted above actually illustrate a relativist epistemology: to be able to understand something (e.g., the concept of "beautiful") one must be able to differentiate between what something is (i.e., being beautiful) and what it is not (i.e., being ugly). The prevalent use of antithesis in ancient Chinese texts, as noted above, reflects such a relativist view in the ancient Chinese way of thinking by stressing a neat arrangement of characters/words that are comparable in certain categories (Yu & Li, 2006).

While there may be evidence leading to our speculation that the systematic use of variation has been fundamental to the ancient Chinese's way of thinking, it is beyond the scope of this chapter to substantiate all the claims implied in the chapter. Our aim has been to offer ideas we find interesting rather than presenting a substantial and academically-grounded argument. What we are suggesting is that focusing on sameness and focusing on differences may constitute two different pedagogical strategies, and that one (focusing on differences) is more powerful than the other (focusing on sameness). In fact, the combination of both may be better than either alone. Furthermore, it is argued that there is a distinct Chinese pedagogy, a pedagogy of Confucian Heritage countries, characterized by the systematic use of variation and invariance, a pedagogy which seems very powerful.

REFERENCES

Biggs, J. B. (1996). Western misperceptions of the Confucian-Heritage Learning cultural. In D. A. Walkins & J. B. Biggs (Eds.), *The Chinese learner: cultural, psychological and contextual influences* (pp. 45–67). Hong Kong/Melbourne: Comparative Education Research Centre.

Bowden, J., & Marton, F. (1998). *The university of learning.* London, UK: Kogan Page.

Brandsford, J. D., Brown, A. L., & Cocking, R. R. (Eds.). (2000). *How people learn: brain, mind, experience and school* (expanded ed.). Washington, DC: National Academy Press.

Bruce, B. C., & Bruce, S. (1997, May, 1997). *Learning from China.* The Peking University Office of Foreign Affairs Newsletter, pp. 4–7.

Chase, W. G., & Simon, H. A. (1973). Perception in chess. *Cognitive Psychology, 4,* 55–81.

Cheng, K. W. (1992). *China educational reform* [in Chinese]. Hong Kong: Commercial Press.

Chik, P. P. M. (2006). *Differences in learning as a function of differences between hierarchical and sequential organisation of the content taught.* Unpublished Ph.D. Thesis, The University of Hong Kong, HKSAR.

Chik, P. P. M., & Lo, M. L. (2004). Simultaneity and the enacted object of learning. In F. Marton, A. B. M. Tsui, P. P. M. Chik, P. Y. Ko, M. L. Lo, I. A. C. Mok, et al. (Eds.), *Classroom discourse and the space of learning*. New Jersey, NJ: Lawrence Erlbaum.

Cortazzi, M. (1998). Learning from Asian lessons: Cultural experience and classroom talk. *Education 3 to 13, 26*(2), 42–49.

Cortazzi, M., & Jin, L. (2001). Large classes in China: "Good" teachers and interaction. In D. Watkins & J. B. Biggs (Eds.), *Teaching the Chinese learners: Psychological and pedagogical perspectives.* Hong Kong & Australia: CERC & ACER.

Crystal, D. (1987). *The Cambridge encyclopaedia of language.* Cambridge, UK: Cambridge University Press.

Dahlin, B., & Walkins, D. A. (2000). The role of repetition in the processes of memorising and understanding. A comparison of the views of western and Chinese secondary school students in Hong Kong. *British Journal of Educational Psychology, 70*, 65–84.

Gu, L. (1991). *Learning to teach* [In Chinese: 學會教學]. Beijing: People's Education Press.

Gu, L. (1994). *Theory of teaching experiment: The methodology and teaching principle of Qingpu* [In Chinese: 青浦實驗的方法與教學原理研究]. Beijing: Educational Science Press.

Gu, L., Huang, R., & Marton, F. (Eds.). (2004). *Teaching with variation: A Chinese way of promoting effective mathematics learning.* Singapore: World Scientific Publishing Co. Pre. Ltd.

Hägglund, J. (2008). *Teaching systems of linear equations in Sweden and China: What is made possible to learn?* Göteborg: Acta Universitatis Gothoburgensis.

Hansen, C. (1989). Language in the heart-mind. In R. E. Allinson (Ed.), *Understanding the Chinese mind. The philosophical roots.* Hong Kong: Oxford University Press.

Hiebert, J., Gillimore, R., & Stigler, J. W. (2002). A knowledge base for the teaching profession: What would it look like and how can we get one? *Educational Researcher, 31*, 3–15.

Hägglund, J. (2008). *Teaching systems of linear equations in Sweden and China: What is made possible to learn?* Göteborg: Acta Universitatis Gothoburgensis.

Holmqvist, M., Gustavsson, L., & Wernberg, A. (2009). Variation theory: An organizing principle to guide design research in education. In A. Kelly (Ed.), *Handbook of design research in education.* Mahwah, NJ: Lawrence Erlbaum Associates, Inc.

Kilpatrick, J., Swafford, J., & Findell, B. (Eds.). (2001). *Adding it up: Helping children learn mathematics.* Washington, DC: National Academy Press.

Ko, P. Y. (2002). *The notion of teaching excellence in People's Republic of China: the case of Chinese Language teachers.* The University of Hong Kong, HKSAR.

Ko, P. Y., & Marton, F. (2004). Variation and the secret of the virtuoso. In F. Marton, A. B. M. Tsui, P. P. M. Chik, P. Y. Ko, M. L. Lo, I. A. C. Mok, et al. (Eds.), *Classroom discourse and the space of learning.* Mahwah, NJ: Lawrence Erlbaum Associates, Publishers.

Lau, D. C. (Trans.). (1979). *Lao Tzu: Tao Te Ching.* London: Penguin Group.

Lee, W. O. (1996). The cultural context for Chinese learner: Conceptions of learning in the confucian tradition. In D. A. Walkins & J. B. Biggs (Eds.), *The Chinese learner: Cultural, psychological and contextual influences.* Hong Kong & Australia: Comparative Education Research Centre and The Australian Council for Educational Research Ltd.

Lo, M. L., & Ko, P. Y. (2002). The "enacted" object of learning. In F. Marton & P. Morris (Eds.), *What matters? Discovering critical conditions of classroom learning.* Goteborg: Acta Universitatis Gothoburgensis.

Lo, M. L., Pong, W. Y., & Chik, P. P. M. (Eds.). (2005). *For each and everyone: Catering for individual differences through Learning Studies.* HKSAR: The HKU Press.

Ma, L. (1999). *Knowing and teaching elementary mathematics: Teachers' understanding of fundamental mathematics in China and the United States.* New Jersey, NJ: Lawrence Erlbaum Associates, Inc., Publishers.

Ma, L. (2000). *A traditional Chinese way of teaching mathematics.* (Periodical from American Mathematical Society: Mathematics Subject Classification 01A25, 97D50)

Marton, F., & Booth, S. (1997). *Learning and awareness.* New Jersey, NJ: Lawrence Erlbaum.

Marton, F., & Chinese Language Research Team. (2009). The Chinese learner of tomorrow. In C. Chan & N. Rao (Eds.), *Revisiting the Chinese learner: Changing contexts, changing education.* Hong Kong: Comparative Education Research Centre/Springer.

Marton, F., Dall'Alba, G., & Tse, L. K. (1996). Memorizing and understanding: the keys to paradox. In D. A. Walkins & J. B. Biggs (Eds.), *The Chinese learner: Cultural, psychological and contextual influences.* Hong Kong & Melbourne: CERC & ACER.

Marton, F., & Morris, P. (Eds.). (2002). *What matters? Discovering critical conditions of classroom learning.* Goteborg: Acta Universitatis Gothoburgensis.

Marton, F., & Pang, M. F. (2006). On some necessary conditions of learning. *The Journal of the Learning Sciences, 15*(2), 193–220.

Marton, F., & Runesson, U. (2003). *The space of learning.* Paper presented at the Improving Learning, Fostering the will to learn, European Association for Research on Learning and Instruction.

Marton, F., Runesson, U., & Tsui, A. B. M. (2004). The space of learning. In F. Marton, A. B. M. Tsui, P. P. M. Chik, P. Y. Ko, M. L. Lo, I. A. C. Mok, et al. (Eds.), *Classroom discourse and the space of learning.* Mahwah, NJ: Lawrence Erlbaum Associates, Publishers.

Marton, F., Tsui, A. B. M., Chik, P. P. M., Ko, P. Y., Lo, M. L., Mok, I. A. C., et al. (2004). *Classroom discourse and the space of learning.* New Jersey, NJ: Lawrence Erlbaum.

Miller, G. A. (1956). The magic number seven, plus or minus two. Some limits on our capacity to process information. *Psychological Review, 63*, 81–87.

Muijs, D., & Reynolds, D. (2000). School effectiveness and teacher effectiveness in mathematics: Some preliminary findings from the evaluation of the Mathematics Enhancement Programme (Primary). *School Effectiveness and School Improvement, 11*(3), 273–303.

Nuthall, G. (2004). Relating classroom teaching to student learning: A critical analysis of why research has failed to bridge the theory-practice gap. *Harvard Educational Review, 74*(3), 273–306.

Nuthall, G. (2005). Cultural myths and realities of classroom teaching and learning: A personal journey. *Teachers College Record, 107*(5), 895–934.

Paine, W. L. (1990). The teacher as virtuoso: A Chinese model for teaching. *Teachers College Record, 92*(1), 49–81.

Pan, K. S. (2007). *Commentary on the thousand character text* (2nd ed.) [In Chinese: 千字文註釋]. Retrieved February 12, 2010, from Cantonese Culture Promotion Society: http://cantoneseculture.org/page_ThousandWords/documents/thousandwords_detail.pdf

Phillipson, S. N. (2007). The regular Chinese classroom. In S. N. Phillipson (Ed.), *Learning diversity in the Chinese classroom: Contexts and practice for students with special needs.* Hong Kong: The HKU Press.

Pong, W. Y., & Morris, P. (2002). Accounting for differences in achievement. In F. Marton & P. Morris (Eds.), *What matters? Discovering critical conditions of classroom learning* (pp. 9–18). Göteborg: Acta Universitatis Gothoburgensis.

Rohlen, T. P., & LeTendre, G. K. (1996). *Teaching and learning in Japan.* Cambridge, UK: Cambridge University Press.

Säljö, R. (1982). *Learning and understanding: A study of differences in constructing meaning from a text.* Göteborg: Acta Universitatis Gothoburgensis.

Siu, M. K. (2004). Official curriculum in Mathematics in ancient China: How did candidates study for the examination? In L. Fan (Ed.), *How Chinese learn Mathematics: Perspective from insiders.* Singapore: World Scientific.

Stevenson, W., & Lee, S. (Eds.). (1997). *The East Asian version of whole-class teaching.* Albany, NY: State University of New York Press.

Stigler, J. W., Gonzales, P., Kawanaka, T., Knoll, S., & Serrano, A. (1999). *The TIMSS videotape classroom study: Methods and findings from an exploratory research project on eighth-grade mathematics instruction in Germany, Japan and the United States* (NCES, 99–074). Washington, DC: US Department of Education, National Center for Education Statistics.

Stigler, J. W., & Hiebert, J. (1999). *The teaching gap: Best ideas from the world's teachers for improving education in classroom.* New York: The Free Press.

Wenglinsky, H. (2000). *How teaching matters: Bringing the classroom back into the discussion about teacher quality.* Princeton, NJ: Educational Testing Service.

Yang, Y. (2009). English translation of antitheses in ancient Chinese poems [In Chinese: 古詩英譯中對偶的處理]. *Zhong Hua Xian Di Jiao Yu,* (39). Retrieved February 12, 2010, from ChinaQking journal database: http://www.chinaqking.com/%E5%8E%9F%E5%88%9B%E4%BD%9C%E5%93%81/2009/33261.html

Yu, Q. Y., & Li, X. L. (2006). A literature review on the relationship between Dui ou and Han culture [In Chinese:對偶與漢文化關係研究綜論]. *Journal of Shenyang Normal University (Social Science Edition),* 5(30).

Pakey Pui Man Chik
Faculty of Education
The Chinese University of Hong Kong

Ference Marton
Department of Education
University of Gothenburg

3. LEARNING TONES

"Two faces of variation" was the title of a paper presented by Marton and Pang at the 8th EARLI Conference in Gothenburg 1999. The paper pointed out the close relationship between two kinds of variations that have been central to Pheno-menography: one was central to Phenomenography in the earlier period of the 1970s and 80s and concerned the different ways of seeing the same thing, while the other was an important feature in the later period of the 1990s and concerned the variations (of the thing) the person experiences. In this chapter, we shall look at these two kinds of variations in relation to a widely acknowledged learning problem, namely, the problem that non-tonal language speakers have in learning lexical tones (in Cantonese). Furthermore, we shall also discuss the problem in light of the more recent works in Phenomenography in the 2000s dealing with the joint working of variation and invariance in learning.

VARIATIONS AND PHENOMENOGRAPHY

According to the paper "Two faces of variation", the first kind of variation studied in Phenomenography was the variation among different ways of seeing (or experiencing, understanding, conceptualizing, apprehending, etc) the same thing (by different persons or by the same person at different points in time). Describing such differences was what the term Phenomenography referred to when it was coined (Marton, 1981). In this initial stage, Phenomenography was entirely a descriptive undertaking, and the description was from the perspective of the researcher, with an underlying ambition to develop an epistemology without an ontological status.

On the basis of the study of variations of the first kind (between the different ways of seeing the same thing), Phenomenography then faced the need to explain "What makes a person experience a particular phenomenon in one way but not the other?" Obviously, the question could not be answered without relation to a theoretical perspective on the structure of awareness of the experiencer. The theoretical perspective taken could be called the "axiom of incompleteness". Were we (humans) capable of seeing (or experiencing, understanding, etc) all there was to see (or experience, understand, etc) of something, then we, all of us, would see the thing in the same way (Marton & Booth, 1997, p. 101). However, we cannot see all there is to be seen: when looking at something, we see certain aspects while failing to see others. Phenomenographic studies in the 1970s and 80s indicated that differ-ences between ways of seeing something can be described in terms of what (different) aspects of the thing are discerned and focused upon simultaneously by the experiencers.

F. Marton, S.K. Tse and W.M. Cheung (eds.), On the Learning of Chinese, 31–51.

So what does it take for an experiencer to see something in a certain way, or what does it take for him or her to see certain aspects of something and not others? The answer is formulated in terms of what we might call "the axiom of difference": Seeing a particular aspect of something amounts to seeing how that thing differs from other things in that particular respect. This means that in order to see that three things are <u>three</u> things (with 3 being an aspect that we are aware of), we must be aware that they are not 2 things, or 4, or 5. Seeing that something is green amounts to seeing that it is not red, or blue, or yellow. Seeing that a country is a democracy amounts to seeing that it is not a dictatorship or under colonial rule. In a world in which everything came in threes, three would not exist (nor would numbers); in a world which was completely green there would be no greenness to be seen (nor would there be colours); and in a world in which all countries were run in the same way, they all would be democracies, and hence there would be no democracy (nor ways of governing countries). People are only aware of aspects of things that they have experienced / are experiencing as variations. This is referred to in the paper "Two faces of variation" as the second kind of variation in Phenomenography – the experienced variations in the thing. Hence, differences between different ways of seeing something (the first kind of variation) can be explained in terms of the differences in what aspects of the object of experience that are being (or have been) experienced by the different experiencers (i.e. the differences in the second kind of variation). Such a relationship is mainly what the Theory of Variation (Marton & Pang, 1999; Pang, 2003) was first about.

On the basis of its descriptive and explanatory accounts of people's different ways of seeing the same thing Phenomenography then faces the question concerning pedagogy: "how can people be helped to learn to see things in new and more powerful ways", or in the language of Phenomenography, "how can people be helped to become able to discern and simultaneously attend to certain critical features (of the thing) that they have not been able to discern or attend to before?"

The challenging fact is that many common ways of seeing, like alternative conceptions, misconceptions, or preconceptions found in psychology and educational studies, although having faults and being less powerful, have repeatedly been shown to be robust and difficult to change. Why then is the existing conception or way of seeing often so difficult to be changed? From the perspective of Phenomenography just described, if variation is indeed the key to discernment and hence the way of seeing something, why is experiencing more instances of the thing though plain immersion often not conducive to the changing over to the more powerful way of seeing?

According to "the axiom of incompleteness" that we named, it is the varying aspect that warrants / attracts a person's attention, and hence, learners cannot possibly be aware of certain aspects of a thing if they have not experienced the variation of the thing with respect to those aspects. However, the converse is not necessarily true (that if a certain aspect of the thing varies, the learner will be aware of it). If indeed, every aspect of the thing varies at the same time in the learner's experience, with no aspects being held invariant (at least temporarily), then every aspect would always be competing for the learners' attention. All of them might attract some attention from the person, but none to a very strong degree. There will not be the differential focus of attention, nor the separation of the different aspects from each other; and not to mention the structuring of these aspects into the any kind of figure-and-ground or structural relationship. What is experienced by the learner is hence more likely a kind of variation among the different wholes (whole instances of the thing) and not much attention of the learner will be drawn to the individual aspects of the thing, including those critical aspects that the learner has NOT been able to discern or attend to before.

In view of this, Phenomenographic studies in the 2000s propose a theory of pedagogy in which variation and invariance work together to produce learning. At a particular stage of learning, we need variation as well as invariance among the learning instances to help in discerning differences, as well as the boundaries between differences. When one aspect changes while the other stay invariant, the aspects can be separated, and as the learner goes from one learning stage to another, there should also be the co-working of variation and invariance to provide reference points, structural relationships and continuity.

To summarize this section, we have briefly described the descriptive, explanatory and pedagogic faces of Phenomenography from the 1970s to the present, and how these different faces can all be dealt with in the same terms – all being about experiencing the variation and invariance of things along their different dimensions. In the remaining parts of the chapter, we will discuss the problem of tone learning from these perspectives of variation and invariance. We shall examine the qualitative differences between the ways of seeing of tonal and non-tonal language speakers, and how such differences can be related to the kinds of variations that the two groups of people have experienced among words in languages. Furthermore, we shall look into the question of why plain immersion is often not very effective for the learning of tones, and discuss how the pedagogy of variation and invariance may help to provide a better affordance for the learning of tones.

WHY CAN'T THEY HEAR THE TONE

Let us begin our discussion of tone learning with a comparatively simple context: We are observing a typical year 9 class in a small Hungarian town close to the Austrian border. The question is – what does it take for this particular group of students to be able to hear the tones in Chinese words?

Now, the teacher is talking about the Chinese language, one of her great interests after having spent 3 years in Hong Kong. (Here, the Chinese she refers to is actually Cantonese, a Chinese dialect commonly used in Hong Kong, and this dialect also has tones).

The teacher says, "Chinese is not an alphabetic language; there are no letters. They have characters instead, each one corresponding to a specific word meaning. Take [瞓], for instance. It means [sleep] and is pronounced /fan$_{33}$/. When I say /fan$_{33}$/ you can hear that I am uttering a special sound <u>and</u> a special tone. Chinese is a so-called tonal language: each word has both a particular sound and a particular tone.[1] The latter has to do with the frequency of the

33

sound, like in songs. The tone can be higher or lower; it may go up or down, etc. So here you can see the particular character, corresponding to a particular meaning, and it is read with a particular sound and tone, which you can hear.

The students object, however, "No, we can't hear any tone".

"That's curious" the teacher says. "OK, I'll give you some other examples: [斜] means [steep] and is pronounced /ce$_{33}$/; [厭] means [dislike] and is pronounced /jim$_{33}$/, and as I said earlier, [瞓] means [sleep] and is pronounced /fan$_{33}$/. These are three different words, corresponding to three different characters and pronounced with three different sounds. But the tone is the same as in my first example. Can you hear it now?"

"No, we can't hear any tone," the students insist. The teacher gets a little bit irritated. "You can't! But there is nothing wrong with your ears, I guess. Why can't you hear the tone?"

Yes, indeed, why can they not hear the tone? They are in fact not playing games with the teacher, nor do they have any problems with hearing in general. Their ears receive exactly the same audio stimulus as the teacher's ears, and the stimulus is relayed from the ears to areas of their brains where sound waves are interpreted. However, she hears the tone and the students do not. Why is it so?

Well, what does it take "to hear" a tone? The thing is that every Chinese word has a sound which is uttered with a certain tone, and just as you can utter different sounds with the same tone (as the teacher actually did just now), you can utter the same sound with different tones. In Cantonese (see above), you can utter a syllable sound with high even pitch, middle even pitch, low even pitch, high rising pitch, low rising pitch and low falling pitch (which can be represented respectively with the pitch level numbers as 55, 33, 22, 25, 23, 21). There are thus 6 tones in Cantonese. Words with the same sound but with different tones are completely different words with different meanings, and every sound may be combined with at most 6 different tones. So, for instance, [分] means [share] and is uttered as /fan$_{55}$/ with a high even tone; [墳] means [tomb] pronounced /fan$_{21}$/ with same sound, but with a low falling tone; and [瞓] means [sleep] again pronounced with the same sound, this time as / fan$_{33}$/ with a mid level tone. This means, in order to be able to understand the spoken Cantonese words, you need to hear the difference in tone. You need to discern this difference in tone, and combine it with the difference in sound in order to differentiating the meaning of the words.

So now what is the problem with these Hungarian year 9 students? Actually, it is not their problem. According to the Theory of Variation (the 'axiom of difference' mentioned earlier), in order to experience (or discern, become aware of, etc) X, the learner must experience ~X (not-X) instead of being exposed to X repeatedly. If this is correct, it is obviously not good enough for the students to have heard only words of the same tone (/ce$_{33}$/ and /jim$_{33}$/, which have the same tone as /fan$_{33}$/). All the words that the teacher said were with the same tone. She did not provide any difference. No, you must not only have heard the same tone; you must have heard the other tones so that you can notice the difference. Furthermore, by limiting the learning instances to the three words with the same tone, the discernment of tone is totally non-functional in their differentiation.

The teacher, instead of saying words with the same tone but with different sounds, could have said words with the same sound but with different tones. Then the students would surely have heard the tone. She could have said, for instance: [分], [墳] and [訓], all three words pronounced with the same sound but with different tones, each with its different meaning; then surely, the students would have noticed the difference and its significance? Hearing a tone amounts to hearing how it differs from other tones, and if you have only heard one tone, you cannot possibly hear how it differs from other tones. Hence, you cannot hear it at all.

LEARNING TONES IN HONG KONG

However, if you live in Hong Kong, you are exposed to Cantonese with its different tones all the time, together with its different sounds. Both tones and sounds vary, as well as the meanings of the words. Nevertheless, interestingly, the general experience is that it is almost impossible for non-tonal language speakers to learn the tones simply by being immersed in such everyday use of Cantonese.

If you are a speaker of a non-tonal language (such as English, German, French, Spanish, Italian, Russian, Hungarian, etc.), you will primarily notice the different meanings of the Cantonese words. Furthermore, you will in all likelihood link the word meanings with one kind of differences in the spoken words, the differences in sound, but NOT the differences in tone. This is so because you have learnt from your mother tongue what it takes to learn new words: you have to find out what they sound like (the consonants and vowels and how they are spelled) and what they mean, of course. This is the way you have learnt to perceive words in your mother tongue. However, in Cantonese, you need to learn to perceive words in a different way: you need to notice how the different words (for different meanings) differ in both sound and tone. Without this, you will never capture the Cantonese words.

The thing is that all peoples are bound to use differences in tones in their languages, but in what we call non-tonal languages, differences in tone are linked to differences in meaning at the sentence level: The intonational pattern of a question, for instance, differs from the intonational pattern of an exclamation. Psychoacoustic experiments have indicated that speakers of non-tonal languages are not less skilled in hearing differences in tone (Stagnay & Downs, 1993), it is just that they do not discern tone as an aspect of the word (Ki & Marton, 2003) and do not focus on it simultaneously with the sound in interpreting the word.

Then why is it almost impossible for non-tonal language speakers in Hong Kong to learn the new way of perceiving spoken words simply by being immersed in the everyday use of Chinese? In some experiments carried out by Ki and Marton (2003), it was shown that when both tones and sounds varied along with meanings, the foreign learners tended to focus on the variation in sounds (and meanings), basically neglecting the variations in tone among words. Also, more importantly, although this method of the foreign learner is not perfect, it does work in most everyday situations. Within a particular situation, there are often only a number of different words of special relevance to the situation, which the foreigner needs to distinguish. These words usually vary both in sounds and tones, and the approach of the foreigner to focusing only on the sounds of words would work, of course, if there are none, among these relevant words, that have the same sound but different tones. In such situations, tones are redundant and can be neglected. Features of words are there for the purpose of distinction, and in the development of language, redundant features tend to disappear while new distinguishing features are added. This is, at least, our reading of de Saussure (1983).

The problems of these foreign learners of Cantonese being unable to pick up tones become conspicuous mostly when the foreigners speak Cantonese. They may pronounce the right sound (consonant and vowel aspects) of a word but the tone of the word will vary according to the sentence level meaning. Then, unlike the case in English that a word with different intonations can still be recognised to be the same word, the native Cantonese speaker just cannot relate to the Cantonese word that the speaker means if it is said in a different tone. To these native ears, the difference in tone matters as much as the difference in consonants or vowels in spoken words – the difference in tone in Cantonese can amount to a gap as much as the difference between 'bit' and 'pit', or 'bit' and 'bat' in English. There is little association in meanings between Cantonese words of different tones. For example, as we have mentioned, /fan$_{55}$/ means [share] [分]; /fan$_{33}$/ means [sleep] [瞓]; and /fan$_{21}$/ means [tomb] [墳] in Cantonese. These spoken words have completely unrelated word meanings, and to the Cantonese listener, on hearing one meaning, there is typically no association he/she would make with the others. When he/she hears /fan$_{55}$/ (and gets the meaning [share]) it is highly unlikely to ring a bell that the speaker might have meant [sleep] or [tomb]. Hence, Cantonese speakers typically find the Cantonese spoken by these foreigners very difficult to understand, while the foreigners just cannot imagine why native speakers cannot understand what they are saying.

WAY OF SEEING AND THE SPACE OF VARIATION

You can say that the native speaker of Chinese and the intonation language speaker see (in a metaphorical sense) spoken words in different ways. The two different ways of seeing constitute a qualitative difference of the kind Phenomenography is intended to describe. Moreover, according to Phenomenography, such differences can be described in terms of what aspects of the thing are discerned and focused on simultaneously by the person.

When any person (of any language) says a word, he or she cannot possibly say it without uttering a particular sound with a particular tone. Thus, both kinds of physical qualities are there. Why, then, do tonal and non-tonal language speakers try to understand the word by discerning different aspects in what is heard? The reason is that the utterance is never heard in isolation. The purpose of the listener here is to identify the word amongst possible words in the experience of the person. It is in relation to this space of possibilities that the instance is perceived.

Tonal language speakers see both sound and tone as critical aspects in the spoken word, because to them, word identity varies according to both sound and tone. A word's particular sound and tone are both important for distinguishing the word among the many others in the space of possibilities. However, in the case of non-tonal language speakers, their space of possibilities for words is different; for them (as experienced in their mother tongue), words are only differentiated from one another by the sound aspect. They therefore contrast the sound of what is heard against the other possible word sounds they know, and leave out the aspect of tone. The tone, to them, belongs to the sentence or utterance (even if it is just a one-word utterance) and is just not a part of the pronunciation of the word. When the word meaning is attended to, the tone is filtered out.

The different ways of seeing can be characterised by what aspects of the thing (the word) are discerned and focused upon simultaneously by the person, and the aspects discerned depend on the dimensions of variations among the possible instances of things (possible words) that exist within the person's experience, against which the particular instance (the particular word) at hand is characterised. Paying attention to a certain aspect of a word amounts to paying attention to how this word differs from other words in this particular respect. Were there no such differences in this particular aspect among words in our experience, we would not discern the particular aspect, nor would the aspect warrant any of our attention.

In the case of the Hungarian classroom, the word instances in the students' experience are like SET A in Figure 3.1. One cannot discern tone if all the words

SET A – The set of words having different sounds with the same tone

Combinations	Sound 1	Sound 2	Sound 3	...	
Tone 1	Word A	Word B	Word C	Word D	...
Tone 2					
Tone 3					
...					

SET B – The set of words being diagonal combinations of tones and sounds

Combinations	Sound 1	Sound 2	Sound 3	...	
Tone 1		Word B		Word D	
Tone 2	Word F				Word J
Tone 3			Word M		
...					

SET C – The set of words being orthogonal combinations of tones and sounds

Combinations	Sound 1	Sound 2	Sound 3	...	
Tone 1	Word A	Word B	Word C	Word D	Word E
Tone 2	Word F	Word G	Word H	Word I	Word J
Tone 3	Word K	Word L	Word M	Word N	Word O
...	Word P	Word Q	Word R	Word S	Word T

Figure 3.1. Experiencing 3 different sets of words.

are of only one tone. In many everyday situations in Hong Kong, and in some experiments of Ki and Marton (2003), the instances that foreigners experience can be like SET B in Figure 3.1. As in this case there are no two words that have the same sound but different tones, the foreigners can continue to survive just by attending to sounds only and not the tone, as they always do in their mother tongue.

Then how about if the non-tonal language speaker is provided with a situation in which he/she has to distinguish a set of words like SET C – the orthogonal combination of different sounds and tones? Is he/she likely to change his/her way of perceiving Cantonese words by experiencing these word instances?

PILOT EXPERIMENT: TRYING WITH ORTHOGONAL COMBINATIONS

A simulation experiment was carried out to study empirically the effect of a learning situation like SET C. It used 9 Cantonese words, which were the orthogonal combinations of 3 tones (the High-level, Mid-level, and Low-falling tones) by 3 sounds (/fan/, /ce/, /jim/), all spoken by the same speaker.

A computer program was produced for non-tonal language speakers to learn these 9 Cantonese words. The subjects first read an English story which embodied 9 word meanings. Then they were provided with a training exercise on the spoken form of the 9 words in Cantonese. The interface of the training exercise is illustrated in Figure 3.2 below. Each item of the training task went as follows: The 9 cards on the right of the screen are the 9 words, with their locations randomised in every item. The subject could click on them to hear the 9 words as many times as he/she liked. Then the subject pressed a button to get a target word (appearing on the top left corner of the screen, with its meaning hidden). The subject could hear this target word as many times as he/she liked by clicking on it. The task was to identify which of the 9 words it was. Once the subject had heard the target word, he/she would not be able to hear the 9 words on the right. So, in order to do the matching, the subject had to rely on his/her knowledge about the association between the meanings and pronunciations of the 9 words. In cases where the subject chose a wrong card on the right, that mis-chosen card would display its meaning and play its pronunciation for comparison, so that the subject could learn from such a mistake. The subject was allowed a maximum of 2 attempts for every item before going onto the next item.

This program was meant to simulate the real life learning situation: the learner was aware of a number of words (meanings) relevant to the situation; the learner was first told the spoken forms of the words and their meanings; the learner then heard one of the words and guessed what it was; and then the learner received the feedback "Yes" or "No, this word (meaning) you have chosen actually should be pronounced like this ....". The learner was expected to learn from the comparison.

The exercise was tried with 4 university students with no prior knowledge of Cantonese. We first let the learner read a story (in English) to have a good idea about the meanings of the 9 words and the representation of their meanings (which were denoted by English translations and pictures) before they worked on the computer program.

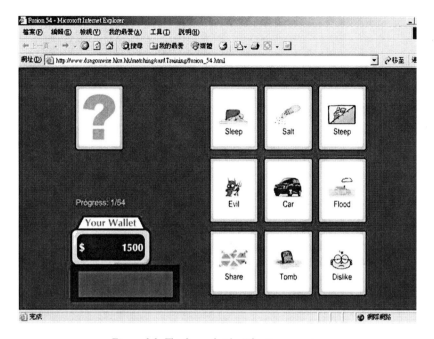

Figure 3.2. The 9 words identification exercise.

The overall observation was that the learning exercise was in fact very challenging and slightly frustrating for the subjects. The learners spent more than an hour laboriously on the program, and still the rate of getting their first choice correct was mostly only around 60%. Only one subject reached a level of around 80%. Their mistakes (confusion) were mostly in the tone. Some errors in sounds also appeared, though people may expect that the discernment of sounds should not be too difficult for them. Perhaps it may be that the subjects were quite overwhelmed by the amount of things to be attended to and remembered at the same time, and it might have been especially cognitively demanding when they needed to attend to tones and sounds which did not conventionally go together as one thing to be attended to or remembered.

The subjects reported that they were able to notice some variation in the pitch of the words, but the levels were not very distinct. Furthermore, the task was judged by all subjects to be very demanding in terms of memory and concentration.

The effect afforded by this set of learning instances of orthogonal combination did not seem satisfactory. It is interesting to note that the one subject who performed well actually used a very clever learning strategy. Before she drew the target word, she clicked on the 9 words to hear them in a special order – She tried to find three words which shared the same sound and clicked on them again to hear the different tones, and she repeated this with the other sounds. Hence, this subject, unlike the others, had taken the initiative to structure her learning experience instead of letting her experience go in random order across the 9 words.

Then why is the provision of these orthogonal combinations to the learner not working well? Do the combinations not provide the necessary variations to the learner for tone discernment and the development of simultaneous discernment and attention to tone and sound in the hearing of Cantonese words? Following are some possible explanations.

First, rote learning of the words without the discernment of key features underlying their differences does not lead to effective grasp of the words. Let us assume the repeated random exposure and comparison provided in the program eventually makes a subject develop some holistic impressions of the 9 words and their pair-wise differences. According to the argument of Jakobson (1961) this will not lead to an effective perception of the words. Because when the subject is asked to identify a given word, he/she would need to do 9 comparisons against the 9 candidates. In contrast, if the subject is able to extract the key features of tone and sound, he/she would only need to do 3 tone comparisons and 3 sound comparisons.

Secondly, the discernment of tone feature is not well supported by the exercise. Randomly encountering 2 of the 9 words which are different in tone is not good enough. The learner needs the simultaneous awareness of certain words which have a special kind of relationship – the words are similar in all other respects and only differ in their tone. These words need to be experienced close to each other in time, and this simultaneity is especially important here because memory tends to be very short when people come to learn a new domain.

Furthermore, the learning of the 3 contrastive values along the tone dimension also imposes a further requirement on simultaneity. Here, there are 3 tones, the high level, middle level, and low level tones. In order to perceive the tone values correctly, we need the presence of all 3 of them (with the same sound) as close as possible in time. Otherwise, if there is only the contrast between the high and middle tones, then the two tones could be wrongly perceived as a high tone and a low tone, or the middle tone and low tones.

In other words, just providing the 3 tones x 3 sounds orthogonal combinations (the 9 words) without providing the right simultaneity structure (appropriate grouping and sequencing of these learning instances) in experiencing them is not good enough. Very often, words will be learnt without the immediate presence of the right cont-rastive instances, and the tonal aspect of the words will not be made salient when they are learnt. In the end, most of the words may be learnt without a clear and correct tone quality. If this is the case, then although the set of words are intended by the teachers to be distinct orthogonal combinations of tones and sounds, what the learner experiences may be something quite different – a lot of the words may just appear be homophones and hence non-contrastive to the learner.

EXPERIMENT 1: SEPARATION OF THE TONE DIMENSION WITH THE CO-WORKING OF VARIATION AND INVARIANCE

Development research indicates that infants less than one year old can discern various contrasts in speech sounds, which are quite universal and include contrasts that are not used in their mother tongues. However, as they grow older, they learn to attend to those contrasts that are used for meaning differentiation in their mother tongues and neglect those which are not. Documentary evidence exists showing that the same applies to the use or non-use of tone contrast for word meaning differentiation (Halliday, 1975). It is with more experience in their non-tonal mother tongues that infants learn not to discern tones as a part of word.

So what can we do in order to help non-tonal language speakers to relearn this way of seeing? We need to create a situation in which they must distinguish between word meanings by means of differences in tones. This situation only occurs when they encounter different words all with the same sound and differing only in the tones. This, interestingly, is not just about variation; it is a combination of variation and invariance. Putting the learner into this situation can only have two results: either they fail to learn to distinguish the words, showing that acculturation in the mother tongue might have led to a permanent loss of the capability in processing tones of words; or they succeed, and demonstrate a new way of hearing words.

A learning experiment was carried out to study empirically the effect of such a situation (Ki & Marton, 2003). It used the 9 Cantonese words, which were the orthogonal combinations of 3 tones (the High-level, Mid-level, and Low-falling tones) by 3 sounds, which had been used in the pilot experiment just described. In this experiment, the 9 words were learnt 3 at a time. A computer program provided an interactive matching exercise for the subjects to learn 3 words in relation to one other with close simultaneity. With each group of 3 words, the matching activities were carried out in 4 different situations as illustrated and explained in the Figure 3.3 below. In all 4 situations, the user's task was the same: to match one of the top cards to the bottom card, but the conditions of the 4 situations were different so as to provide gradual steps for the learner to learn the right association between the 3 word meanings (represented by picture and English text on the 'card' on the screen) and the 3 pronunciations. In the two earlier situations, the subjects could do the matching simply by direct comparing what they heard (when they clicked on the cards), but in the two later situations, they would need to remember the spoken forms of the 3 words, and their association with the 3 word meanings to accomplish the task. The matching exercise was carried out for all 4 situations with one group of 3 words, before moving onto another group of 3 words. The learning exercise had altogether 144 items to cover the 9 words in 3 groups.

The grouping of the same 9 words was done in two different ways to provide two tone learning conditions: In one condition (good learning condition), the 3 words to be learnt at the same time shared the same sound, but had different tones; and in the other condition (poor learning condition) the 3 words to be learnt at the same time shared the same tone but had different sounds. Two groups of 8 subjects learnt the same 9 words under the two different conditions. All subjects were university exchange students newly arrived in Hong Kong, with no prior knowledge of Cantonese or any tonal languages. They generally did not find the exercise difficult. The exercise typically took the subjects about 45 minutes to finish.

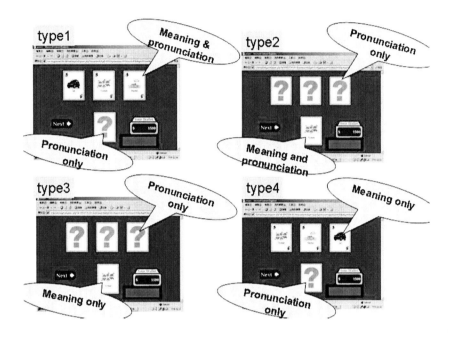

Figure 3.3. The 4 types of situations in the 3-words matching exercise.

Explanatory Note: Type 1 situation: The top cards, besides displaying the meanings of the words (picture and English text), would also sound the pronunciations of the words when the user moved the mouse over them. The bottom card would sound the pronunciation of a word when the user moved the mouse over it, but the meaning was not shown. Type 2 situation: The top cards would sound the pronunciations of the words when the user moved the mouse over them. The bottom card, besides displaying the meaning of a word, also would sound its pronunciation when the user moved the mouse over it. Type 3 situation: The top cards showed no pictures or text of the word meanings. They only sounded the pronunciation of the words when the user moved the mouse over them. The bottom card displayed the meaning of a word, but did not give the sound of the word. Type 4 situation: The top cards displayed the meanings of the words (pictures and English text), but did not give the sounds of the words. The bottom card showed no picture or text of the word meaning. It only sounded the pronunciation of the word when the user moved the mouse over it.

Post-test was then used to test how well the subject could remember the tone and sound aspects of the 9 words – The subjects were given the word meaning (a picture with English text, identical to what had been used in the training) and then a spoken word, and were asked to decide whether the latter correctly matched the former. The computer interface of the test is given in Figure 3.4. Table 3.1 is a summary of the results.

The results indicated that the ways of seeing of these non-tonal speaker subjects could easily be modified according to the variation and invariance pattern among the words to be learnt and distinguished at the same time.

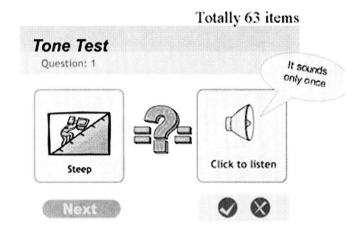

Figure 3.4. Interface of the post-test.

Table 3.1. Post-test performance of the 2 groups of subjects

	Average percentage of correct responses in different types of post-test items in which the pictures matched with ...			
Learning conditions	Right sounds and right tones (18 items)	Right sounds and wrong tones (18 items)	Wrong sounds and right tones (18 items)	Wrong sounds and wrong tones (9 items)
'good learning condition' Variation in Tone and invariance in sound	85%	**85%**	79%	94%
'poor learning condition' Invariance in Tone and Variation in sound	85%	56%	**97%**	97%
Sig. level indicated by t-test on the difference of means of the 2 groups, each with 8 subjects	0.92	**0.03**	**0.01**	0.31

On the <u>post-test items in which both tone and sound of the word were right</u> (the first column in the table), the two groups did equally well. Of course, for these items, there would not be any difference in performance between someone who could remember the right tone and someone who could not remember any tone at all. Their performance, however, would differ on the post-test items, in which the words had the right sounds, but the wrong tones. Indeed, the results on these items (the second column of the table) indicated that such a significant difference in performance existed between the two groups. For the 'poor learning condition' group, the average correct rate was 56%, which was quite close to 50%, the level people could attain by mere chance. In contrast, the 'good learning condition' group was able to notice on average 85% of these mismatches in tone.

More importantly, further experiments indicated that after having worked under the 'good learning condition' for the 9 words, some transfer effect could be observed when the subjects came to work on the second round of the experiment, in which they learnt another 9 words (which were the orthogonal combination of the same 3 tones, but other different 3 sounds) under the 'poor learning condition'. Their average correct response rate in noticing tone mismatch in the post-test (for items in which the sounds of the words were right, but the tones were wrong) was 76%. Although it was lower than the 85% correct rate mentioned above that they achieved under the 'good learning condition', it was still much higher than 50%, and the level one could get by chance. This indicated that once the subjects were sensitized to the relationship between tone and word meaning, they began to pay attention to the tones of words on learning them, even if the grouping of the words did not make it immediately necessary. This is really an encouraging result – one can make a qualitative change in one's way of seeing within less than an hour of training!

BEYOND THE SEPARATION OF TONE

In the above discussion, we have mainly talked about the importance of separation in learning, and that the variation in tone and invariance in the other aspects (among the words to be learnt at one time) can work together to produce a powerful effect for the perceptual separation of the tone aspect from the spoken words. However, we would argue that there might be a number of other variation and invariance patterns in the 'good learning condition' that might have contributed to the strong learning effect.

In most cases, qualitative changes in people's way of seeing things involve the breaking of old connections and the creation of new ones. Under the 'good learning condition'), the learning was not just about the separation of tones from what was heard. It was also about breaking the learner's conventional connection between tone and sentence level meaning – under this learning condition, tone varied, but obviously, there was no variation in sentence level meaning; hence, the tone became separated from the sentence level meaning. Simultaneous to this separation, there was the creation of the new connection of tones to word level meanings, which was abnormal to these learners. How was that connection made? The Theory of Variation suggests that the aspect that varies enters into the person's focal awareness; and when several aspects are varying at the same time, all the varying aspects will enter into the person's focal awareness, and the effect can be a perceptual fusion of these aspects (as connected aspects belonging to the same overall thing or phenomenon).

Under the 'good learning condition', when tone varied, there was simultaneous co-variation in word meanings, and the two aspects (tone and word meaning) would therefore be attended to at the same time and became perceptually fused (linked) to each other.

Another important thing that happened was about <u>the contrastive relation between the different tones and its generalisation to new words</u> (with different sounds). Under the 'good learning condition', the learner experienced the contrast of the 3 tones (the variation in value along the tonal dimension) in the context of one sound among the first group of words. Then, the learner experienced the same contrast in the context of another sound with the second group of 3 words, and so on. Here, with the same contrast occurring in the different contexts, the learner was afforded the opportunity to learn the contrastive pattern as something generalisable into other sound contexts, and indeed the transfer was observed in the second round of the experiment.

ATTENDING TO BOTH TONE AND SOUND

Interestingly, the results of Experiment 1 also indicated that awareness of the sound dimension was also affected by the pattern of variation and invariance. The subjects under the 'good learning condition' were only able to only notice 79% of the sound mismatches as compared to 97% in the 'poor learning condition' group.

One interpretation could be that it was a kind of 'mutual inhibition' (similar to what we have already discussed in the pilot experiment): to these non-tonal language speakers, tone and sound were conventionally aspects pointing to meanings of different kinds, and hence the non-tonal language speakers felt it difficult or unnatural to attend to these aspects simultaneously as one kind (pointing together towards one things – the word meaning). In their mother tongue, sound belongs to word level meaning, while tone belongs to sentence level meaning. When you reach for the word level meaning, the sound comes to the foreground and the tone recedes to the background; and when you reach for the sentence level meaning, the tone comes to the foreground and the sound recedes to the background. Although the learner can switch instantly between the two meanings (sentence and word), and combine the two to get the overall message, the two still belong to different basic 'meaning slots', not to be pressed into one. They are not like consonants and vowels, which can be put together on the same level.[2]

The lack of fusion between tone and sound among non-tonal language speakers in their learning of Cantonese words was first observed in Ki & Marton (2003). In their study, 4 non-tonal language speakers had already been trained to distinguish the 6 tones of Cantonese. They were trained with one sound after another. For each sound, they were trained to discriminate and to identify the 6 tones. They first worked with the 2 tones furthest apart, and then other intermediate tones were added gradually. In the end, after about 12 hours of training, they were able to distinguish the different tones. In addition, when given a sound with the high level tone, they were able to produce the other tones by themselves. These results all seemed very pleasing. However, on one simple post-test task, it was incidentally revealed that their structural relationship between tone and sound was still fundamentally different from that of native Cantonese speakers – of the 4 subjects, 3 still had the tone and sound unconnected in their consciousness.

The post-test task went as follows. The researcher said two words, one following the other, and the subject was asked to make two utterances: first to copy the two words, and then to swap the two words around in order. It was found that 3 of the 4 subjects just swapped the sounds around, but left the tones as they were, with the result that the 2 words were broken up and became completely changed (in meaning). Interestingly, rarely were we able to we find a native Cantonese who could do this separation – to them the tone and sound are joined together tightly as the integral unit of the spoken word. Even more interesting is that on hearing the audio recording of the speech (the erroneous production made by the subjects), not even one native Cantonese speaker was able to notice that the overall tonal pattern across the two words (i.e. the tune across the two words) remained the same. The native speakers simply could not see the overall tune across the two words! Their perception of tone (pitch) co-terminates with the word and is totally fused into the word. It was only when the researcher substituted all the sounds with 'aa' while keeping the tones untouched, did the native ears then began to hear the overall invariance in the tune.

We believe that the tight fusion of the tone and sound as one thing is crucial for efficient operation of the Cantonese language. It is a fusion of the two into an entity – zi-yin (字音), pronunciation of the monosyllabic Cantonese word. This Zi-yin which forms the basic unit used to generate the whole spoken language of Cantonese. The Zi-yin has to be a robust unit for flexible and efficient constructions, and one cannot afford to allow the tone and sound of this basic unit to fall apart easily and for the Zi-yin to be mutated.

Hence, in order that the learner can really learn to make use of tone, just learning to discern tones and sounds is not enough, the learner must move on – to develop the capability to discern and attend simultaneously to both the tone and sound aspects and to fuse the two aspects into one in looking for word meanings. To develop this capability, the Theory of Variation predicts that it is necessary for the learner to experience the simultaneous variation of tone and sound; and that brings us back to the orthogonal combinations we discussed earlier on. Paradoxically, though orthogonal combinations are not suitable when the learner has yet learnt to discern tone as a salient feature of the spoken word and the connection of tone to word meaning, they are highly useful for affording this later stage learning.

EXPERIMENT 2: SEPARATION-THEN-FUSION

One further experiment was therefore carried out to explore the effect of a two-stage learning model. Stage 1 was concerned with the separation of tones and their fusion with word meanings; and Stage 2 was concerned with the fusion of tones and sounds and word meanings (Ki, Ahlberg & Marton, 2006). The experiment was carried out with 20 Swedish university students with no prior knowledge of Cantonese – 10 were in the experimental group, and 10 were in the control group.

They all learnt the same 9 words used in Experiment 1 reported above. It generally took the subjects 60 to 90 minutes to go through the two stages of learning.

Stage 1: The subjects learnt 3 words at a time with a matching exercise on the computer. The form of the exercise was same as the one used in Experiment 1 reported above, but the number of items was reduced to 54. For the experimental group subjects, words were grouped for the separation of tones (The 3 words to be learnt at the same time had the same sound, but different tones, as in the 'good learning condition' in Experiment 1). For the control group subjects, the 3 words were grouped to create a 'neutral learning condition' – under this condition all words to be learnt at the same time had different tones and different sounds. Therefore, the subjects were free to choose to attend to tone or sound. Either way would be sufficient for distinguishing the 3 words. After learning a group of 3 words, the exercise was repeated with another group of 3, and then still another group of 3 to cover all the 9 words.

Stage 2: Both experimental and control group subjects came to do the same Stage 2 exercise – the 'Fusion Exercise'. This was an identification exercise on the computer, the same as the one in the Pilot Experiment reported above. The exercise involved the same 9 words as in Stage 1, but now the subjects had to handle the 9 words all at the same time and hence, had to pay attention to both tone and sound in order to distinguish the words. The identification exercise had 54 items.

The learning outcome of the two groups of subjects was examined on the basis of how accurate they were in their in their identification of the words on their first attempts for every item of the Fusion Exercise in Stage 2. There are 54 items in the Exercise, and the table below shows the performance of the subjects.

As a whole, both groups in the end were able to distinguish the 9 Cantonese spoken words above chance level after the training (by mere chance, the percentage of correct identification should be around $1/9=11\%$). However, the effectiveness of the training in the control group did not appear to be encouraging: they learnt 9 words for more than an hour, yet only slightly more than half of the words they identified were correct. The results also indicated a significant advantage of the experimental group treatment over the control group (Table 3.2). With the first half of Second Training program

Table 3.2. Performance of subjects in the fusion exercise of experiment 2

	No. of items answered correctly on the 1st attempt ...	
	for items 1 to 27 of the 'fusion exercise'	for items 28 to 54 of the 'fusion exercise'
Experimental group average	17.5 (65%)	20.6 (78%)
Control group average	12.6 (47%)	15.6 (56%)
Level of significance (t-test for difference between the group averages)	p<0.02	p<0.04

questions, the experimental group already achieved better than the control group, and this lead was maintained throughout the latter half of questions in the program.

The results are in total agreement with the prediction of the Theory of Variation. For the experimental group, the training was designed first to help learners discern the tone aspects in Cantonese spoken words through variation of the tone whilst holding the other aspects invariant, together with the co-variation of word meaning. This choice (of tone and not sound) was made as it was presumed that the subjects were already accustomed to experiencing words based on sound variations, it was the discernment of tone which was difficult for them in learning Cantonese words. The results indicated that the greater ability to discern tone developed in this early part of the training then benefited the experimental group subjects more than the control group in their subsequent training, when they had to attend to both the tone and sound aspects simultaneously in forming an integrated perception of the spoken words that points to the different word meanings. Looking at it the other way round, the results indicates the difficulty of the control group in developing an effective grasp of the Cantonese syllables when all aspects kept varying all the time. Without a proper structuring of the variation and invariance, boundaries between aspects could not be established, and simply having repeated exposure or immersion into the undifferentiated wholes did not lead to very effective learning of the wholes.

Ki (2007) repeated the experimental group treatment in Experiment 2 with 99 native English language teachers in Hong Kong schools. These teachers generally knew some Cantonese words, but they all felt the mastering of tones to be very difficult. Results indicated that after the same such separation-then-fusion training as described above, the subjects' were able to identify the 9 words correctly 89% of the time. More importantly, after such training the subjects were able to display quite good transfer to perceiving these Cantonese words (both in terms of their sounds and tones) when they appeared as constituting units in bi-syllabic compound words. This kind of perception task has generally been experienced as extremely hard, but the subjects were able to reach an average correct identification rate of around 70% after the separation-then-fusion exercise, before they received any further training in the bisyllabic contexts.

SUMMARY

To summarize, so far we have described the qualitative difference in how spoken Cantonese words are "seen" by native speakers and by speakers of non-tonal languages, and how the difference can be characterized in terms of what aspects of the spoken words are discerned and focused on simultaneously. Furthermore, we have also pointed out that each of these discerned and attended aspects correspond to a dimension of variation in the space of possible words that was experienced by the two groups of people (as illustrated diagrammatically in Figure 3.5(a)). This is thus an example of how the different ways of seeing the same thing can originate from the variations they experience.

Then we come to explore the question of pedagogy – How can non-tonal language speakers be helped to see spoken words in the new way. In answer to this, we have also pointed out that simply immersing non-tonal language speakers into the variation pattern that the native Cantonese speaker experiences (as listed in the bottom row of Figure 3.5(a)) does not readily help the discernment of tone. Variation and invariance have to work together to separate dimensions of variations which the learner has not been originally aware of. The discussion points to the need for a 'separation' stage (Stage 1) at the beginning, when the tones vary among the learning instances and become discerned, separated from sounds (which are hold invariant), and linked to the variation in meanings, before the 'fusion' stage (Stage 2), when tones, sounds and meanings vary all at the same time (Figure 3.5(b)). It is interesting to note that for the case of tone learning, the same framework of dimensions of variation (the patterns of variation and invariance in the dimensions) can be used for describing the different ways of seeing as well as the design of learning experiences.

Finally, we wish to highlight one subtle but major characteristics of the research described in the chapter. All along this research, the learners were learning Cantonese words and tone was learnt as something for the identification of the word meaning. This contrasts against that most other researchers working on the topic of tone learning have focused on training subjects to perceive the particular tones of Chinese, in anticipation that these subjects would transfer this knowledge of tones (or apply what they have learnt) to their future learning of Chinese words. In such kind of training experiments, the subjects were typically asked to respond by saying whether they had heard Tone 1 or Tone 2 and so on (or High-level tone, rising tone, etc). In contrast, the experiments described in this chapter have their unique characteristics – all the time the learner is learning to differentiate Cantonese words – The instruction emphasize how the aspects of what is heard relate to what is meant. This is because we think it is this relation that has caused the problem – non-tonal language speakers conventionally relate tone in what they hear to the sentence and

	the variations experienced among different words		
	Sound	Tone	Meaning
Speakers of non-tonal languages	V	–	V
Native speakers	V	V	V

Figure 3.5 (a) A dimension of variation experienced among different words.

	Variation/invariance of aspects among the learning instances provided to the learners		
	Sound	Tone	Meaning
Stage (1)	I	V	V
Stage (2)	V	V	V

Figure 3.5 (b) Variation and invariance of aspects among the learning instances.

not the word level meaning. Therefore, we need to change their ways of seeing words, and we change their way of seeing a word (in terms of what aspects are being foregrounded or suppressed in hearing for the word meaning) through the simultaneous presence of other words. The variation and invariance among these words can afford a change in how the learner sees them, and such a change is precisely what we tried to bring about.

NOTES

[1] In this chapter, the word 'sound' is used to refer to the segmental pattern, i.e., the consonant and vowel pattern, of a spoken word; and 'tone' the pitch pattern of the spoken word.

[2] Another interpretation could be labeled as the law of 'conservation of attention': under this 'good learning condition', when the words all had the same sound, but different tones, the difference in tone was functional in distinguishing the words, but the sound was not. Moreover, attention is like a limited resource; when attention was allocated to the functional aspect (tone) that varied, less attention was given to the other aspect that was invariant (sound) (although the subjects still paid some attention to it as they conventionally did). This interpretation could also be a reasonable one when a learner comes to handle a new situation and gets overwhelmed.

ACKNOWLEDGEMENT

The authors acknowledge the important contribution of Professor Amy Tsui and Professor K.K. Luke in providing their insights for the research, Dr Ho-cheong Lam, Mr Anthony Lai and Mr Samson Lai in producing the computer programs, and Dr Kristina Ahlberg and Mr Eddie Lau in operating many parts of the experiments.

REFERENCES

De Saussure, F., et al. (1983). *Course in general linguistics.* Originally published: London, UK: G. Duckworth, 1983. Translation reprinted by Open Court Publishing, 1986.

Halliday, M. A. K. (1975). *Learning how to mean: Explorations in the development of language.* Baltimore, UK: Edward Arnold.

Jakobson, R. (1961). *Structure of language and its mathematical aspects.* Providence, RI: American Mathematical Society Bookstore.

Ki, W., & Marton, F. (2003). *Learning Cantonese tones.* Paper presented at EARLI 2003: 10th European conference for research on learning and instruction: Biennial meeting. Padova, Italy: European Association for Research on Learning and Instruction.

Ki, W. (2007). *The enigma of Cantonese tones: how intonation language speakers can be assisted to discern them.* Unpublished PhD thesis. Hong Kong: The University of Hong Kong.

Ki, W., Ahlberg, K., & Marton, F. (2006). *Computer-assisted perceptual learning of Cantonese tones.* Paper presented at ICCE 2006: 14th International conference on computers in education. Beijing, China: Asia-Pacific Society for Computers in Education (APSCE).

Marton, F., & Booth, S. (1997) *Learning and awareness.* Hillsdale, NJ: Lawrence Erlbaum Ass.

Marton, F. (1981). Phenomenography—Describing conceptions of the world around us. *Instructional Science, 10*(2), 177–200.

Marton, F., & Pang, M. F. (1999). *Two faces of variation.* Paper presented at EARLI 1999: 8th European conference for research on learning and instruction: Biennial meeting. Goteborg, Sweden: European Association for Research on Learning and Instruction.

Pang, M. F. (2003). Two faces of variation: on continuity in the phenomenographic movement. *Scandinavian Journal of Educational Research, 47*(2), 145–156.

Stagnay, J. R., & Downs, D. (1993). Differential sensitivity for frequency among speakers of a tone and a nontone language. *Journal of Chinese Linguistics, 21*(1), 143–163.

Wing Wah Ki and Ming Fai Pang
Faculty of Education
The University of Hong Kong

Ference Marton
Department of Education
University of Gothenburg

HO CHEONG LAM

4. ORTHOGRAPHIC AWARENESS

In this chapter, I discuss a theoretical framework for investigating the teaching of Chinese characters, which draws mainly on the theory of learning proposed by phenomenographic studies of learning (See Chapter Two; Marton, 1981, 1988a, 1988b; Marton & Booth, 1997; Marton, et al., 2004; Marton & Pang, 2006).

In brief, the aim of phenomenographic studies is to find out the qualitatively different ways in which people experience or think about a phenomenon and to find out how to change their way of experiencing the phenomenon. Thus of particular interest here is the central question of how children experience the reading of Chinese characters (i.e. the phenomenon) and how to develop or contribute to developing their way of reading the characters.

To this end, I draw on the Theory of Variation, which emerged from Marton's phenomenographic studies. According to this theory, in order to experience the characters in a powerful way, children need to develop a structure of awareness, i.e. to direct their focal attention to certain critical aspects of the characters and to be simultaneously aware of them. By "critical aspects," I mean aspects that are essential for children to fully understand the characters. It also means that children do not focus their attention on aspects of the characters that are not essential or irrelevant to their understanding, for example, the size of the characters.

Since the experience of reading the characters primarily has to do with the written form and not the spoken form of Chinese words, aspects that are important here are basically orthographic in nature, i.e. those aspects in the written form 媽 maa1 [1] that signify its connection to the lexicon of 'mother.' For this reason, I proposed the term orthographic awareness in the current theoretical framework (Lam, 2006, pp. 46–70).

The next chapter, Chapter Five, is also going to discuss another approach of teaching Chinese characters as inspired by the phenomenographic theory of learning, which also sees learning to proceed as an increased differentiation of the understanding of a whole. But, a whole in that chapter often refers to something larger than the unit of a character, for example, a whole lesson or a whole text as analysed in the sample lesson to be mentioned in the chapter. In contrast, this chapter differs from Chapter Five in referring a whole only to the unit of a character. Thus, in this chapter, I am going to discuss how to help children to learn certain orthographic aspects of the characters, while Chapter Five will look at a bigger picture of analysing a whole lesson for teaching the characters.

In the rest of the chapter, I shall first present a linguistic analysis of the characteristics of Chinese characters. Next, the various orthographic aspects that children

F. Marton, S.K. Tse and W. M.Cheung (eds.), On the Learning of Chinese, 53–73.
© 2010 Sense Publishers. All rights reserved.

need to be aware of in learning the characters will be discussed, which is followed by a discussion on how we can possibly bring about such orthographic awareness in teaching the characters to children.

LINGUISTIC ANALYSIS OF CHINESE CHARACTERS

Semantic radical versus phonetic radical. The overwhelming majority of Chinese characters (about 90%) fall into the category of semantic-phonetic characters (形聲字 in Chinese; Li, 1986, p. 21)[2]. These characters are made up of one semantic radical (義符) and one phonetic radical (聲符)[3, 4], which respectively contribute to the meanings and sounds of the characters. For example, the characters 榕 jung4 'banyan,' 根 gan1 'root,' 椰 je4 'coconut' and 柴 caai4 'firewood,' sharing the same semantic radical 木 'tree,' are all associated with the meaning of 'tree.' Similar to this, all of the characters 嗎 maa1 'an indicator of a question,' 媽 maa1 'mother,' 螞 maa5 'ant' and 罵 maa6 'to scold' share the common phonetic radical 馬 maa5 'horse,' and their sounds are close to each other.

Functioning position. Certain components can only function as a semantic radical at their specific functioning position in a character. For example, when the character 木 muk6 'tree' is used as a semantic radical, it should be located either on the left of those characters with a left-right configuration (e.g., the 木 in 榕 jung4 'banyan'), or at the bottom of a top-bottom configured character (e.g., the 木 in 柴 caai4 'firewood;' See Liang, 1959, pp. 139–141; Chiu, 1995, pp. 278–280). But when located elsewhere, the 木 stops functioning as a semantic radical. For example, the 木 muk6 in 沐 muk6 'bath' only functions as a phonetic radical to the character. As another example, the character 鳥 niu5 'bird' can only function as a semantic radical on the right such as in the characters 鴨 aap3 'duck,' 鵝 ngo4 'goose,' 鴿 gap3 'pigeon' and 鴉 aa1 'crow.' In these characters, the components on the left, namely, 甲 gaap3, 我 ngo5, 合 hap6 and 牙 ngaa4, function as a phonetic radical.

Hierarchical analysis. Of particular importance is that some phonetic radicals are themselves compound characters, which consist of two or even more components (Gao, 1996, pp. 51–52). For example, the character 淅 sik1 'the sound of raining' has the phonetic radical 析 sik1, which as a character (i.e. 析 sik1 'to analyze') is made up of the two components – 木 'tree' and 斤 'axe'[5]. As another example, the character 照 ziu3 'to shine' has the phonetic radical 昭 ciu1. The 昭, as a character 昭 ciu1 'to make clear,' has the phonetic radical 召 ziu6. The character 召 ziu6 'to invite' in turn consists of 刀 'knife' and 口 'mouth.' In this case, the characters can be analyzed into a hierarchy as shown in Figure 4.1 below, which is in fact in congruent with the historical development of the characters from their components (Wang, 2002, pp. 44–48; Wang & Zou, 1999, pp. 103–104).[6, 7]

Figure 4.1. Hierarchical analysis of the characters 媽 maa1 'mother,' 淅 sik1 'the sound of raining' and 照 ziu3 'to shine'.

Such analysis of the characters is different from the conventional approach of categorizing the characters into certain typical configurations (Fu, 1999, p. 65; 1993, pp. 108–113; Gao, et al., 1993, pp. 60–61; Liang, 1959, pp. 85–87; See Figure 4.2 from Ki et al. (1994) as an example). In this conventional approach, the historical development of the characters is neglected and the characters are merely treated as a flat plane structure. As such, the previous characters 淅 sik1 'the sound of raining' and 照 ziu3 'to shine' will just be considered as nothing more than having the same configuration as the characters 街 gaai1 'street' and 忘 mong4 'to forget' as indicated in Figure 4.2 below. However, the historical analysis of the characters 街 and 忘 (analyzed as 行 hang4 'to walk' and 圭 gwai1 'a piece of jade,' and as 心 'feeling' and 亡 mong4 'to lose' respectively) actually differ greatly from that of the two characters 淅 and 照.

Figure 4.2. Fifteen typical configurations of the characters.

Constituent component versus sub-component. As mentioned above, some characters such as 淅 sik1 'the sound of raining' and 照 ziu3 'to shine' can be analyzed into a hierarchical structure with several levels. Components at different levels in a character actually take on completely different functions with regard to their constituency to the character (See Halliday, 1994, pp. 3–36; 1961; Eggins, 1994, pp. 114–145 for the idea of constituency). For example, the 氵 'water' in the character 淅 constitutes the character meaning while the 木 in the middle is only part of 析 sik1 and has nothing to do with the whole character 淅 sik1 'the sound of raining.' A distinction is made here between these two types of functionally different components, i.e., those constitute the characters (called constituent components) versus those do not (called sub-components). Thus, both the 氵 'water' and the 析 sik1 in the character 淅 sik1 'the sound of raining' are constituent components while the 木 and 斤 are sub-components. Notice that this constituency of a component does not solely depend on the component itself but is about the relation between the component and the character. For example, 木 is a sub-component in the character 淅 sik1 'the sound of raining' but the same 木 'tree' is a constituent component in the character 椰 je4 'coconut.'

Put more explicitly, constituent components contribute to either the meanings or the sounds of the characters. Accordingly, the 氵 'water' in the character 淅 sik1 'the sound of raining' is said to function[8] as a semantic radical while the 析 sik1 functions as a phonetic radical to the character. Constituent components are similar to the morphemes in English words in the sense that they are the atoms with which the characters are built. But, different from the morphemes, some constituent components purely function as phonetic radicals and in no way contribute to the meanings of the characters. For example, the meaning of the constituent component 析 sik1 'to analyze' as a character cannot be broken down from the meaning of the character 淅 sik1 'the sound of raining.' Thus, the components in the characters are organized around not only the meaning but also the sound.[9]

Rank shift. Now we have set up a rank of scale, i.e., characters are composed of constituent components, which are in turn composed of sub-components. Thus a larger unit is made up of one or more smaller units. For example, the character 淅 sik1 'the sound of raining' is composed of the two constituent components 氵 'water' and 析 sik1, the latter of which is in turn composed of two sub-components 木 and 斤, as diagrammed in Figure 4.3 below.

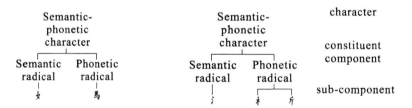

Figure 4.3. Analysis of semantic-phonetic characters 媽 maa1 'mother' and 淅 sik1 'the sound of raining'.

When a unit of a given rank functions as a unit in the next rank down, changes occur in the unit. This is called rank-shifted (Halliday, 1994, p. 188; Eggins, 1994, pp. 135–138). For example, when the characters 女 neoi5 'female' and 馬 maa5 'horse' become the constituent components of the character 媽 maa1 'mother,' the 女 loses its sound neoi5 while the 馬 loses its meaning 'horse.' In another example of the character 淅 sik1 'the sound of raining,' the character 木 'tree' muk6 first loses its sound muk6 as a constituent component in the character 析 sik1 'to analyze,' then further loses its meaning 'tree' as a sub-component in 淅 sik1 'the sound of raining.' Thus neither the sound muk6 nor the meaning 'tree' of the character 木 is related to those of the character 淅 sik1 'the sound of raining.'

Opaque constituency.   Some constituent components may appear to be unrelated to both the sounds and the meanings of the characters, for example, the constituent component 金 'metal'[10] in the character 錯 co3 'error.' This is due to historical changes, which have caused the constituent functions of the components to become opaque, i.e. not transparent. Though the character 錯 is now commonly used to mean 'error,' it still has the 金 'metal' function as a semantic radical because the original meaning of the character 錯 refers to 'the crossing on the surface of metal' as the meaning of 錯 now used in the word 交錯 gaau1co3 'crossing.'

On the basis of the above linguistic background, I shall move to discuss the various orthographic aspects necessary for learning the characters, i.e. what constitute the object of learning in the current theoretical framework.

CRITICAL ORTHOGRAPHIC ASPECTS

Take what happens to children when they encounter an unknown character 椰 in the context of 椰子 je4zi2 'coconut' as an example (Figure 4.4) (See Lam (2008) for an exploratory study on the various ways that children read unknown characters). In order to guess what it means, they need to be focally aware of the following orthographic aspects of the character.

Figure 4.4. The experience of reading an unknown character.

Part-whole relation.   As mentioned above, the semantic radical and phonetic radical in a character contribute to respectively the meaning and the sound of the character. These are the two types (i.e. semantic and phonetic) of part-whole relation between the components and the characters. In our example, if children's attention is drawn to the presence of the component 木 'tree' in the character 椰 je4 'coconut,' they will probably be able to guess that 椰子 je4zi2 'coconut' refers to something associated with 'tree' (i.e. 木). More generally, certain components in a character can provide clues to the semantic field to which the whole character belongs. For example, having the same 木 'tree,' the characters 林 lam4 'forest,' 桃 tou4 'peach,' 枝 zi1 'branch' and 橙 caang4 'orange' are all in the same semantic field of 木 'tree.' An awareness of the semantic part-whole relation between the component and the character is a critical aspect of orthographic awareness.

Another type of part-whole relation is of a phonetic kind. If children focus their attention on the other part (i.e. 耶 je4) of the character, the children may speculate that the sound of the character 椰 je4 'coconut' should be close to those of the characters 耶 je4 'used in interrogation,' 爺 je4 'grandfather' and 揶 je4 'to tease'[11] because 耶 je4 serves as a phonetic radical in the latter two characters. In light of the speculated sound je4zi2, the children, who probably have heard of this sound in everyday speech, is likely to be able to associate the word with 椰子 which means 'coconut.' In other words, the phonetic part-whole relation is another critical aspect of orthographic awareness that will help children to determine the sound of the character and in some cases to deduce meaning of the character via the sound.

The following excerpt from my previous interview study illustrates how a boy in Grade Two made use of his knowledge of spoken Chinese as well as that of the above two types of part-whole relation to figure out the precise meaning of the character 聾 lung4 'deaf' unknown to him. Preceding the conversation, the boy had indicated that he did not know the character 聾.

1	Researcher:	Can you make a guess of how this character (pointing at the character 聾 *lung4* 'deaf') is pronounced?
2	Boy:	Hm… pronounced as *lung4*?
3	Researcher:	What *lung4* are you referring to?*
4	Boy:	The *lung4*, that is to say, the *lung4* of *lung4zo2*** 'to have become deaf' or cannot hear anything.
5	Researcher:	How do you know that? Have you seen the character before?
6	Boy:	No, I have never learned the character before. Never seen it before. I just guessed. Because there is a 龍 *lung4*, and there is a 耳 'ear.' It should be related to 'ear.'

The sound lung4 in Cantonese can mean a number of different things such as 龍 lung4 'dragon,' 籠 lung4 'cage,' 隆 lung4 'prosperous,' 聾 lung4 'deaf,' etc.

**lung4zo2 is spoken Cantonese, which can be expressed in written form as 聾了 lung4liu5 'to have become deaf.'*

It can be clearly seen that the boy from the component 龍 lung4, arrived at the sound of lung4 and from the component 耳 'ear,' inferred that the character had something to do with 'ear' (in line 6). He also recalled that in speech lung4 can mean 'deaf' as in lung4zo2 'to have become deaf' (in line 4), thus he eventually arrived at the correct answer that 聾 is the character lung4 for 'deaf.' This suggests that being aware of the part-whole relation is of crucial importance to the learning of Chinese characters.

Part-part relation.   One extremely important question, which is often left unexamined in other research studies, is how children can see the character 椰 je4 'coconut' as composed of the two constituent components 木 'tree' and 耶 je4, but not in any other ways. This suggests that there is another critical aspect of orthographic awareness, which is the relation between the various parts of the character (i.e. the part-part relation). Which part(s) of a character will come together to form a constituent component (as either a semantic or phonetic radical), which in turn combines with another constituent component to form the whole character?

Theoretically the character 椰 je4 'coconut' can be divided in a number of different ways, for example, 木, 耳 and 阝, 木 and 耶, 栭 and 阝, 椰 as one unit and even as thirteen individual strokes. Indeed, some children do make errors in their division of characters and in assigning meanings to the divided parts. For example, some children in the Experiment 1 of Lam (2006, pp. 71–80) were found to mistake the character 椰 je4 'coconut' as related to the meaning of 耳 'ear.' It was highly likely that they took the 耳 in the middle of 椰 as a constituent component rather than just part of the component 耶 je4. The children thus erroneously guessed that the character 椰 je4 'coconut' had something to do with 耳 'ear.'

So the part-part relation is about whether children have developed a powerful way of seeing the orthographic structures of the characters. Characters such as 椰 je4 'coconut' being configured as three components arranged in a row are divided by linguistics into the leftmost 木 'tree' and the remaining 耶 je4, which function as a semantic and phonetic radical respectively[12, 13]. Such linguistic analysis of the composition of the characters has been taken on board by teachers and that from a very early age, children are taught to differentiate the structures as composing of components in different ways. Thus, to look for a clue to the character meaning, those children who correctly analyze the character 椰 je4 'coconut' will focus on the leftmost part of the character (i.e. the 木 'tree' in this case) but not elsewhere.

The other children who fail to analyze the character 椰 je4 'coconut' see the orthographic structure in a different way such that they mistake the component 耳 'ear' in the middle by itself as a constituent component that contributes to the meaning of the whole character. But, as discussed previously, in the character 椰, the sub-component 耳 is only part of the phonetic radical 耶 je4 and does not function as a semantic radical to the whole character. As such, in order for children to realize that the 耳 'ear' is not related to the meaning of the character 椰 je4 'coconut,' they need to understand the part-part relation of the 耳 and 阝, that they are parts of the constituent component 耶 je4 to the character rather than the 耳 'ear' on its own as one constituent component.

Put it in another way, in order to appropriately analyze the orthographic structure of a character, children should discern and attend to the location of a component in the orthographic structure and understand that only when a component is located in a particular place in the orthographic structure, it functions as a constituent component (e.g. the 木 'tree' in 椰 je4 'coconut') and provides a clue to the meaning of the character. When the component is located in other places in the orthographic structure, it functions as a sub-component (e.g., the 耳 'ear' and 阝 'town' in 椰 je4 'coconut'), and does not provide such clues. In other words, children must understand the significance of the location of a component in the orthographic structure of the character to determine whether or not the component functions as a semantic radical to the character. This way of seeing the orthographic structure of a character is of critical importance to the understanding of the composition of the character.

In schools, children are commonly taught the typical configurations of Chinese characters (such as those in Figure 4.2) with the aim of improving the legibility of writing or calligraphy. However, this is not sufficient. It is also necessary for children to perceive the different ways of dividing the characters as relevant to the task of making sense of unknown characters. In other words, the object of learning here is not the legibility of writing but the understanding of the relation between the meaning of a character and its orthographic structure.

Besides this, it should also be pointed out that the part-part relation discussed here involves more than a relation just among the components. It actually bears a relation with the character as a whole. For example, the sub-components 女 and 又 in the character 怒 nou6 'angry' have a part-part relation that they are part of the same constituent component 奴 nou4. However, in another character such as 娶 ceoi2 'to marry a wife,' the part-part relation of the two components 女 and 又 is totally different. The 女 'female' is a constituent component while the 又 is part of another constituent component 取 ceoi2. Thus, the part-part relation, as well as the part-whole relation, is only specific to the character concerned.

As an example to demonstrate how children understand the part-part relation, the following interview excerpt of a Grade Two boy gives a flavor of an advanced understanding that the component 扌 'hand' does not provide a clue to the meaning of the character 誓 sai6 'swear' due to its location in the orthographic structure. The interview was conducted after a lesson in which the ways to analyze the orthographic structures of characters were taught.

1	Researcher:	What have you learned during the lesson?
2	Boy:	I have learned that … Hm… Before [the lesson], I believed that whenever a character contained a certain component, the character would be one of those characters.
3	Researcher:	One of those characters being related [to the meaning of the component]?
4	Boy:	Yes. But now I believe it is not.
5	Researcher:	You mean, all those characters are not related [to the meaning of the component]?
6	Boy:	No. Sometime related, sometime not related. (Pointing at the character 誓 *sai6* 'swear.') For example, this character is not related to 扌 'hand' but is related to 言 'speech.' However, if the 言 is taken away from the character, that means (Covering the 言 'speech' and leaving the character 折 *zit3* 'to break'), it will be related to 扌 'hand.'

In the above excerpt, the boy talked about how he analyzed the orthographic structure of the character 誓 sai6 'swear.' He obviously understood which part of the character he should focus on in order to find a clue to its meaning, i.e. the 言 'speech' at the bottom but not the 扌 'hand' at the top left (in line 6). He also demonstrated his understanding that if 扌 occurred in the character 折 zit3 'to break,' then attention should be focused on the component 扌 'hand' to guess the meaning (also in line 6). This suggests that he realized the difference in the locations of the component 扌 in the orthographic structures and that this makes a difference to whether the component 扌 'hand' provides a clue to the meanings of the characters (i.e. the part-part relation).

Up to this point, two critical orthographic aspects essential to the learning of Chinese characters have been discussed, namely the part-whole relation between the constituent components and the whole characters (i.e., what a constituent component signifies in a character?) and the part-part relation among the components (i.e., which components are part of the same constituent component to a character?). These are the orthographic aspects that children need to be aware of in order to see or experience the characters in a powerful way. In other words, these critical orthographic aspects constitute the object of learning in the present theoretical framework.

DEVELOPING ORTHOGRAPHIC AWARENESS

The question that naturally follows from here is how we can help children to develop such a powerful way of seeing or experiencing the characters. According to the Theory of Variation, children must discern the critical orthographic aspects so that they are likely to see other characters (whether the characters are familiar to them or not) in terms of these orthographic aspects. To discern these aspects, children have to simultaneously (in a diachronic sense) experience how each of these aspects vary among different characters. To do this, characters should not be taught in an individual manner but in pairs or sets with variation in a certain orthographic aspect. This is because, as Bowden & Marton (1998, p. 24) have argued, "Discernment springs from the experience of variation; … what does not vary cannot be discerned."

Teachers in everyday practice do show children sets of characters that share common semantic or phonetic radicals. This is why some children are able to divide the characters according to these semantic and phonetic radicals. However, this is only done intuitively and not systematically enough. More importantly, the teaching is not guided by any theories of learning. Thus the characters that they present in pairs do not necessarily vary explicitly in the critical orthographic aspects. For example, they may present pairs or a list of characters with the same semantic radical 女 'female' such as the characters 媽 maa1 'mother,' 妹 mui6 'younger sister,' 姊 zi2 'elder sister' and 她 taa1 'she,' and say that these characters all have to do with 'female.' However, this is not sufficient. As Marton and Pang (2006, p. 199) point out, "We cannot discern quality X without simultaneously experiencing a mutually exclusive quality ~X." This means that the teachers must also show the children characters without the semantic radical 女 'female' such as 螞 maa5 'ant' together with 媽 maa1 'mother,' and 味 mei6 'taste' together with 妹 mui6 'younger sister.'

Therefore, what this theoretical framework is trying to do is to structure the learning experience in a way that is motivated by the Theory of Variation. As the theory suggests, by varying a certain critical aspect while holding the other aspects constant, one can focus children's attention on the aspect that varies. Thus certain characters are paired up together to bring out variations in certain critical orthographic aspects so as to focus children's attention on those aspects essential to learning the characters. In other words, by drawing on the Theory of Variation, I systematically vary the characters in the instruction, which is further explained below.

Teaching part-whole relation. Take as an example the teaching of the characters' part-whole relation. That is, a component of a character signifies the semantic field to which the character belongs. As such, the object of learning is to help children to recognize that characters having the component 木 'tree' are likely to have a meaning associated with 'tree,' but not with 'water,' for instance, or whatever. The following Table 1 illustrates two methods of teaching this with the same eight characters being paired up in different ways. The two methods are called Contrastive Pair and Generalization Pair[14].

Table 4.1. Two ways of teaching the meaning that the component 木 'tree' signifies in a character

No.	Pairs of characters shown to children	Explanation of teacher
	Contrastive Pair	Question: Are the two characters related to the meaning of 樹木 *syu6muk6* 'tree'?
1	椰 揶	Answer: The first character 椰 *je4* 'coconut' is related to 樹木 *syu6muk6* 'tree' while the second character 揶 *je4* 'to tease' is not because only the first character contains the component 木 'tree.'
2	挑 桃	Answer: The second character 桃 *tou4* 'peach' is related to 樹木 *syu6muk6* 'tree' while the first character 挑 *tiu1* 'to pick out' is not because only the second character contains the component 木 'tree.'
3	揚 楊	Answer: The second character 楊 *joeng4* 'poplar' is related to 樹木 *syu6muk6* 'tree' while the first character 揚 *joeng4* 'to wave' is not because only the second character contains the component 木 'tree.'
4	棒 捧	Answer: The first character 棒 *paang5* 'stick' is related to 樹木 *syu6muk6* 'tree' while the second character 捧 *pung2* 'to hold up with both hands' is not because only the first character contains the component 木 'tree.'

Table 4.1. (Continued)

	Generalization Pair	Question: Are the two characters related to the meaning of 樹木 *syu6muk6* 'tree'?
1	椰 桃	Answer: Both of the characters 椰 *je4* 'coconut' and 桃 *tou4* 'peach' are related to 樹木 *syu6muk6* 'tree' because both of them contain the component 木 'tree.'
2	捓 挑	Answer: None of the characters 捓 *je4* 'to tease' and 挑 *tiu1* 'to pick out' is related to 樹木 *syu6muk6* 'tree' because none of them contains the component 木 'tree.'
3	楊 棒	Answer: Both of the characters 楊 *joeng4* 'poplar' and 棒 *paang5* 'stick' are related to 樹木 *syu6muk6* 'tree' because both of them contain the component 木 'tree.'
4	揚 捧	Answer: None of the characters 揚 *joeng4* 'to wave' and 捧 *pung2* 'to hold up with both hands' is related to 樹木 *syu6muk6* 'tree' because none of them contains the component 木 'tree.'

Each of the four pairs in Contrastive Pair contrasts characters in different semantic fields due to a difference in the component on the left while the other components of the pair are identical. In contrast, the characters of each pair in Generalization Pair are both in the same semantic field owing to an identical component on the left but the other components of the pair are different.

According to the Theory of Variation, one will predict a better learning outcome of those children receiving Contrastive Pair than those receiving Generalization Pair, with all other things being equal. Each contrastive pair of characters varies in the orthographic aspect of the component on the left of the characters (i.e. 木 – 'tree' and 扌 – not 'tree'). This focuses the children's attention on what varies, that is the semantic radicals of the characters. This helps the children to connect whether a character belongs to the semantic field of 'tree' to whether the character contains the component 木 'tree.' On the contrary, there is no variation of this sort in each of the generalization pairs. Instead, what vary are the components on the right of the characters, which are the phonetic radicals of the characters. The children's attention will be drawn to these components that do not contribute to the meanings of the characters. Therefore, if the object of learning is about the meanings of characters, children who learn from Contrastive Pair should outperform those who learn from Generalization Pair.

This prediction is not obvious and in fact is falsifiable. One can argue that Generalization Pair should yield a better result as the children can recognize the part-whole relation by analogical reasoning. Indeed, Ho et al. (1999) taught children character pairs, such as 嫂 sou2 'the wife of elder brother' and 媳 sik1 'daughter-in-law,' and later found that the children could successfully draw analogies from the characters in identifying the semantic field of unknown characters with a 女 'female' on the left. Thus it is not absolutely impossible that Generalization Pair can be found to be more effective than Contrastive Pair.

Indeed, in classroom practice, most teachers tend to adopt an approach in line with Generalization Pair. For instance, as mentioned previously, to illustrate the nature of the semantic radical 女 'female,' teachers commonly give examples of characters with a 女 'female' such as 媽 maa1 'mother,' 妹 mui6 'younger sister,' 姊 zi2 'elder sister' and 她 taa1 'she' and explain that the persons referred to by these characters are all female. The rationale underlying this agrees with that of Generalization Pair, i.e., children learn by making analogies. This raises the question of whether the Theory of Variation does apply to the learning of characters given that the intuitive practice of teachers appears to work well.[15]

To find out which of the above two instructions is more effective than the other requires more empirical evidence. In what follows, I shall illustrate the design of the teaching of the part-part relation as guided by the Theory of Variation, which has been empirically put to test in Lam (2006, pp. 91–122).

Teaching part-part relation. Suppose that the object of learning is the characters' part-part relation, i.e., which components are part of the same constituent components to the characters. Again there are two possible ways of teaching this, namely using Contrastive Pair and Generalization Pair, with the same set of eight characters as shown below in Table 2.

Table 4.2. Two ways of teaching the orthographic structures of the characters

No.	Pairs shown to children	Explanation of teacher
	Contrastive Pair	Question: Are the two characters related to the meaning category in brackets?
1	椰　蜥 (樹木)　(樹木)	Answer: The first character 椰 *je4* 'coconut' is related to 樹木 *syu6muk6* 'tree' while the second character 蜥 *sik1* 'lizard' is not. In the first character, the component 木 'tree' is located on the leftmost and thus functions as a semantic radical, while in the second character the component 木 is part of the component 析 *sik1* on the right and thus does not function as a semantic radical.
2	渺　瞅 (眼睛)　(眼睛)	Answer: The second character 瞅 *cau2* 'to cast a look' is related to 眼睛 *ngaan5zing1* 'eye' while the first character 渺 *miu5* 'very small' is not. In the second character, the component 目 'eye' is located on the leftmost and thus functions as a semantic radical, while in the first character the component 目 is part of the component 眇 *miu5* on the right and thus does not function as a semantic radical.

Table 4.2. (Continued)

3	袈 (水)　溶 (水)	Answer: The second character 溶 *jung4* 'to dissolve' is related to 水 *seoi2* 'water' while the first character 袈 *saa1* 'cassock' is not. In the second character, the component 氵 'water' (a variant form of the character 水) is located on the left and thus functions as a semantic radical, while in the first character the component 氵 is part of the component 沙 *saa1* at the top and thus does not function as a semantic radical.
4	傭 (人)　煲 (人)	Answer: The first character 傭 *jung4* 'maid' is related to 人 *jan4* 'people' while the second character 煲 *bou1* 'cooker' is not. In the first character, the component 亻 'people' (a variant form of the character 人) is located on the left and thus functions as a semantic radical, while in the second character the component 亻 is part of the component 保 *bou2* at the top and thus does not function as a semantic radical.

Generalization Pair

1	椰 (樹木)　瞅 (眼睛)	Question: Are the two characters related to the meaning category in brackets? Answer: The two characters 椰 *je4* 'coconut' and 瞅 *cau2* 'to cast a look' are related to 樹木 *syu6muk6* 'tree' and 眼睛 *ngaan5zing1* 'eye' respectively. The components 木 'tree' and 目 'eye' are both located on the leftmost and thus function as semantic radicals.
2	蜥 (樹木)　渺 (眼睛)	Answer: The two characters 蜥 *sik1* 'lizard' and 渺 *miu5* 'very small' are not related to 樹木 *syu6muk6* 'tree' and 眼睛 *ngaan5zing1* 'eye' respectively. The components 木 and 目 are both part of the components 析 *sik1* and 眇 *miu5* respectively on the right and thus do not function as a semantic radical.
3	溶 (水)　傭 (人)	Answer: The two characters 溶 *jung4* 'to dissolve' and 傭 *jung4* 'maid' are related to 水 *seoi2* 'water' and 人 *jan4* 'people' respectively. The components 氵 'water' (a variant form of the character 水) and 亻 'people' (a variant form of the character 人) respectively are both located on the left and thus function as semantic radicals.
4	袈 (水)　煲 (人)	Answer: The two characters 袈 *saa1* 'cassock' and 煲 *bou1* 'cooker' are not related to 水 *seoi2* 'water' and 人 *yan4* 'people' respectively. The components 氵 and 亻 are both part of the components 沙 *saa1* and 保 *bou2* respectively at the top and thus do not function as a semantic radical.

In each of the contrastive pairs, the same component varies in its location and in whether it functions as a semantic radical in the two characters. For example, the component 木 'tree' functions as a semantic radical on the leftmost of the character 椰 je4 'coconut' but not in the middle of the character 蜥 sik1 'lizard.' Actually, in principle, here the components other than the 木 'tree' in the two characters (i.e. the 耳 and 阝 in 椰, and the 虫 and 斤 in 蜥) should be held constant. But this is not practically feasible because there is no such real character, which can be used to illustrate the variation in the location of the component while, at the same time, have all the other components the same (e.g., 耶阝 is not a real character.).[16]

In contrast to the contrastive pairs, both of the characters in each generalization pair have the components in question located at the same place and function (or not function) as a semantic radical at the same time. For example, the components 木 'tree' and 目 'eye' both function as a semantic radical on the leftmost of the characters 椰 je4 'coconut' and 瞅 cau2 'to cast a look' respectively.

According to the Theory of Variation, one will predict a better performance of those children who receive Contrastive Pair than those who receive Generalization Pair. The two instructions are analyzed as follows. In order to understand why the character 椰 je4 'coconut' is related to the meaning of 木 'tree' but the 蜥 sik1 'lizard' is not, children must simultaneously (in a synchronic sense) discern and attend to both the part-whole and part-part relations. This means that children must know the part-whole relation that the component 木 signifies a meaning of 'tree' in a character. Moreover, they must also realize the part-part relation that when a component is not located on the leftmost part of a character of a left-right configuration, it becomes part of a constituent component to the character (i.e. a sub-component and not a constituent component in the orthographic structure) and loses its semantic function in relation to the character.

According to the Experiment 1 of Lam (2006, pp. 71–80), children in Grade Two or above were found to be well aware of the part-whole relation. Thus, if we assume that children who receive the above instruction are in Grade Two, they should realize that whether or not a character is related to the meaning of 'tree' somehow has to do with the component 木 'tree' in the character. On the basis of this, in Contrastive Pair, what varies of the component 木 in the characters 椰 je4 'coconut' and 蜥 sik1 'lizard' is in its location in the orthographic structure of the two characters. This focuses the children's attention on the difference in the location of the component 木. That is, when the component 木 'tree' is located on the leftmost, it functions as a semantic radical. The character 椰 je4 'coconut' is thus related to the meaning of 'tree.' When the 木 is located in the middle of the character 蜥, it becomes part of the component 析 sik1 which functions as a phonetic radical, and the 木 loses its semantic function. The character 蜥 sik1 'lizard' is thus not related to the meaning 'tree.' In other words, in the contrastive pair of 椰 je4 'coconut' and 蜥 sik1 'lizard,' children can simultaneously experience the variation in the location of the component 木 'tree' in the orthographic structure.

Unlike the contrastive pair, the generalization pair such as 椰 je4 'coconut' and 瞅 cau2 'to cast a look' has the components 木 'tree' and 目 'eye' respectively located in the same leftmost position of the characters. What vary of the components 木 and 目 in the two characters are the components themselves. They are two different semantic radicals. This focuses the children's attention on this difference of the components, which is however not helpful to the understanding of the significance of the location of the components in the orthographic structure (i.e., both components are located on the leftmost and function as a semantic radical.). In other words, since there is no variation in the location of the component 木 or 目, the children cannot simultaneously experience how the component varies in its location in Generalization Pair.

Taken together, what the Theory of Variation predicts is that children who learn from Contrastive Pair should have a greater improvement than those who learn from Generalization Pair with regard to their capability of analyzing the ortho-graphic structures of the characters. In the Experiments 3 and 4 of Lam (2006, pp. 91–122), empirical data have been sought on this issue and the results show that Contrastive Pair is generally superior to Generalization Pair. Thus this supports the claim that the Theory of Variation is powerful in explaining the effectiveness of the two methods.

This empirical result is also in congruent to the findings of the Experiment 1 previously reported in Chapter Three. In that experiment, variation in tone and invariance in other aspects was found to produce a powerful effect on non-tonal language speakers for a perceptual separation of the tone aspect from other aspects in spoken Cantonese words. Such learning experience as provided in the experiment was designed on the basis of the same theoretical foundation (i.e. the tenet of the Theory of Variation) as the Contrastive Pair discussed here.

The above argues for what kind of instruction that can possibly help children to discern the critical orthographic aspects for learning the characters. To further clarify this concept of the discernment of an orthographic aspect, I shall contrast this with a similar concept in another very influential theory of instruction in the next section.

DISCERNMENT VERSUS DISCRIMINATION

Discrimination. The concept of discernment in the Theory of Variation can be brought to contrast with the concept of discrimination in Robert M. Gagné's Condi-tions of Learning. In his own words, "A discrimination is a capability of making different responses to stimuli which differ from each other along one or more physical dimensions" (Gagné & Briggs, 1979, p. 63).

This means that discrimination primarily has to do with identifying something as belonging to a certain concept (i.e. recognizing a part as itself, regardless of the whole). This is illustrated in the exercise that follows (Figure 4.5) (from Tse, 2002, p. 177).

Please add other components to the 口 'mouth' to turn it into a meaningful character.
(你可以在「口」字加上其他部件，成為一個有意義的字詞嗎？)

Figure 4.5. Discrimination of characters with and without a 口 'mouth'.

This exercise has been tried out in a school. As the school reports, a child in response to it came up with a list of 76 unrelated characters in total. Part of the list is reproduced below (Figure 4.6) (from School-based Curriculum (Primary) Section, 2001, Appendix xxxii).

味加叨只故吆向吞吥吽吹呔吻合回[17]

Figure 4.6. Part of the response of a child to the above discrimination exercise.

It can be seen that the child has produced quite a lot of characters that have met the requirement of the exercise. In this sense, the result of the child is satisfactory and it seems that the child has successfully acquired the skill to discriminate those characters with a 口 'mouth' from those without.

However, under the theoretical framework discussed here, this child has barely accomplished a full understanding of the part-whole relation between the 口 'mouth' and the characters (i.e., why those characters have a 口?). A closer look at the child's response reveals that the child has in fact produced several non-real characters and some others were unlikely to be known to the child, namely, 叨, 吆, 吥, 吽 and 呔. Further to this, the roles of the 口 'mouth' in other characters such as 只 zi2 'only,' 故 gu3 'of the past,' 向 hoeng3 'face a direction,' 合 hap6 'to get together' and 回 wui4 'to return' are rather opaque and are difficult for the child to understand. Perhaps, this leads to the conclusion that the child only blindly and mechanically generated as many characters as possible without ever giving a thought to why the 口 is a part of these characters. Thus it may be worthwhile to redesign this exercise in light of the concept of discernment.

Discernment.　Perhaps, to test whether children can discern a 口 'mouth' in the characters, the above exercise can be modified to the following (Figure 4.7).

Please add other components to the 口 'mouth' to turn it into a character with a meaning related to 'mouth.'
(你可以在「口」字加上其他部件，成為一個與「口」意義有關的字詞嗎？)

Figure 4.7. Discernment of 口 'mouth' from the characters[18].

By so doing, children are directed to consider only those characters like 味 mei6 'to taste,' 喝 hot3 'to drink,' 吃 hek3 'to eat,' 叫 giu3 'to shout' and 吐 tou3 'to spit,' all of which belong to the same semantic field of 'actions by mouth.' As such, if children can attend to the relation between having a component 口 'mouth' and having a character with meaning related to 'mouth,' they should perform better in the exercise. In other words, it is about how the component 口 'mouth' functions as a semantic radical in the characters. Once the children realize this part-whole relation, the reason why there is at the first place a component 口 'mouth' in the characters such as 味 mei6 'to taste' will become clear, i.e., we use the mouth 口 to taste 味 food.

Taken together, apparently both of the concepts of discrimination and discernment involve learning through the differentiation of different things. But the key essence of discrimination is to identify the parts in a whole as what the parts are on their own (i.e., the focus is on the parts). For example, a part of the character 味 is 口. By contrast, discernment emphasizes how one can meaningfully understand the whole from its parts (i.e., the focus is on the whole). For example, we can dissect a 口 'mouth' out of the character 味 mei6 'to taste' because the 口 'mouth' contributes to the meaning of the character.

To take this point a step further, the exercises to be mentioned in the Appendix D of Chapter Five are instructive. In these exercises, children have to come up with as many characters as possible from a given list of components. For example, the second exercise in the chapter presents children first with 4 x 4 = 16 components and then asks the children to write down as many characters that are made up of these components as they can. What are first given to the children are the components, while next they have to come up with the characters. In other words, the experience of the children goes in such an order from the parts (i.e. the components) to the wholes (i.e. the characters). The exercise in essence requires children to identify the components as what the components are individually and then to apply them for use in various situations, i.e. in other characters. It is the components that the children act upon, and thus of primary importance are the parts, which as I argued above is what characterizes the concept of discrimination.

By contrast, an instruction seriously drawing on the concept of discernment is likely to begin with presenting the characters (i.e. the wholes) to children. The children may then be called upon to find out what component the characters have in common. Here the children have to act upon the characters (i.e. finding out the commonality among the characters), and thus primacy is given to the wholes. And only in relation to these wholes, the children learn to discern a common part from the wholes. It is in this way that the principle that the wholes should come first is upheld.

This distinction between the concepts of discernment and discrimination further opens up the question of how far children have to know the functions of the components in the characters. For some researchers, being able to realize the characters as simply the "and-sum" of their components is more than sufficient, i.e., 榕 = 木 + 容 (Tse, 2002, pp. 132–142). But, as I argue throughout this chapter, this merely requires children to identify the components in the characters as what they are and neglects the functions of the components in relation to the characters as a whole, i.e. the part-whole relation and the part-part relation, or in other words 榕 jung4 'banyan' = 木 'tree' + 容 jung4. One critical difference of the concept of discernment from discrimination is thus its special emphasis on the significance of the discerned parts in relation to the whole.

SUMMARY

In sum, I have discussed in this chapter a theoretical framework that draws on the Theory of Variation to investigate the teaching of Chinese characters. First, a linguistic distinction has been made between the constituent components (e.g. the 木 'tree' and the 耶 je4 in 椰 je4 'coconut') and the sub-components (e.g., the 耳 'ear' and the ß 'town' in 椰 je4 'coconut') in a character. After that, the notion of orthographic awareness has been put forward, which in brief states that in order to see or experience a character in a certain powerful way, children must be focally aware of certain critical orthographic aspects. These orthographic aspects include the part-whole relations between the constituent components and the character (i.e., what a constituent component signifies in the character?) and the part-part relations among the components (i.e., which components are part of the same constituent component to the character?). Then, I have moved on to discuss that in order to discern each of the orthographic aspects, children have to simultaneously experience how the orthographic aspect varies. This is empirically supported by the result of the superior effectiveness of Contrastive Pair (in which a critical orthographic aspect varies in the instruction) over Generalization Pair (in which the orthographic aspect is kept constant). Finally, in contrast with discrimination, the concept of discernment has been characterized as having a special emphasis on the significance of the discernment of the parts in relation to the whole. On the whole, the present theoretical framework forms a basis for future empirically based research towards a theory of learning Chinese characters.

NOTES

[1] The sounds of the characters in this chapter are in Cantonese, which is a dialect of Chinese language widely spoken by 90% of people in Hong Kong. The sounds are transcribed using the Cantonese romanization developed by the Linguistic Society of Hong Kong (2002).

[2] However, many of the most frequently used characters are not semantic-phonetic characters. As Gao (1988) points out, in the top 50 most frequently used characters, only 9 of them are semantic-phonetic characters, i.e. only 18%. But if we take into account all characters, the vast majority of the characters are semantic-phonetic characters.

[3] Several Chinese linguists (Tang, 1949, pp. 107–108; Qiu, 1993, pp. 177–181; Chiu, 1995, pp. 253–256; Gao, 1996, pp. 53–54) have strongly argued against the analysis of some semantic-phonetic characters as having more than one semantic or phonetic radical. For example, the character 寶 bou2 'treasure' should not be analyzed as consisting of three semantic radicals 宀 'house,' 玉 'jade' and 貝 'sea shell' and one phonetic radical 缶 fau2 (i.e. 三形一聲 in Chinese; as in Yang, 1988, pp. 239–240). This is because it was once found in some ancient texts the rarely known character 寚, which is

made up of the three components 宀, 玉 and 貝. This character as one should instead be the semantic radical in forming the character 寶.

[4] There is no consistent way to describe these linguistic units of the characters in English. Semantic-phonetic characters are also given the names of picto-phonetic characters, phonetic compounds, phonograms, phono-semantic compounds and many others. Some researchers also refer semantic radicals to as semantic components, morphological components or simply radicals while phonetic radicals are referred to as phonetic components or in short phonetics.

[5] The character 斤 gan1 originally meant 'axe' though it now more commonly denotes the meaning of 'catty.'

[6] In this chapter, the historical analysis of the characters is based on the dictionary of Gu (2003).

[7] Note that Su (2001, p. 77) also adopts a hierarchical analysis of the characters, which however does not follow the constituent functions of the components in the characters and is for the purpose of breaking down the characters into the smallest reusable parts.

[8] In this context, the verb "function" is interchangeably used with "act" and "serve."

[9] In the analysis here, the relation between the phonetic radicals and the whole characters has only to do with the sounds of the characters, which makes the notion of constituency here different from that of Halliday (1994), whose analysis only concerns the meaning.

[10] The meaning of the character 金 gam1 is 'metal' as in the word 金屬 gam1suk6 'metal' but it is also commonly used to mean 'gold' now.

[11] as in the word 揶揄 je4jyu4 'to tease'

[12] There are a few exceptional cases among the early formed characters such as 街 gaai1 'street,' apparently with the same configuration as 椰, is however divided into the two constituent components 行 'walk' (from the leftmost and the rightmost components in the character) and 圭 gwai1 (the component in the middle). But characters like this are rare in comparison to those analyzed into the leftmost and the remaining components as the semantic and phonetic radicals respectively.

[13] Linguists call this 從木耶聲 cung4muk6je4sing1, i.e. 木 'tree' as a semantic radical and 耶 je4 as a phonetic radical.

[14] I use the term "Contrastive Pair" (with the first letters in upper case) as the general name of this method while "a contrastive pair" (in lower case) refers to a particular pair of characters used in this method. The same applies to "Generalization Pair."

[15] One could argue that Contrastive Pair tells children that the two adjacent characters are different in some valuable aspect, and asks them to identify which aspect changes across the two characters. That is, it requires them to look for what varies in what appears to be similar (i.e. 同中求異 in Chinese). In contrast to this, children in Generalization Pair are told that the two different characters have an important aspect being the same, and thus the children look for such an aspect that is the same in both characters. That is, it requires them to look for what is invariant in what appears to be different (i.e. 異中求同).

[16] One may also wonder why the variation in the location of the component 木 'tree' in the orthographic structure of the characters with a ▮▯ configuration here only includes the cases of the leftmost and middle positions, but not that the 木 is located on the rightmost, which is in principle also possible. The reason is that actually the component 木 is rarely found on the rightmost of a character. For instance, out of the 2600 characters listed in the curriculum (Curriculum Development Council, 1990), 148 characters contain the component 木 but there is only one exception, i.e. the character 淋 lam4 'to water,' which has the component 木 located on the rightmost. Thus I have decided not to include the rightmost position in the variation in the location of the component 木 in the characters.

[17] The characters can be explained as follows: 味 mei6 'to taste,' 加 gaa1 'to add,' 只 zi2 'only,' 故 gu3 'of the past,' 向 hoeng3 'to face a direction,' 吞 tan1 'to swallow,' 吹 ceoi1 'to blow,' 吻 man5 'to kiss,' 合 hap6 'to get together' and 回 wui4 'to return;' while the rest of the rarely used characters 叨, 呚, 呧, 咩 and 呟 are unlikely to be known.

[18] Actually, this modified exercise can only be used as an assessment of whether children can discern the part-whole relation in the characters. If the purpose is to raise children's awareness of the part-whole relation, according to the Theory of Variation, the children must experience the contrast

between characters with and without the component 口 'mouth,' for example, 味 *mei6* 'to taste' and 妹 *mui6* 'younger sister.' Only in such case, the children can possibly realize that only one of the two characters has a meaning related to 'mouth,' i.e. 味 *mei6* 'to taste' but not 妹 *mui6* 'younger sister.' The children's attention can then be drawn to the relation between having a component 口 'mouth' and having a meaning related to 'mouth.'

REFERENCES

Bowden, J., & Marton, F. (1998). *The university of learning – Beyond quality and competence.* London,UK: Kogan Page.

Chiu, T. S. (1995). *Wenzixue xintan* [New investigation in the study of Chinese characters]. Taipei: Ho Chi.

Curriculum Development Council. (1990). Fenji changyongzibian [List of frequently used Chinese characters by grade levels]. In Curriculum Development Council (Ed.), *Syllabus for Chinese (primary 1–6)* (pp. 69–76). Hong Kong: Government Printer.

Eggins, S. (1994). *An introduction to systemic functional linguistics.* London, UK: Pinter.

Fu, Y. H. (1993). Hanzi jiegou he gouzao chengfen de jichu yanjiu [Basic study of the composition and constituent components of Chinese characters]. In Y. Chen (Ed.), *Xiandai hanyu yongzi xinxi fengxi* [Analysis of the information about the use of characters in modern Chinese] (pp. 108–169). Shanghai: Shanghai Educational Press.

Fu, Y. H. (1999). *Zhongwen xinxi chuli* [Chinese information processing]. Guangzhou: Guangdong Educational Press.

Gagné, R. M., & Briggs, L. J. (1979). *Principles of instructional design.* New York: Holt, Rinehart, and Winston.

Gao, J. C. (1988). Luetan xingshengzi de landian he qita [Some thoughts on the difficulty of semantic-phonetic characters and others]. In Institute of Applied Linguistics (Ed.), *Proceedings of the conference on Chinese characters* (pp. 100–107). Beijing: Yu Wen.

Gao, J. Y., Fan, K. Y., & Fei, J. C. (1993). *Xiandai hanzixue* [Modern study of Chinese characters]. Beijing: Higher Education Press.

Gao, M. (1996). *Zhongguo guwenzixue tonglun* [Introduction to ancient Chinese characters]. Beijing: Peking University Press.

Gu, Y. K. (2003). *Hanzi yuanliu zidian* [Dictionary of the evolution of Chinese characters]. Beijing: Hua Xia.

Halliday, M. A. K. (1961). Categories of the theory of grammar. *Word – Journal of the Linguistic Circle of New York, 17,* 241–292.

Halliday, M. A. K. (1994). *An introduction to functional grammar* (2nd ed.). London, UK: Arnold.

Ho, C. S. H., Wong, W. L., & Chan, W. S. (1999). The use of orthographic analogies in learning to read Chinese. *Journal of Child Psychology and Psychiatry, 40*(3), 393–403.

Ki, W., Tse, S. K., Law, N., Lau, F., & Pun, K. H. (1994). A knowledge-based multimedia system to support the teaching and learning of Chinese characters. In T. Ottman & I. Tomek (Eds.), *Proceedings of ED-MEDIA 94-World conference on educational multimedia and hypermedia* (pp. 323–328). Charlottesville, Virginia: Association for the Advancement of Computing in Education.

Lam, H. C. (2006). *Orthographic awareness in learning Chinese characters.* Unpublished doctoral dissertation, The University of Hong Kong, Hong Kong SAR, China.

Lam, H. C. (2008). An exploratory study of the various ways that children read and write unknown Chinese characters. *Journal of Basic Education, 17*(1), 73–97.

Li, H. T. (1986). *Hanzi de qiyuan yu yanbian luncong* [The origin and evolution of Chinese characters]. Taipei: Linking.

Liang, D. H. (1959). *Hanzi de jiegou ji qi liubian* [Structure and evolution of Chinese characters]. Shanghai: Shanghai Educational Press.

Linguistic Society of Hong Kong. (2002). *Yueyu pinyin zibian (dierban)* [Guide to LSHK Cantonese romanization of Chinese characters (2nd ed.)]. Hong Kong: Linguistic Society of Hong Kong.

Marton, F. (1981). Phenomenography – Describing conceptions of the world around us. *Instructional Science, 10,* 177–200.

Marton, F. (1988a). Phenomenography: Exploring different conceptions of reality. In D. M. Fetterman (Ed.), *Qualitative approaches to evaluation in education: The silent scientific revolution* (pp. 176–205). New York: Praeger.

Marton, F. (1988b). Describing and improving learning. In R. R. Schmeck (Ed.), *Learning strategies and learning styles* (pp. 53–82). New York: Plenum Press.

Marton, F., & Booth, S. (1997). *Learning and awareness*. Mahwah, NJ: Lawrence Erlbaum Associates.

Marton, F., & Pang, M. F. (2006). On some necessary conditions of learning. *The Journal of the Learning Sciences, 15*(2), 193–220.

Marton, F., Runesson, U., & Tsui, A. B. M. (2004). The space of learning. In F. Marton & A. B. M. Tsui (Eds.), *Classroom discourse and the space of learning* (pp. 3–40). Mahwah, NJ: Lawrence Erlbaum Associates.

Qiu, X. G. (1993). *Wenzixue gaiyao* [Essential study of Chinese characters]. Taipei: Wan Juan.

School-based Curriculum (Primary) Section. (2001). *Jinxiu zhongwen jihua: xiaoben shizi jiaoyuxue xingdong yanjiu* [Jinxiu Chinese project: School-based action research on the teaching and learning of Chinese characters]. Hong Kong: Curriculum Development Institute, Education Department.

Su, P. C. (2001). *Xiandai hanzixue gangyao* [Essential study of modern Chinese characters]. Beijing: Peking University Press.

Tang, L. (1949). *Zhongguo wenzixue* [Study of Chinese characters]. Hong Kong: Hong Kong Taiping.

Tse, S. K. (2002). *Zonghe gaoxiao shizi jiaoxuefa* [Integrated highly effective pedagogy for teaching Chinese characters]. Hong Kong: Greenfield Educational Centre.

Wang, N. (2002). *Hanzi gouxingxue jiangzuo* [Lectures on the study of the composition of Chinese characters]. Shanghai: Shanghai Educational Press.

Wang, N., & Zou, X. L. (Eds.). (1999). *Hanzi* [Chinese characters]. Hong Kong: Peace Book.

Yang, S. D. (1988). *Zhongguo wenzixue gaiyao* [Study of Chinese characters essentials]. Shanghai: Shanghai Guji.

Ho Cheong Lam
Department of Early Childhood Education
The Hong Kong Institute of Education

AUTHOR'S NOTES

I want to acknowledge that the ideas reported in this chapter were developed during my PhD study (See Lam, 2006) under the supervision of Professor Tsui, Bik May Amy, the University of Hong Kong. Professor Tsui has truly inspired me a lot on the development of the theoretical framework reported here. Special thanks must also go to Dr. Ki, Wing Wah who introduced me to this area of children's learning of Chinese characters.

SHEK KAM TSE, FERENCE MARTON, WING WAH KI
AND ELIZABETH KA YEE LOH

5. LEARNING CHARACTERS

INTRODUCTION

There are two major language systems in the world: alphabetic languages and ideographic languages. Alphabetic languages, like English, use letters in an alphabet to represent sounds; and ideographic languages, like Chinese, use characters to represent meanings. The number of letters (symbols) is limited in alphabetic languages like English; but the number of characters is huge in the ideographic language of Chinese. Due to the large number of characters in Chinese, students need to learn the meaning, sound and form of each character. Generally speaking, Chinese learners need to memorize at least 2,500 characters in order to read a newspaper or magazine of average difficulty (National Education Commission & National Language Construction Committee, 1993, p. 99; Ministry of Education, PRC, 2001). In order to reproduce Chinese characters accurately, Chinese learners need to read each character aloud, copy it many, many times then try to write it down from memory. The learning is out of any literary context and the children may not even really understand the meaning of the character in question. The whole learning process is usually exhausting, boring and frustrating.

Inspired by the phenomenographic theory of learning and awareness, an approach to the learning of characters with focus on the learners' awareness has been developed by the authors. We believe that this new learning approach will help to make the learning of Chinese characters easier and more pleasurable and shorten the overall learning process. The approach draws upon and incorporates various innovative teaching methods first tried out in Mainland China.

CHARACTERISTICS OF THE CHINESE WRITTEN LANGUAGE

Each Chinese character occupies an imaginary square of space. Some are pictographs that stand for objects or they indicate abstract meaning by having additional marks put on the pictographs (for example, 雨 = rain and 雲 = cloud; 月 = moon and 明 = bright [adding up the light of sun and moon]). Although these characters have ideographical origins, they are not pictures. The transformation of orthographic form is somewhat arbitrary (Bloomfield, 1935), and may not even be at all apparent. The character 月 (moon) has a pictorial origin of the moon on the wane, but the moon can never take the form of a square!

Most Chinese characters are composite characters made up of multiple utilizable components. Some components can stand on their own as characters and some cannot;

F. Marton, S.K. Tse and W. M.Cheung (eds.), On the Learning of Chinese, 75–102.

and simple components can be combined to form more complex components (Ki et al., 2003). These compositions usually follow some 15 or so different patterns of spatial configuration (Zhang, 1987; Tse, 2000; Huang, 2003; Ki et al., 2003). For example, the characters 跑 (run), 咆 (roar), and 泡 (bubbles) have the left-right configuration, and the characters 囚 (prisoner) and 困 (besiege) have the outer-inner configuration (口 + 人 = 囚 and 口 + 木 = 困). Figure 5.1 shows other common patterns. Each Chinese character consists on average of some 12.7 strokes (Yang, 2000, p. 138) imposes considerable strain on working memory according to theorists such as Miller (1956), Sweller (2004), Merriënboer & Ayres (2005) and Yang et al. (1994), a load that is facilitated by the learner perceiving and combining nested components as units in linguistic structures and meanings.

i.	Upper and lower structure	白 white +水 + water = 泉 = spring
ii.	Outer (left and bottom) and inner structure	辶 + 軍 = 運 (walking + army = transport)
iii.	Outer (left and top) and inner structure	尸 + 出 = 屈 (corpse + exit = bend)
iv.	Left, middle and right structure	米 + 古 + 月 = 糊 (rice + old + moon = glue)
v.	Upper, middle and lower structure	日 + ㅁㅁ + 又 = 曼 (sun + four + again = graceful)

Figure 5.1. Other examples of spatial configurations of Chinese characters.

Generally speaking, components provide cues about the meaning and sound of the character. For example, the common component 木 carries the meaning wood and appears in the characters 椅 (chair), 桌 (table) and 床 (bed). This kind of component that stands for an element of meaning in the character is called the *morphological component*. The element in the character that represents the sound of the character is called the *phonetic component*. For example, the characters 晴 (sound: cing4), 請 (sound: cing2), 淸 (sound: cing1), 睛 (sound: zing1) all have similar sounds, and their sounds relate to the sound of 青 (a character on its own that means green and has the sound cing1). 青 is the phonetic component of all these characters. Over 90% of modern Chinese characters are morpho-phonetic compositions (Lee, 1989), 晴, 請, 淸 being common examples of morpho-phonetic characters:

i. 日 (sun) + 青 (sound: cing1) = 晴 (sunny)

ii. 言 (speech) + 青 (sound: cing1) = 請 (request)

iii. 氵 (water) + 青 (sound: cing1) = 淸 (clear)

iv. 目 (eye) + 青 (sound: cing1) = 睛 (eye)

In many circumstances, people can guess a character's meaning or sound from its components (Zhang, 1987). However, the situation is complicated since the phonetic component does not always indicate the sound of the character. Using the above case as an example, the component 青 is a meaningful character with the sound /cing1/, but the characters making up the component are not all pronounced exactly the same. In other words, orthography-phonology correspondence is neither always straightforward nor always consistent.

It is very important for learners to acquire awareness of the structural features of Chinese characters when learning to write in Chinese. Psycholinguistic studies of Chinese provide evidence about the importance of an awareness of part-whole relations in the processing of Chinese text. Chen at al. (1996) and Liu (1995) provide evidence of how knowledge about components is used in the processing of Chinese characters and text. Research by Tzeng et al. (1986) into the writing produced by brain-damaged Chinese patients indicates that Chinese characters are processed as symbols that carry structures possessing different levels of graphic complexity. Chan and Nunes (2001) show that children are often aware of aspects of the whole character in relation to its textual context before developing sensitivity to the internal structure of the individual characters. For example, they can differentiate drawings from characters; each character can be seen as occupying an imaginary square; and they note that one character corresponds to one syllable in speech. (For readers who want to learn more about Chinese characters, please refer to Chapter 4 of this book.)

TRADITIONAL APPROACHES TO TEACHING CHINESE CHARACTERS

The difficulty in learning Chinese characters carries profound implications for the way Chinese is taught and for the complexity of teaching materials. Traditionally, Chinese children are taught in a bottom-up manner that starts from learning how to write individual characters; characters are then placed in the context of sentences then paragraphs; then the character is read in the context of the whole passage. In writing a character, students are required to follow a strict sequence of stroke order and the exact position of each stroke is strictly prescribed (Ministry of Education, Taiwan, 1996). In order to ensure that students memorise how to write correctly the characters being taught, teachers ensure that they practise writing every character many times until its recall is automatic. Sometimes, students are made to write each character up to 100 times in a single lesson (Ministry of Education, PRC, 2001).

The most frequently used classroom procedure for assessing how well students have memorized characters they are supposed to have learnt is dictation. Students are required to write down what they hear without error. If they make mistakes, they are required to do a 'correction' by writing the characters without error at least ten times, and to practise writing the wrong words again and again until they are securely learnt.

The traditional learning of Chinese characters via endless copying and frequent dictations is very tough and most youngsters find the whole process very tedious indeed. The relationship between strokes and characters is often opaque and their memorisation is often very difficult. Children find it difficult to discern different Chinese characters that contain similar components but have dissimilar sounds.

Conversely, they mix up words that have similar sounds but quite dissimilar characters (and meanings). It is no wonder that most learners are exhausted by dictation exercises.

Chinese teachers are all too aware of students' errors due to the confusion between characters and every week they assign at least one dictation exercise. The imminence of the ordeal is a nightmare for many young children and their parents. In order to meet dictation requirements, parents have to rehearse over and over again with their children the characters the school has asked them to learn. The students spend so much time on dictation preparation that they relinquish time supposed to be spent in the library or in participating in extra-curricular activities. It is not unusual for parent-child relationships to be severely strained. From time to time there are reports in the media of parents and students committing suicide due to the torture of frequent dictation exercises, for parents feel fraught about what they can do to improve their child's dictation performance (A Mother, 2002).

In order to make teaching and learning less stressful, teachers avoid teaching characters containing many strokes or complicated structures in the beginning stage. This imposes constraints on the range and choice of language used and explored in class. It seems logical for the characters students are asked to learn to be simple and easy to write, and for students to have to learn only a few at a time. However the syllabus for the mid and later years of primary education imposes the criterion that words to be taught are those of high frequency in adult media usage. This results in upper primary teachers, like their lower primary colleagues, having to use words that are irrelevant to the students' daily life and world. The teaching materials are often dull and the language curriculum lacks appeal (Tse & Li, 2001). Progress is slow and the learning materials are contrived and artificial.

The traditional approach to teaching and learning Chinese characters is quite restrictive. The scope of teaching content is quite narrow and its interest level for the child is poor. The material used in Chinese language lessons with beginner readers only features words that have been formally taught. Progress is slow and very laboured.

NEW APPROACHES TO TEACHING CHINESE CHARACTERS

In the past decades, various regions in China have experimented with ways to teach students to read and write Chinese more effectively. These methods are not exclusively confined to particular regions, but it may help the reader if the regional origin of each initiative is identified.

Emphasising the Meaning of Characters

This strategy (see Huang, 1952) was most strongly advocated in Anhui province in the 1980s. It aims at helping students learn the meaning of characters through teaching materials that relate to their own daily life experiences. Characters are classified into two main categories: scientific perspective and social perspective. Students learn characters and content language simultaneously, chiefly in Chinese language lessons but also in any lesson where new characters are introduced. New words are relevant for curriculum content and the teaching of characters through a language-across-the-curriculum approach has been found to be effective.

Explicit Instruction about the Structure and Form of Characters

Teachers in Hebei province of China were prominent in adopting this approach. They teach their students to analyze the structure of Chinese characters into two broad components, morphological and phonetic. The teaching of a character consists of three tiers: whole character, components and strokes. And component is the core and the base for the formation of a Chinese character (Le, n.d.; *Teaching Reading*, n.d.; Tse, 2001). This strategy emphasises accurate pronunciation of syllables and analysis of Chinese characters through teaching the order of strokes, the shape of components, explanation of meaning in context, and the copying of characters. It aims at developing students' ability to pronounce the characters and explain their components instantly.

Emphasising the Association between Character, Form and Meaning

This is a popular strategy adopted particularly by teachers in Hunan province. Students are encouraged to add associations to the character and its forms using their imagination and creative thinking (Li, 1989). Guessing games and the copying of characters are also common elements of this strategy (Dai, 1998).

Emphasising Speech and Text Association

This method is widely used in Tianjin province. Students listen to a spoken text repeatedly and memorise it. They then read the text and match the sound and meaning they hold in memory to the characters one by one. They listen to their teacher's speech, and finger-touch or trace each character synchronously with the syllable in speech. They read the characters until they can recognise them in isolation, integrating the sound and meaning of words with the form of the character (Gu & Tian, 1999).

Phonic Systems

This strategy, in one form or another, is the most widespread approach used all over China. It enables learners to access the sound of characters and how they are pronounced via "Pinyin". It is expected that once learners know the Pinyin sound of a character, they are better able to attach sound to the ideographs (individual or in combination) and to the meaning. Every student in China is supposed to master the skills of pronunciation using *Pinyin*, and how to pronounce accurately the sound transcription of text, including nouns, vowels, consonants and tones (Ministry of Education, PRC, 2001, p. 5). Pinyin equivalents are printed alongside the characters in textbooks to tell students how to read aloud the characters in question.

Pinyin provides support for children who know spoken Putonghua to learn new characters. However, in places where the lingua franca is a local dialect of Chinese, the effectiveness of the method is reduced. In Hong Kong, over 90% of the residents speak the Cantonese dialect. Schools generally find that students learn Chinese characters more effectively through their mother tongue without the support of a phonic transcription system[1]. Tse (2000) points out that the shape (character), the sound and the meaning constitute a combined unit of language, and he proposes that all three elements should be learnt simultaneously. Very importantly, the learning of phonic symbols should not be put before the learning of shapes (characters).

Strategies Emphasising the Use of Character Clusters: Teaching Character Clusters with Similar Radicals

This practice is commonly employed in Liaoning province. The strategy follows the principle of "learning characters before reading text" (Editorial Board of Central Educational Science Research Centre, 1980; Kwok & Cheung, 1991; Zhang, Chen, & Li, 1995). Students learn to read clusters of characters with similar or the same radicals with the help of Pinyin. They then read several texts to consolidate the characters they have learnt.

Teaching Characters Possessing the Same Rhyme

This strategy is advocated and particularly used by teachers in Liaoning province. It aims at enabling students to learn a large number of words within a short period of time and begin reading and writing as soon as possible. Students memorise rhymes and learn the characters used in the rhyme (National Institute of Educational Research & Liaoning Province Donggang City Experimental School, 1996; Jiang, 1997).

Teaching Text that Contains Character Clusters

This strategy is widely used by teachers in Sichuan province. Students read a text containing characters with similar sounds, character shape/form or meaning. They are first taught to read the text and associate sound and meaning to the characters. They then search for clusters of characters that are similar in some way. They recite the text until they can recall it without error, and use this to memorise other characters (Dai, 1998; Yan et al., 1994).

Each of the above teaching methods has some appeal. No single approach has been commonly adopted because the identification of the *best* method is unresolved. The various methods tend to focus with different stress on particular features of the written language. What is generally lacking is a theory that draws upon the benefits of each and every method. At the same time, what is needed is a theory that adequately addresses and embraces the relationship between parts and wholes, such that Chinese language teachers are able to cover all aspects of character learning.

THE PHENOMENOGRAPHIC THEORY OF LEARNING
AND PERCEPTUAL LEARNING

Gibson and Gibson (1955) point out that a fundamental question about learning concerns the roles of doing and perceiving. The traditional approach to teaching Chinese characters builds clearly on the primary role of doing: the learner learns through copying characters until they know them by heart. However, the many writing errors and the obvious confusion of characters demonstrated by students clearly indicate that doing does not guarantee that learners have perceived the critical features of the characters. It is necessary to investigate how students perceive the Chinese characters and how these perceptions develop, so that an effective strategy of teaching Chinese characters can be developed.

Partly inspired by Phenomenography, a perception oriented approach to the learning of Chinese characters has been developed. It integrates enhancement of the *way of seeing* (perception of the meaning and structures of the language) into the process of doing (the reading, writing and the using of language). This approach emphasises the meaningfulness of the text being taught, and the discernment of part-whole relationships. In effect this is predominantly a top-down approach that sees reading as commencing in the mind with a search for meaning.

Phenomenography and its empirical research provide evidence that there exist different ways among people of seeing the same thing. A person's experience about variations of the phenomena and the associated consequences affect the way that the person attends to the phenomenon (Bowden & Marton, 1998).

Central to the phenomenographic theory of learning is discernment. With the experience of variation, parts are discerned *from* the whole, and at the same time *in relation to* the whole, and this is a process that goes from the whole to the parts. Marton and Booth (1997) see this as an organic development that follows Werner's *orthogenetic law* (1948), is typically a change from an undifferentiated whole towards a more complex whole with increasing differentiations of its part, their organisation and integration. The whole precedes the parts. The meaning of the whole guides the search for the meanings of the parts. Therefore, the under-standing of what is learnt generally goes from the whole to the parts or from general to specifics.

To summarise, Phenomenography emphasises that in order to experience a pheno-menon in different ways one needs to discern its structure and meaning from and within its context; for people to discern these aspects, variations of these aspects should be experienced; perception of a phenomenon generally goes from the whole to the parts. The implications of Phenomenography on the perceptual learning of Chinese characters are discussed in the next section.

PHENOMENOGRAPHY AND THE LEARNING OF CHINESE CHARACTERS

Phenomenography questions the effectiveness of the traditional idea that children should learn by memorising and reproducing the forms of characters perfectly one at a time. In contrast, it is suggested that the learning of Chinese characters should comprise the simultaneous discernment of their structural and referential (meaning) aspects. Chan and Nunes (2001) point out that children's learning should start from focusing simultaneously on the structure and meaning of the whole character. This includes discerning structural aspects, as well as differentiating the overall shape of the character from that of its neighbours.

As well as discernment of the appearance of the character, emphasis should also be placed on the meaning of the character and how it corresponds to a unit of spoken language (the syllable). In the early stage of character learning, the learner will look for the meaning and sound of characters. As a result, it is important to ensure that the character appears in meaningful text and that the text contains the child's own lexicon of familiar words.

The teacher should make it clear that characters follow certain "*position on the page*" conventions. As teachers help students simultaneously to attend to the shape, pronunciation and meaning of characters, they should emphasise that, as the message in the text unfolds, characters and sound may change. The role of the character in the message in the text should be emphasized rather than features of its appearance in isolation. This is in contrast with traditional approaches that insist that the student must be able to produce the character from memory without error before learning how to use it in a meaningful context.

Furthermore, the teaching process should start with characters that the student already knows in terms of meaning and pronunciation. Where possible, the context in which the character appears should also relate to the student's own life experience. Through this, the student will learn how meanings are associated with components of individual characters and distinctive features of their shapes. An awareness of the inner structures of characters should be highlighted in the form of related characters in clusters, through the experiencing of their similarities and differences. The importance of variation highlighted by Phenomenography explains why the incremental learning to read and to copy correctly one Chinese character at a time cannot bring about a student's personal perception of the internal structures of characters. In the traditional approach, a talented reader may very well be able to discern the critical features (i.e. similarities and differences) between characters and important variations of each newly learnt character to be recognised. However, this very much depends on the ability and insight of the individual child rather than intentional instruction from the teacher.

The basic ideas of variation and discernment provide a useful insight into the on-going debate among language educators about structural awareness instruction. One objection against structural awareness instruction is that analysis of the structure of language requires a considerable amount of meta-language that may constitute an additional burden for the language learner. However, according to the theory, the structural features of the language are something learners can feel by themselves and be engendered through the learners' own experience of the relevant variations. Discernment is experienced by learners rather than being *told* about by others. Using meta-vocabulary to teach the structure is insufficient for the development of this sensitivity. Meta-language, if at all introduced, should be taken as secondary to the learner's primary experience.

Another objection to explicit structural awareness instruction is that the learning of the language can become very analytical and may actually become an obstacle to integration and fluency in using language. However, according to the principles of discernment and orthogenetic development, parts should always be discerned from and in relation to the whole. Hence the learning of components should be experienced as variations in the context of whole characters, and not as things that stand on their own. If one varies a part within the context of the whole, differentiation and integration (analytic view and synthetic view) should come into being at the same time. In fact, in structural awareness training of Chinese characters, parts (e.g. components) are always discerned in the context of a whole (e.g. character) and not in isolation.

A COMPREHENSIVE AND INTEGRATIVE PERCEPTUAL APPROACH TO CHINESE CHARACTER LEARNING: INTEGRATING LANGUAGE LEARNING AND LANGUAGE AWARENESS DEVELOPMENT

The meaning of characters as perceived by the learner helps determine the level of difficulty the student will encounter in learning the characters. Word meaning implies two senses. First, it refers to the meaning of the characters derived from the context. Second, it refers to the characteristics and structural aspects of characters when they are set against related characters in the language. Learners need to deal with both senses of meaning at the same time.

Unlike practice in the traditional approach, the comprehensive and integrative perceptual approach uses spoken language as a starting point with meanings familiar to the learner. The teaching material used is usually based upon spoken language that students have already learnt at home, in the kindergarten and in school. The new approach deliberately incorporates nursery rhymes and children's' games as teaching materials because many parents like to teach their children nursery rhymes and children's' games as family activities. As a result, most students know the content and meaning of the nursery rhymes and games when they are young, and have a secure knowledge of the language and the meanings involved. This helps teachers to stimulate students' awareness that characters actually represent meanings.

The new approach places major emphasis on the learning of characters within realistic and meaningful language contexts. The lesson usually begins with a meaningful situation that the text describes and typically goes from whole to parts. Teachers are encouraged to draw upon familiar language games or nursery rhymes when developing new teaching materials. The students use the words in meaningful contexts and are thereby interested in knowing how they are written. Looking at the text while playing the game or singing nursery rhymes, they associate structures and sounds with meanings. Learning to read is a natural progression. The written forms and sounds of words are linked to their meaning in an enjoyable context.

Once students recognise characters and their sounds, teaching switches to the form and features of the characters. Attention is drawn to samples of related characters in the text. The similarities and differences between these characters are discerned and critical attributes are highlighted and explained: components, structures and strokes. Awareness of the internal structure of Chinese characters is enhanced at the same time. Other features of the teaching approach are illustrated in the sample lesson that follows.

A SAMPLE LESSON FEATURING COMPREHENSIVE AND INTEGRATIVE LANGUAGE INSTRUCTION

Below is a lesson illustrating principles of the perceptual approach to teaching that aims to integrate language learning and structural awareness development. The lesson took place in a Grade 1 classroom, when students had been at school for about two months. The text (Tse, 2006, p. 75) used in the lesson is the rhyme below:

Siu Baau with his schoolbag on his shoulder,	小鮑背着大書包，
Carries a pineapple bun in his hand,	手中拿着菠蘿包，
Met a roaring wolf,	遇見狼狗在咆哮，
He ran back in fright,	嚇得立刻往回跑，
Breathless and footsore,	氣喘如牛腿兒酸，
There was a blister on his foot and it hurt.	腳板疼痛起水泡。

The lesson outlined below lasted 50 minutes.

i. The teacher told the story first so that the students had an overview of the content. The students listened attentively.

ii. With guidance from the teacher, the students read the text line by line (text shown as a PowerPoint file). Then, the teacher asked the students to *read* the text themselves with body movements matching the rhyme. They enjoyed the reading.

iii. The teacher played the character of *Siu Baau* (a little boy), and another student played the *wolf*. The other students read the text aloud. When the teacher invited them to join in, they held their hands up high to attract her attention. Most of the students wanted to participate in the drama. All the students read out loudly in chorus. They also laughed when they were watching the drama. The students enjoyed the learning process.

iv. The teacher asked two students to participate in the instant drama and it was repeated twice. The other students read the text aloud in chorus. They laughed loudly. The excitement of the students was rising. Some students stood up and acted characters in their seats.

v. The teacher highlighted four target characters 鮑, 咆, 跑 and 泡 in the text which are related in form, and asked the students to identify the invariant (包) and variable (魚, 口, ⻊, 氵) components of characters. Most of the students were able to identify the invariant components quickly and spoke out loudly.

vi. The teacher took out the variable components of each character. Students were asked to trace the correct components of the characters with the cue of the whole words (i.e. 鮑魚, 書包, 麵包, 咆哮, 跑步, 水泡), and the meanings of the words.

vii. The teacher asked the students to explain their answers, and then wrote the correct components (i.e. 魚, 口,⻊ , 氵) on the board.

viii. The teacher showed the class the pictorial origins of the morphological components (魚, 口,⻊ , 氵) which corresponded to the meaning of fish, mouth, foot and water (see Figure 5.2).

Figure 5.2. Pictorial origins of morphological components:
fish, mouth, foot and water

ix. The teacher told the students that these components (魚, 口,⻊ , 氵) can combine with other parts to form different characters and the shapes will change a little. The students were then asked to identify the variant components in the characters listed in Exercise Two (see Appendix A).

x. As the story mentioned eating a pineapple bun, one of the most common foods for breakfast, the teacher asked students to share their life experiences about eating buns and the bun they liked the most. Most of the students put up their hands high to attract the teacher's attention. More than ten students related their experience about eating buns. As the students told their experiences, the teacher wrote down related words used by them on the board.

xi. The teacher asked students to copy at least three words relating to their own experience from the board into their textbook, Exercise Three (see Appendix A). Many students wanted to write down more than three words.

xii. The teacher identified target words from the text, and made some flash cards. Students were divided into groups, and the teacher distributed the flash cards to each group. The students were asked to read the words on the flash card one by one (see Appendix B). Students who could read the words correctly were given one mark. The student with the highest marks was the winner of the game. The students enjoyed the game very much.

xiii. Then, the teacher summed up the whole lesson and gave the students a worksheet. The target words of the text, and other words with similar shape or meanings of the target words, were printed on the worksheet. The teacher read aloud the target words and the students were asked to identify and circle the correct words from the worksheet (see Appendix C).

Discussion of the Lesson

This lesson provides an example of a comprehensive and integrative perceptual approach that deliberately houses the structural understanding of components and the structure of characters within a meaningful language context. It first looks at the overall meaning of the poem, then targets a number of characters and words that contain invariant and variable components. It then uses these as a springboard to focus on an aspect or theme that highlights the structure of selected Chinese characters. Finally, the lesson links up the students' own life experiences, the meanings present in the overall text and the fun of combining thoughts and physical actions in drama. Language learning and language awareness are taught simultaneously, and the lesson illustrates how teachers can help children experience both.

Deriving the Meaning of the Characters from the Context

The lesson moves from *whole* to *parts* in a smooth and natural manner. Traditionally orientated teachers may question the wisdom of having students *read* the text without having first been taught the characters in detail. The rhyme contains about forty characters, of which the students previously knew only a few. The students were able to *read* because the meaning in the poem touched on their daily life experiences, their own spoken language and their prior knowledge of the vocabulary involved. The lesson forcefully uses contextual cues to bring out the meaning of the characters and words. As the students look at the characters, sing them out aloud and act out their meaning in a sort of charade, they are simultaneously matching speech to character to meaning. The sequence begins with meaning, moves onto the sound, then onto the overall shape, then the components and structure of the character. Once students are able to recognise the sound and critical features of the shape, the two are combined, all set against the meaning of the character arrived at earlier. To speed up the learning progress, it is essential that the teaching material is based upon spoken language that students have already been taught at home, in the kindergarten and in school. Crucially, the learning of reading and writing is build on students' own grasp of the language and the meanings involved. When reading the text and joining in the game, students have opportunities to associate structures and sounds with meanings. Learning to read is natural, easy and pleasurable.

Relating the Meaning of the Character to Similar Characters in the Language

Once students match and recognise characters and their sounds, the teaching switches to a pre-selected set of target characters in the text, and to highlighting their structural features. Simultaneously attending to character clusters and the variations between them induces structural awareness that the teacher is conscious of stressing. Through the various activities and steps in the lesson, similarities and differences between strokes, structures, components and the pronunciation of characters are discerned and explained, and critical features are emphasised, all in an enjoyable ambiance. The various levels of components, characters and words are brought closely together, one embedding the other. The dynamics of the learning situation provide space for possibilities, anticipation and ways of thinking which are absent from the traditional incremental approach. Within this *space of learning* (c.f. Marton et al., 2004), the number of characters and words covered can be huge. At the same time, since their critical features are easy to identify, the students can make contrasts and generalisations. Furthermore the fresh insights are extended as students make connections to their previous word knowledge and life experiences.

Unlike the traditional approach, the new approach does not expect students to learn in one fell swoop all the precise knowledge about and details of every character form they encounter. It is no surprise that the students in the lesson setting described are able to "read" and recognize characters they would stumble over if presented out of context. The pleasure of discovering meanings by themselves is a key learning objective of the lesson and helps students memorize the variant and invariant features of the target characters and the meaning of the text with ease. According to the principle of orthogenetic development (Werner, 1948), students will gradually make progress in getting to know these characters when they later encounter them repeatedly in different texts.

In the initial stages of such learning, students can read many more words than they can write. However, it is important to stress that, when highlighting structural principles and/or components, the teacher makes a clear distinction between those characters that students should learn to write and those they only need to be able to read in context. The number of reading texts covered in the year is greatly increased, and exposure to characters used in meaningful contexts and text is hugely expanded. In contrast to practice in the traditional approach, students are not systematically required to write without error from memory all the characters in the initial stage. Such slavish learning makes learning like a chore, ineffective and painful.

PRINCIPLES OF THE COMPREHENSIVE AND INTEGRATIVE APPROACH

In terms of the principles of the comprehensive and integrative perceptual approach, the pedagogy of integrating language learning and structural awareness in Chinese characters can be summarised as follows:

i.   Character learning must start from real text that relates meaningfully to the students' own life experiences and their own spoken language.
ii. All texts used in class are selected with the objects of learning in mind. These include the varying and invariant components of characters, particular structural features of characters or words, and consideration of which characters to learn to write and which characters to learn to read in context. It should be noted that not all characters will be learnt to the same depth.
iii. Common nursery rhymes, children's games and rhyming text well known to the students are good choices of passages to be used in the early stages of character learning. Characters may also be categorised according to similarities and differences in the visual appearance of their component parts.
iv. The instructional process typically goes from whole to parts: from text to words to characters, and from characters to their component parts.
v.   Structural awareness is brought about through learning characters in related clusters. Characters are categorised according to their components, structure or sound to form clusters. Teachers can highlight the similarities and differences among features to encourage meaningful learning that is easier to retain.

vi. When the students are being guided to discern the structural features of characters, the relationship between the form, pronunciation and meaning of the characters is concurrently brought to their attention.

vii. Students are encouraged to link up current characters and text to their previous knowledge and life experiences. Their banks of known words are valuable resources that teachers can use to help them integrate sound, meaning and written forms.

viii. Character analysis and composition games are good choices for the consolidation of students' structural awareness about components and the structure of characters. New tasks may also be created to assess students' knowledge of characters (see Figure 5.3), especially since the traditional dictation does not have this capacity.

Figure 5.3 shows how a Grade 1 student explored his own lexicon around the theme "科學" (science). The students had been asked to write down as many words they could remember relating to the theme.

Figure 5.3. An alternative to the traditional dictation task.

THE EFFECTIVENESS OF THE COMPREHENSIVE AND INTEGRATIVE PERCEPTUAL APPROACH: A CLASSROOM-BASED STUDY

Research Approach

A small-scale quasi-experiment was carried out. Although it is difficult and rarely feasible to conduct strictly controlled experiments in the complexity of real classrooms, it is entirely possible to study the merits and weaknesses of innovations by comparing the responses of matched groups (Brown, 1992; Collins, 1992).

Research Design

The new approach was introduced and tried out in three primary schools in Hong Kong for a whole academic year. In order to avoid objections from parents about splitting children into groups within the same year so that some are taught using different (special) approaches and teaching materials, an entirely separate and distant comparison group was selected. This group consisted of Grade Two students who had been taught entirely via traditional methods the year before. All the Grade One students learnt through the new approach and materials in the Chinese Language lessons for two out of the eight lessons they had each week. In the other six lessons, they used conventional textbook materials. Teaching was carried out over one academic year. All Grade One and Grade Two students in the three primary schools participated.

Procedure

All Grade One students completed a pre-test in September at the very beginning of the academic year. The same test was given to all Grade Two students at the same time. Teachers taught all Grade One students Chinese characters and Chinese Language by using traditional textbooks (six out of the eight lessons per week), supplemented by the new approach and teaching materials (the other two of the eight lessons per week). The total instructional time (eight lessons per week) was the same duration the Grade Two students had received the previous year when they were in Grade One. A post-test (the same test given to all of the students before the start of the project) was given to all of the Grade One students when they entered Grade Two at the beginning of the next academic year.

Research Instruments

The test consisted of four sections and took 40 minutes.

Reading comprehension. This section examined students' ability to decode words, make inferences, organise information, present their own ideas and evaluate text. The 130 characters in the reading comprehension test were carefully chosen from all those present in the new teaching material. Text content was congruent with the characters suggested for Grade One students by the Hong Kong Curriculum Development Council (1990), and in traditional textbooks used in Grade One (Chan, 1995; Editorial Board of New Asia Cultural Enterprises [EBNACE], 1995). This ensured that the Grade Two students would not be disadvantaged as a result of having been taught a different set of characters when in Grade One. Although 14 of the 130 characters were not in the Grade One word list, experienced Primary teachers gave the assurance that the 14 new characters were regularly used in other subjects in Grade One. All the characters had definitely been taught to the students and the teachers were convinced that the test material would offer no advantage to either group.

Writing down words related to pictures. This section assessed the number of words the students were able to write down from memory. Three simple pictures were presented and the students were given three minutes to write down as many words as possible they thought related to the content of each picture. The words could be nouns, verbs, adverbs, adjectives and so on. These pictures described the family life (a family dining in the living room), school life (students studying in the classroom and playing in the playground) and daily life in society (people walking in the street). The content of the pictures had no obvious relationship to either the content of traditional textbooks or the materials used in the experimental materials, so did not favour or disadvantage any group of students.

Identifying correct characters. This section evaluated the students' structural awareness of characters. Structural variations of five characters were shown and the students were asked to identify the correct one out of 15 characters (with 75 structural variations) chosen randomly from the new teaching materials. The list of characters was shown to the junior grade teachers in the school and compared with traditional word lists (Hong Kong Curriculum Development Council, 1990; Chan, 1995; EBNACE, 1995). Although six out of these 15 characters were not included in the recommended word lists, the teachers confirmed that all six characters were used very regularly in different subjects throughout Grade One and would not grant any advantage to the students taught using the new approach.

Matching characters to sounds. This section assessed students' sensitivity to the pronunciation of characters. Students listened to the teacher read aloud the correct answer then picked out the correct pronunciation from five options. The choice of words was from those taught specifically in the new approach, and the words were not included in the official Grade One word list (Hong Kong Curriculum Development Council, 1990; Chan, 1995; EBNACE, 1995). The experienced junior grade teachers assured the research team that the words had been used frequently in Grade One classes and that it would be known to all students now in Grade Two.

ANALYSIS OF DATA

The pre-test and post-test scores for the experimental group learning by the new approach were compared (see Table 5.1). Then, the post-test results of the experimental group were compared (see Table 5.2) against those of the control students tested a year earlier (when they had just entered Grade Two).

RESULTS

In Table 5.1, the pre- and post-test performance of the students who had experienced the new teaching approach was compared. Paired-sample t-testing revealed that all the gains were highly statistically significant (p< .001 and p< .01). The effect sizes (c.f. Cohen, 1977; Glass et al., 1981; Hedges, 1981; Curlette, 1987; Hattie, 1992) of different parts of the test vary between 1.04 and 2.11^2.

Table 5.1. Attainment of the experimental group at pre and post-test (N = 503)

Testing items	Full marks	Pre-test (Sept., 1998)		Post-test (Sept., 1999)		t	d
		M	SD	M	SD		
1. Reading comprehension	20	6.66	3.66	14.23	2.95	-36.76***	2.07
2. Writing down words related to pictures							
a. Family	14	6.78	4.22	11.31	3.39	-22.17***	1.07
b. School	14	4.60	3.11	10.46	3.23	-32.29***	1.88
c. Society	14	6.17	3.52	11.46	3.10	-27.49***	1.50
3. Identifying correct words	15	5.24	2.93	11.43	3.16	-37.69***	2.11
4. Matching correct characters to sounds	15	10.87	3.35	14.36	1.55	-23.27***	1.04

*** indicates a level of statistical significance at <.001 level

A comparison between Grade One students (experimental group) who had received both the new and traditional teaching against that of the Group Two students (control group) who had received traditional teaching alone was made (see Table 5.2). It is apparent that the experimental group had significantly outperformed the control group on all parts of the test. The analysis indicates a large and significant effect in favour of the group that had been taught using both traditional and new approach teaching.

Table 5.2. Comparison of attainment of the two broad groups of students

Testing items	Full marks	Grade 1 (n = 503) New + Traditional teaching		Grade 2 (n = 496) Traditional teaching		F	d
		M	SD	M	SD		
1. Reading comprehension	20	14.23	2.95	9.30	3.03	679.70***	-1.67
2. Writing down words related to pictures							
a. Family	14	11.31	3.39	11.00	3.77	1.89	-0.09
b. School	14	10.46	3.23	9.2	4.33	27.39***	-0.39
c. Society	14	11.46	3.10	8.29	4.95	148.18***	-1.02
3. Identifying correct words	15	11.43	3.16	7.63	3.07	372.72***	-1.20
4. Matching correct characters to sounds	15	14.36	1.55	14.29	1.75	.50	-0.05

*** indicates a level of statistical significance with $p < .001$

Preliminary Discussion

The results suggest that the students who had received both new and traditional teaching had made better progress than their counterparts taught using the traditional approach alone. Their gains were impressive, taking this group to a level of performance higher than that of their counterparts taught using conventional teaching alone. The research instruments used had been carefully designed and examined so as not to build bias into the data. Even though it may be argued on *a priori* grounds that the test included items that might be more familiar to the new teaching group, the very experienced junior grade teacher consultants had assured the authors that the research instruments were comprehensive and fair to both groups of students.

Great care was taken to avoid any Hawthorne effect brought about by the students knowing that they had been taught in ways out of the ordinary and that they were in experimental groups. Hattie (1992) indicates that the Hawthorne effect can be suspected if the effects of any intervention exceed significantly the gains that can be expected by conventional teaching. Although the effect sizes obtained in the present study are far above the levels predicted by Hattie (.4 of a standard deviation) for all four sections of the test used, the intervention was deliberately very low key. Indeed, teachers using the traditional approach were intent on showing its positive impact.

Although the results support the new teaching approach, caution is needed in interpreting the data. One possible source of error is the learning effects of testing. The experimental group had been tested twice using the same test. However, it has to be pointed out that Hong Kong students, even at Grade One, are tested very much more frequently than counterparts in the West. Having received no feedback about performance on the pre-test, they were unlikely to remember the format and content of a single test taken a year ago. Why should students remember the format and content of a test taken 12 months earlier, particularly when no feedback had been given? In these circumstances, the extent of the gain scores (c.f. Hattie, 1992) is quite exceptional.

Another source of error is the possibility that the two groups of student in the same school might differ in terms of intellectual capability. However, the schools' attainment test results in all subject areas clearly indicate that the profiles of the two groups are entirely comparable in all of the three schools involved. At the same time, Hattie (1992) claims that if effect size is greater than .4 of a standard deviation, then it should be taken seriously. All of the effect size were greater than the level indicated by Hattie.

It is suggested that further research on a more extensive scale is needed before one can claim that any difference in attainment between the two ways of teaching Chinese characters is truly valid. More controls over variables such as sampling, teaching and testing are necessary to ensure that data are reliable and valid.

DISCUSSION AND CONCLUSION

Comparison of the two experimental groups suggests that the students who had received traditional teaching supplemented by new approach teaching had made better progress than counterparts taught entirely using the traditional approach. The gains in performance of the students taught using the dual approach were impressive. The test used had been carefully constructed to avoid incorporating bias into the data. Even though it may be argued on *a priori* grounds that the test included items that tended to favour the new approach teaching group, the very experienced primary school consultants assured the researchers that test was comprehensive and fair; that all groups had covered exactly the same areas of study; and that all had studied the Chinese language for the same length of time.

The comprehensive and integrative perceptual approach to teaching Chinese characters reported in this paper was a response to students' and teachers' dissatisfaction with the traditional approach used so consistently in Hong Kong. It was prompted by the need to introduce new and alternative approaches to the teaching of Chinese characters. Based on Phenomenography, the approach makes learners aware of crucial differences and similarities between characters, and helps them discover for themselves the meaning of vocabulary and grammar. Instead of teaching and learning the characters one at a time in artificial isolation, the approach seeks to make learning natural and pleasurable.

A major concern of the traditional approach to teaching Chinese characters is on how characters are written. Students are expected to learn the parts that make up the whole, and in a fixed sequence that is inflexibly constant. Each character is learned as a unit. In contrast, the new approach emphasises reading characters as a search for meaning and as a means of communication. In order to discern how characters relate to one another, attention is drawn to clusters of characters that possess similar or related features. Knowledge of characters helps the reader to perceive literal meaning and to use language as a means of thinking and refining thinking.

The phenomenographic theory of learning and awareness holds that an important goal of education is to develop powerful ways within the learner of seeing the world around them, especially in terms of variations and co-variations. Variations in meaning and structure are fundamental aspects of learning in general. Meaning and structure fuse when they co-vary together (Marton & Booth, 1997; Marton et al., 2004).

The results of the empirical study reported here support the effectiveness of the new approach. The remarkable results emanating from experience with the new approach are persuasive evidence. The teachers participating in the study recognised the merits of the approach, especially when they saw for themselves that their students had made very good progress; Chinese lessons were more popular than ever before; much of the chore of memorising characters was eased; and a springboard was established early on in the children's schooling for making language a tool for learning, rather than an objective in itself.

Many teachers and parents have shown great interest in the approach. More than 60 seminars have been organised since 1999, with over 16,000 participants. The innovation has had a sweeping impact on primary schools in Hong Kong. Since 2000, over 250 primary schools and two special schools have been adopted the new approach. Furthermore, 70% of the leading publishers in Hong Kong were marketing teaching materials based on the new approach, either redesigning existing materials or producing entirely new materials based on it. The teaching methodology and materials are now used in schools that teach Chinese in Singapore, San Francisco, the Netherlands, Toronto, Australia, Sweden and Taiwan. (For learning tones, please refer to chapter 3; for learning orthographic awareness in learning Chinese characters, please refer to chapter 4).

NOTES

[1] There is a phonic system developed by the Hong Kong Language Association to transcribe Cantonese dialect using the Roman alphabet. The symbols are the same as those used in pinyin but interpreted differently. The usage of this system in schools is minimal.

[2] The calculation of effect sizes of different parts of the test employed in the experiment is based on the following formula:

(Mean of post-test − mean of pre-test) / SD of pre-test

REFERENCES

A mother wants to commit suicide with her son for her son's poor academic results. (2002, January 22). *Singtao Daily Newspaper*.

Bloomfield, L. (1935). *Language*. London, UK: Allen and Unwin.

Bowden, J., & Marton, F. (1998). *The university of learning: Beyond competence*. London, UK: Kogan.

Brown, A. L. (1992). Design experiments: Theoretical and methodological challenges in creating complex interventions in classroom settings. *The Journal of the Learning Sciences, 2*, 141–178.

Chan, L., & Nunes, T. (2001). Explicit teaching and implicit learning of Chinese characters. In L. Tolchinsky (Ed.), *Developmental aspects in learning to write* (pp. 33–53). Dordrecht, The Netherlands: Kluwer Academic Publishers.

Chan, W. L. (Ed.). (1995). *Qisi Zhongguo Yuwen, Diyice* [Oxford Chinese language, Book one]. Hong Kong: Oxford University Press (China) Co. Ltd.

Chen, Y. P., Allport, D. A., & Marshall, J. C. (1996). What are the functional orthographic units in Chinese word recognition: The stroke or the stroke pattern? *Quarterly Journal of Experimental Psychology, 49A.*

Cohen, J. (1977). *Statistical power analysis for the behavioral sciences* (Rev. ed.). New York: Academic Press.

Colaizzi, P. F. (1973). *Reflection and research in psychology: A phenomenological study of learning.* Duquesne: Kendall/Hunt.

Collins, A. (1992). Toward a design science of education. In E. Scanlon & T. O. Shea (Eds.), *New directions in educational technology* (pp. 15–22). Berlin, Germany: Springer.

Curlette, W. L. (1987). The meta-analysis effect size calculator: A basic program for reconstructing unbiased effect sizes. *Educational and Psychological Measurement, 47,* 107–109.

Dai, R. Q. (1998). Zhongguo neidi zhizi jiaoxiao [Teaching Chinese characters in mainland China]. In R. Q. Dai, S. K. Tse, & J. J. Hao (Eds.), *Hanzi jiao yu xiao* [The teaching and learning of Chinese characters] (pp. 110–307). Shandong: Shandong Educational Press.

Editorial Board of Central Educational Science Research Centre. (1980). *Jizhong shizi jiaoxiao jingyan xuan* [Experience of the teaching and learning of "Learning characters in cluster"]. Beijing: Educational Science Publication.

Editorial Board of New Asia Cultural Enterprises. (Eds.). (1995). *Xiaoxue zhongguo yuwen, diyice* [Primary school Chinese language, book one]. Hong Kong: New Asia Cultural Enterprises Co. Ltd.

Gibson, J. J., & Gibson, E. J. (1955). Perceptual learning: differentiation or enrichment? *Psychological Review, 62,* 32–41.

Glass, G. V., McGaw, B., & Smith, M. L. (1981). *Meta-analysis in social research.* Beverly Hills, CA: Sage.

Gu, J. P., & Tian, B. N. (1999). *Gu Jin Ping tingdu shizi yanjiu* [Research on Gu Jin Ping's learning Chinese characters through listening and reading]. Jinan: Shandong Educational Publisher.

Gurtwitsch, A. (1964). *The field of consciousness.* Pittsburgh, PA: Puquesne University Press.

Hattie, J. (1992). Measuring the effects of schooling. *Australian Journal of Education, 30,* 5–13.

Hedges, L. V. (1981). Distribution theory for Glass's estimator of effect size and related estimators. *Journal of Educational Statistics, 6,* 107–128.

Ho, C. S. H., & Bryant, P. (1997a). Development of phonological aware of Chinese children in Hong Kong. *Journal of Psycholinguistic Research, 26,* 109–126.

Ho, C. S. H., & Bryant, P. (1997b). Phonological skills are important in learning to read Chinese. *Developmental Psychology, 33,* 946–951.

Ho, C. S. H., & Bryant, P. (1997c). Learning to read Chinese beyond the logographic phase. *Reading Research Quarterly, 32,* 276–289.

Hong Kong Curriculum Development Council. (1990). *Chinese language: Curriculum framework for primary one to primary six.* Hong Kong: Hong Kong Government.

Huang, H. S., & Hanley, R. (1997). A longitudinal study of phonological awareness, visual skills and Chinese reading acquisition among first-graders in Taiwan. *International Journal of Behavioral Development, 20,* 249–268.

Huang, J. J. (1952). Shenghuo jiaoyu fenlei shizifa [Learning Chinese characters through daily living]. In *Scientific categorization of Chinese characters teaching materials.* Anhui: Anhui Institute of Education.

Huang, P. R. (2003). *Hanzi jiaoxuo de lilun yu shijian* [Theories and practise of teaching of Chinese characters]. Taibei: Lexis Bookstore Co. Ltd.

Jiang, Z. C. (1997). *Xiaoxue jiaoxue "kexue, gaoxiao" tansuo* [Investigation on primary education 'efficient science']. Jinan: Shadong Educational Publisher.

Ki, W. W., Lam, H. C., Chung, A. L. S., Tse, S. K., Ko, P. Y., Lau, C. C., et al. (2003). Structural awareness, variation theory and ICT support. *L1 – Educational Studies in Language and Literature, 3,* 53–78.

Kwok, L., & Cheung, T. Y. (1991). *The theories and practice of "learning characters in cluster"*. Beijing: Educational Science Publication.

Le, X. Y. (n.d.). *Xiaosxue shizi jiaoxue lilun weitan* [Investigating the theories of teaching Chinese characters in primary schools]. Chekiang: Chekiang Normal University. Retrieved October 24, 2003, from http://www.learn.vip.sina.com/jylt/yxy00/131218.htm

Lee, C. M. (Ed.). (1989). *Lee's zhongwen zidian* [Lee's Chinese dictionary] (p. 1). Hong Kong: Hong Kong Chinese University Press.

Li, W. M. (1989). *Qite lianxiang shizifa de tansuo yu shijian* [The investigation and implementation of 'creative thinking learning Chinese characters']. Beijing: People's Education Publisher. Retrieved October 24, 2003, from http://www.pep.com.cn/20021201/ca48825.htm

Liu, I. M. (1995). Script factors that affect literacy: Alphabetic vs. logographic languages. In I. Taylor & D. R. Olson (Eds.), *Scripts and literacy: Reading and learning to read alphabets, syllabaries and characters* (pp. 145–162). Dordrecht, The Netherlands: Kluwer Academic Publishers.

Tan, L. H., & Perfetti, C. A. (1999). Phonological activation in visual identification of Chinese two-character words. *Journal of Experimental Psychology: Learning, memory and cognition, 25*, 382–393.

Marton, F., & Booth, S. (1997). *Learning and awareness*. Mahwah, NJ: Lawrence Erlbaum Associates, Publishers.

Marton, F., Runneson, U., & Tsui, B. M. A. (2004). The space of learning. In F. Marton & B. M. A. Tsui (Eds.), *Classroom discourse and the space of learning* (pp. 3–42). Saskatchewan: Lawrence Erlbaum Associates, Inc.

Miller, G. A. (1956). The magical number seven, plus or minus two: Some limits on our capacity for processing information. *The Psychological Review, 63*, 81–97.

Ministry of Education, People's Republic of China. (2001). *Yuwen kecheng biaozhun* [Standards of Chinese language curriculum]. Beijing: Beijing Normal University Publisher.

Ministry of Education, Taiwan. (1996). *Changyong guozi biaozhun ziti bishun shouce* [Guidebook of common use Chinese characters standard shapes and sequence of strokes]. Taibei: Ministry of Education, Promotion of Chinese Characters Committee.

National Education Commission and National Language Construction Committee. (1993). Xiandai hanyu changyong zibiao [A list of common used modern Chinese characters]. In *Yuyan wenzi guifan shouce*. Beijing: Yuwen Chubanshe.

National Institute of Educational Research and Liaoning Province Donggang City Exprimental School. (Eds.). (1996). *Yunyu shizi keben, yi zhi e ce* [Textbooks of learning Chinese characters through rhymes and rhythms, Book 1 and 2]. Beijing: Educational Science Publisher.

Teaching Reading and Writing of Chinese Characters. (n.d.). *Bujian zhizifa shiyan shuyao* [Learning Chinese characters by 'word components': Research summary]. Beijing: People's Education Publisher. Retrieved October 24, 2003, from [http://www.pep.com.cn/20021201/ca69176.htm]

Tse, S. K. (2000). *Yukuai xue hanzi* [Pleasurable learning of Chinese characters]. Hong Kong: Education Department, Hong Kong SAR Government.

Tse, S. K. (Ed.). (2001). *Gaoxiao hanzi jiao yu xue* [Effective teaching and learning of Chinese characters]. Hong Kong: Greenfield Enterprise Ltd.

Tse, S. K. (2006). *Zonghe gaoxiao shizi, yi zhi si ce* [Comprehensive and effective teaching and learning of Chinese characters, Book 1 and 2)]. Hong Kong: Greenfield Education Centre.

Tse, S. K., & Li, H. (2001). Singapore huawen shizi jiaoxue [Teaching of Chinese characters in Singapore]. In S. K. Tse (Ed.), *Gaoxiao hanzi jiao yu xue* (pp. 333–351). Hong Kong: Greenfield Enterprise Ltd.

Tzeng, O., Hung, D., Chen, S., Wu, J., & His, M. (1986). Processing Chinese logographs by Chinese brain damaged patients. In H. Kao, G. van Galen, & R. Hoosain (Eds.), *Graphonomics: contemporary research in handwriting*. Amsterdam: North-Holland.

Werner, H. (1948). *Comparative psychology of mental development*. New York: International Universities Press.

Yan, W. J., Lu, Z. T., & Xie, F. Y. (Eds.). (1994). *Zizuwen shizi jiaoxue* [Word family teaching Chinese characters]. Beijing: People's Education Publisher.

Yang, R. L. (2000). *Xiandai henzixuo tonglun* [General introduction to modern Chinese characters]. Beijing: The Great Wall Publisher.

Zhang, T. R., Chen, L. H., & Li, W. M. (1995). *Zhongguo dangdai hanzi rendu yu Shuxie* [Contemporary reading and writing of Chinese characters in China]. Chengdu: Sichuan Educational Publisher.

Zhang, Z. G. (1987). Chinese characters and reading. *Reading News, 8,* 7–8. Retrieved February 4, 2003, from Zhungwen.com Web site: Chinese characters and culture. (n.d.). *Does Chinese have an alphabet?* Web site: [http://zhongwen.com]

Shek Kam Tse, Wing Wah Ki and Elizabeth Ka Yee Loh
Faculty of Education
The University of Hong Kong

Ference Marton
Department of Education
University of Gothenburg

AUTHORS' NOTES

The authors would particularly like to acknowledge Professor Terry Dolan for his input to this article, and Professor Hazel Francis, London for her critical comments on an earlier version of this paper. We also want to thank the principals and teachers of the pilot schools, and the researchers, Wilson Tang, Leung Ngai Yi, Rex Ng, Kitty Tam, for their contribution in the research. We wish to express our gratitude to the Language Fund, Education and Manpower Bureau of Hong Kong SAR Government, for their financial support in this project.

APPENDIX A

Exercises Completed by the Students in the Sample Lesson

Exercise 1: Find out meaningful components
Please use the hints provided to find the components representing the meaning from the characters.

1. Abalone (鮑魚) is a kind of seafood (魚) with a great taste.
2. Please put all your belongings in you schoolbag (書包).
3. Among all kinds of bun (包), pineapple bun (菠蘿包) is one of my favourites.
4. Shut your month (口) and never shout (咆哮) at me again.
5. Your big feet (足) make you run (跑步) very fast.
6. The blister (水泡) filled with water (水) and hurt me.

Exercise 2: Mental Lexicons

Have you ever eaten bread? What kind of bread do you like most? Can you write down at least three lists of words describing the bread you like to eat? (If you do not know how to write the word, you may draw a picture to represent it).

_____

_____

_____

(Students write their own words on the lines)

APPENDIX B

Example of the Flash Cards

咆	泡	包	鮑	跑
Roar	Bubble	Bag	Abalone	Run

咆哮	水泡	手提包	鮑魚	跑步
To roar	A vesicle	Handbag	Abalone	Running

APPENDIX C

Worksheet Completed by the Students in the Sample Lesson

Please read the following words, and listen to the teacher's instructions carefully. Then circle the correct answers.

1. 小 ____ (*Siu Baau*)
            a. 鮑 (abalone)   b. 跑 (run)   c. 咆 (roar)

2. ____步 (running)
            a. 鮑 (abalone)   b. 包 (bread)   c. 跑 (run)

3. 水 ____ (water)
            a. 咆 (roar)   b. 泡 (vesicle)   c. 包 (bread)

4. ____哮 (cry out in a loud voice)
            a. 咆 (roar)   b. 鮑 (abalone)   c. 跑 (run)

APPENDIX D

Example of New Dictation Task for Learning Chinese Characters

In order to help students perceive similarities and variations in characters, find out underlying structure and relationships between characters, new exercises have been designed. Below are some examples:

1. Using specific component to form different characters
   氵: 泡, 河, 洗, 清, 海, 湯
   (water: blister, river, wash, clear, ocean, soup)

2. Use different components that form different characters (students may use any components in the table and form meaningful characters)

亻	口	忄	言
足	可	氵	虫
扌	木	食	青
火	白	包	日

   亻 + 白 = 伯 (human + white = old man)
   虫 + 青 = 蜻 (insect + green = dragonfly)
   氵 + 可 = 河 (water + permit = river)

3. Adding components to form different characters (students can put any components in the box that they think can form a meaning character)
   食 + 包 = 飽 (eat + bread = satisfy)
   氵 + 古 + 月 = 湖 (water + old + moon = lake)

4. Subtract component(s) from a character so that it becomes another character (students can put any components in the box that can be subtracted to form a meaningful character)
   頑 – 元 = 頁 (play – coin = page)
   火 – 包 = 炮 (fire – bread = cannon)
   胡 – 古 = 月 (northern – old = moon)

APPENDIX E

Pre-Test and Post-Test Results of each Pilot School

Table C1. School A (n = 145)

Test items	Full marks	Pre-test		Post-test	
		M	SD	M	SD
1. Reading comprehension	20	4.68	2.13	15.36	3.36
2. Writing down words related to the pictures					
a. Family	14	6.87	3.78	13.25	0.77
b. School	14	5.01	3.14	13.12	0.95
c. Society	14	6.00	3.39	13.12	0.88
3. Identifying correct words	15	5.41	3.21	11.81	1.98
4. Matching correct characters to sounds	15	11.22	3.30	14.51	0.76

Table C2. School B (n = 299)

Test items	Full marks	Pre-test		Post-test	
		M	SD	M	SD
1. Reading comprehension	20	7.04	3.67	15.33	4.02
2. Writing down words related to the pictures					
a. Family	14	5.48	4.03	12.99	1.53
b. School	14	4.55	2.95	12.81	1.79
c. Society	14	6.07	3.31	12.62	1.80
3. Identifying correct words	15	5.05	2.83	10.09	2.26
4. Matching correct characters to sounds	15	11.13	3.47	14.74	0.65

Table C3. School C (n = 59)

Test items	Full marks	Pre-test		Post-test	
		M	SD	M	SD
1. Reading comprehension	20	9.54	3.95	14.41	3.87
2. Writing down words related to the pictures					
a. Family	14	11.82	2.96	12.95	1.77
b. School	14	7.13	3.43	12.43	1.96
c. Society	14	8.64	3.96	12.50	2.01
3. Identifying correct words	15	5.39	3.15	8.92	2.78
4. Matching correct characters to sounds	15	10.02	3.36	14.39	1.29

PAKEY PUI MAN CHIK, ALLEN LEUNG AND FERENCE MARTON

6. LEARNING WORDS

INTRODUCTION

Learning words - the basic and smallest units of meaning in spoken language - is fundamental to the acquisition of language and literacy in all languages. Compared to words in other writing systems, for example abugidas languages such as Indo-Aryan and alphabetic languages such as English, all word units in Chinese are unique. Words in Chinese are monosyllabic and logographic, whereas the basic word unit in other writing systems is primarily made up of symbols or letters representing a sound or combination of sounds that constitute words. In Chapter Three, the authors reported a research study aimed at helping non-native speakers of Chinese to master the tones of spoken, monosyllabic words in Cantonese which is a branch or dialect of the Chinese language and is mainly spoken in Southern China. The learners approached the task using a computer-assisted learning program premised on the Theory of Variation advanced by Bowden and Marton (1998), Marton and Booth (1997), Marton and Morris (2002), and Marton et al. (2004). There were two groups of participants in the study. Members of one group learnt some Cantonese words in a particular sequence of variation, first experiencing the separation of the tonal and segmental aspects of each word, then the fusion of these aspects and corresponding changes in the meaning of the word. Members of the other group learnt the same words in a random manner. The results suggested better performance by the first group in terms of mastering the pronunciation of the target words.

In this chapter, we use the same theoretical framework as a tool for exploring how two classes of Grade 2 primary school students in Hong Kong learnt new words in Chinese language lessons. Unlike the above study where all the participants were non-native speakers of Chinese with no prior experience of the language, the students in this study had five to six years of daily life experience in Hong Kong and had received one year of formal education through the medium of Cantonese in school. In terms of learning words in Cantonese, the first study focused on learning the complex tones of Cantonese words in a highly controlled and artificial setting, whereas the study reported below explored how young students learnt pertinent words in the classroom, where communication in the target language was live and much more dynamic than the learning via an inanimate computer.

Unlike the case in studies reported in other chapters in this book, the teachers in the present study were not familiar with the Theory of Variation. Nor did anyone who understood the theory have any input into the teachers' lesson planning. In fact, the Theory of Variation was used only for analysing the teaching and

F. Marton, S.K. Tse and W. M.Cheung (eds.), On the Learning of Chinese, 103–122.

learning and had no influence whatever on the ways the teachers chose to deal with the lesson. On the assumption that all teachers knowingly or unknowingly use variation and invariance all the time, the analysis focused on the importance of what varies and what is kept invariant in subject matter on students' learning. The background of the two lessons is presented next, together with a theory-based analysis from the perspectives of the teacher, researcher and students. The chapter concludes with a discussion of the significance and implications of the outcomes of the study.

BACKGROUND TO THE TWO LESSONS

The data referred to in this chapter was gathered from lessons in two half-day sessions in schools under the same administration in Hong Kong. The lessons were taught to two classes by different teachers on the same day, one in the morning session (Class 2A) and one in the afternoon (Class 2B). Classes in the schools were grouped on a mixed ability basis, post hoc checking of the mean scores of students in the two classes on the annual public attainment test in Chinese language revealing that the ability levels in the classes were very similar. In Class 2A the mean score was 61.09 (SD = 15.90) and in Class 2B it was 60.71 (SD = 13.13). The two teachers involved were experienced primary school teachers, each having over six years experience of teaching Chinese language.

Both lessons were the first in a series that dealt with a text in the school text-book and were about teaching the vocabulary in the text. The text was entitled "A Polite Little Guest" and is translated into English and appears below:

"Father wishes to take us as guests to a friend's house. He asks, "What must one do in order to be a polite little guest?" My younger brother says, "We should greet people when we meet them." My younger sister says, "When we are eating, do not pick and choose food in the dish." My elder sister says, "When talking to someone, you should face him. Do not look around. When other people are talking, do not interrupt as you like." I say, "On leaving, we must say goodbye." Father is very pleased on hearing these suggestions. He promises to give us the chance to be polite guests."

The underlined words in the text were words in Chinese that both teachers, though planning the lesson separately, had in common on their chosen list of vocabulary to be dealt with in the lesson. In the next section, we analyse what the two teachers intended to bring about in the learning of the new words and how they intended to run the lesson.

TEACHER PERSPECTIVE: WHAT WAS INTENDED TO BE LEARNT AND HOW IT WAS TO BE TAUGHT IN THE LESSON

Despite independently having the same intended object of learning as to teach new words in a text, post-lesson interviews with the teachers revealed that they differed markedly in their ideas about how to teach new vocabulary, their planning and their aims for the lesson. The Class 2A teacher said her aim was to teach the central theme of the text through developing students' understanding of specific words:

"The main point was the vocabulary. … Another point was to let the students know the theme of the text. For example, it's about a polite child. I wanted them to be able to grasp the theme of the text once they had learnt the vocabulary" (translated interview transcript).

In the interview, this teacher also expressed an enthusiasm for the evolution of Chinese characters from the ancient to modern forms and a wish to foster in her students a sense of admiration of the beauty in such evolution through the teaching of vocabulary selected for study.

"In fact, I am very fond of the evolution of Chinese characters in pictographs … I think this is beautiful. … What else should children learn apart from the form of a character? I think it is this kind of beauty. … So, when I prepared this lesson, I looked up information about the evolution of the characters on the word list to see if there was a story behind their evolution" (translated interview transcript).

When planning the lesson, this teacher carefully picked out words critical to students' understanding of the main theme of the text. The meaning of the words chosen and how they could contribute to the main theme of the text thus became the critical aspects for students to acquire the intended object of learning. The teacher also paid attention to how she might use those words to teach the evolution of Chinese characters.

The Class 2B teacher had different ideas about the choice of teaching focus and the selection of vocabulary. She said she believed that it is of the utmost importance for students in the early years of primary schooling to be able to master the attributes of form, pronunciation and meaning of some 500 to 1000 characters. She believed that the number of characters learnt at this stage form the foundation for students' learning of Chinese at a higher level as far as reading is concerned. Therefore, her lesson focused on teaching attributes of the words selected in the text.

"In the main, I wanted to teach them the words … their form, pronunciation and meaning. … because this is the basic knowledge that students in the early years of primary schooling should grasp. If they can establish a rich vocabulary bank … 500 to 1000 words for Grade Two students … this should help them a lot in reading" (translated interview transcript).

In this light, her criterion for selecting vocabulary was not whether the words were related to the theme of the text, as it had been for the teacher of the other class, but whether the words were new to students and would present students with difficulty in learning the three attributes. Thus, the objects of learning intended for students were the three word attributes and specific features of the chosen words that may confuse students in learning those attributes became critical. Accordingly, the Class 2B teacher made arrangements she thought would facilitate the learning.

The first concerned the sequence of teaching. As revealed in both the lesson plan and the post-lesson interview, the teacher had in mind a specific sequence for her students to learn, from a more basic level (recognising the forms, or the order of strokes of the chosen words) to a more advanced level (exploring the meaning of the words).

> "In this lesson ...I focused initially on teaching the forms of some words. Students have to recognise this (the form) first. ... I chose to highlight the order of strokes in teaching the forms because I want the students to at least recognise and write the forms correctly. ... Then, we can come to the meaning of words" (translated interview transcript).

The teachers' comments show that, although using the same text, teaching the same level and apparently sharing the same objective of teaching the new words in the text, each teacher had different intended objects of learning and thus different critical features or aspects to be addressed in her lesson. They planned for the children to learn what the teacher considered important for students to learn about the vocabulary in the text. They also had different ways to present the intended objects of learning to their students in the lesson.

THEORETICAL PERSPECTIVE: WHAT WAS ENACTED AND WHAT WAS POSSIBLE FOR STUDENTS TO LEARN

Both lessons lasted about 30 minutes. There was whole class teaching in Class 2A, with the teacher asking questions and individual students answering. Discussion between students was minimal. The lesson in Class 2B was also class taught for a period but there was more interaction between students, especially in the second half of the lesson, with children correcting or commenting on each other's work. Students in Class 2B worked in groups for part of the lesson and the teacher only intervened at this stage to provide feedback if the students were unable to arrive at an appropriate answer or disagreed over answers. The course of each lesson closely kept to the teacher's lesson plan. In the accounts below, we look at each lesson separately showing how the framework derived from the Theory of Variation applied: aspects that remained invariant in the various activities and those that varied; and how patterns of variation and invariance afforded by the structure of the lesson served to define certain possibilities for learning in the lessons.

The Patterns of Variation and Invariance Enacted in the Two Lessons

Lesson 2A. After an introductory nomination activity used to introduce the theme *of the lesson and talk about the meaning of the word "polite", the teacher* identified seven words from the text for closer study and dealt with each one in turn. The words singled out included "作客 [zok3 haak3 / be a guest]"[1], "打招呼 [daa1 ziu1 fu1 / greet]", "挑來挑去 [tiu1 loi4 tiu1 heoi3 / pick and choose]", "東張西望 [dung1 zoeng1 sai1 mong6 / look around]", "準備 [zeon2 bei6 / prepare]", "插嘴

[caap3 zeoi2 / interrupt]" and "隨便 [ceoi4 bin6 / as one likes]". To help the students understand each of the words, the teacher employed various methods that allowed different patterns of variation and invariance to be enacted in order to highlight the meaning of the words. For words like, "挑來挑去 [tiu1 loi4 tiu1 heoi3 / pick and choose]", "東張西望 [dung1 zoeng1 sai1 mong6 / look around]" and "準備 [zeon2 bei6 / prepare]", the teacher invited the students to look for the word that best described the meaning of certain pictures or actions shown to them. This resulted in patterns of variation and invariance in the form of representing words that varied in written and pictorial forms. For words like "隨便 [ceoi4 bin6 / as one likes]" and "插嘴 [caap3 zeoi2 / interrupt]"), she asked students to provide explanations or contexts, thus helping them to generalise the meaning of the word concerned from the various contributions from students who offered brief or more *elaborate descriptions of the same word. When students mixed up the meanings of* words, for example "作客 [zok3 haak3 / be a guest]", "打招呼 [daa1 ziu1 fu1 / greet]") or provided an inappropriate explanation for the word, for example "插嘴 [caap3 zeoi2 / interrupt]"), the teacher used contrasts to help students see the *correct meanings and distinguish these from incorrect explanations of words.*

For each word studied, the teacher asked students to find a sentence in the text that included and used the word. When all the sentences for each word were found, the teacher told the students that if they could do all those things that were described by the sentences, they were polite little guests, the main theme of the text. The excerpt below is taken from the lesson transcript and shows how the teacher handled this part of the lesson with reference to the word "插嘴 [caap3 zeoi2 / interrupt]":

Lesson Excerpt

T: "I want you to take a look at this picture (referring to Picture 1 below) and find a character in the text to match it with.

Picture 1

S30: "插嘴 [caap3 zeoi2 / Interrupt]".

(Literally, the word means 'interrupt' and is made up of two Chinese characters: 插 [caap3 / insert] and 嘴 [zeoi2 / mouth].)

T: "Okay, just one character. Alright, Yin."

S31: "插 [caap3 / insert]."

T: "Why do you think it is 插 [caap3 / insert]?" (Posting another picture, Picture 2, on the whiteboard, see below.)

Picture 1   Picture 2

"Let's take a look at another picture, this one…" (pointing to Picture 2 on the whiteboard.) "If I convert this picture (Picture 1) into the form of lines, will it look like this (Picture 2)? It will probably look like this, won't it? … Remember I have told you something about Chinese characters? How did they evolve?"

Ss: "Pictographs."

T: "Right, … let's see how this Chinese character evolved." (posting Picture 3 on the whiteboard.) "Do they (Pictures 2 and 3) look alike?"

Picture 1   Picture 2   Picture 3

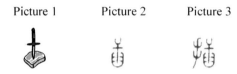

S32: "Yes, they do."

T: "They are alike, aren't they? …… I have also told you that, when we want to insert something, which body part do we use? Can we use our feet to do it?"

S33: "Hands."

T: "We have to use our hands... Correct. … These are what the character looked like in ancient times (referring to Pictures 1, 2 and 3 posted up earlier). And this … (holding up a word card showing the character 插 [caap3 / insert] and referring to the radical component of hand) … this is a hand, isn't it? By putting something (referring to the component '千' of the character) into the meat (referring to the component of '臼' of the character) … Finally, it becomes the modern form of insert."

T: "O.K., now you know that the character, insert, looks like something stabbing into a piece of meat … but what has that to do with our conversation?" (posting the word card of '插嘴 [caap3 zeoi2 / interrupt]' on the whiteboard.)

T: "Who can try to explain it?" (students raising their hands.) "O.K. Man."

S34: "When father and mother are talking to other relatives, you also listen."

T: "You can listen to it, but what can't you do?" (Putting her index finger in front of her lips.) "When people are talking and you add your words in the middle of the conversation, is it just like you have inserted something into it? This is interrupt, understand? Do you understand the meaning of '插嘴

[caap3 zeoi2 / interrupt]'? … Just now when we were talking, for example, when I was talking with Hang, someone interrupted our conversation by inserting his words, what was that?"

C: "插嘴 [caap3 zeoi2 / interrupt]."

…

T: "Tell me, … in which sentence in the text can the word '插嘴 [caap3 zeoi2 / interrupt]' be found?"

…

S44: "別人談話時，不要隨便插嘴 [bit6 jan4 taam4 waa6 si4, bat1 jiu3 ceoi4 bin6 caap3 zeoi2 / When people are talking, do not interrupt as you like]."

T: "Correct. '不要隨便插嘴 [bat1 jiu3 ceoi4 bin6 caap3 zeoi2 / Do not interrupt as you like.]' … (Putting the sentence strip on the whiteboard and likewise, she put up all the sentences each word was found.)… "Okay, let's look at all these sentences (referring to the sentence strips put on the board)… if you can do all these, what kind of child are you? … Sung?"

S45: "A polite child."

T: "Right, a polite child. This is also the theme of today's lesson."

(translated lesson transcript 2A)

Here, the teacher first created a pattern of variation and invariance on the word "插 [caap3 / insert]", the meaning of which remained unchanged while its form varied from a picture to ancient characters, and to its modern form. Then she introduced another pattern of variation and invariance by changing the language context: the meaning of the character on its own; the meaning of the character as embedded in a word, "插嘴 [caap3 zeoi2 / interrupt]"; the meaning of the word as embedded in a sentence in the text, "別人談話時，不要隨便插嘴 [bit6 jan4 taam4 waa6 si4, bat1 jiu3 ceoi4 bin6 caap3 zeoi2 / When people are talking, do not interrupt as you like]"; and its meaning when embedded in the main theme of the text, being a polite little guest. Likewise, the teacher taught with reference to other words identified for the teaching.

In this way, the enacted patterns of variation and invariance in the words taught and the sentences that these words form made it possible for students to see the structure and part-whole relationships in the Chinese language: Characters, which are made up of components and radicals, are the component parts that make up words; words are the component parts of sentences; and sentences are the component parts of paragraphs, which in turn, contribute to the main theme of the whole text. Figure 6.1 below illustrates the part-whole relationships in the Chinese language thematized by the patterns of variation and invariance enacted in Lesson 2A.

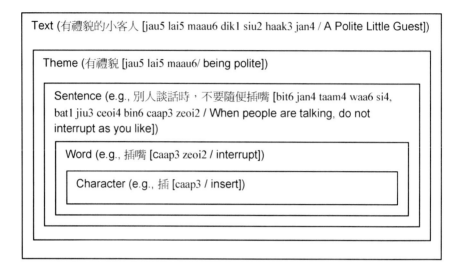

Figure 6.1. An illustration of the part-whole relationships shown in lesson 2A.

Within such a complex and hierarchical lesson structure in which different aspects of the words were closely linked together, the patterns of variation and invariance enacted in the teaching facilitated the function of fusion. This made it possible for students to discern the significance and meanings of the selected words (which remained constant throughout the lesson) in different language contexts (which varied from being a character, a word, a sentence and the theme of the text). At the same time, they helped students to see the relationships between different parts (a character as part of a word; a word as part of a sentence; and so on) that finally contributed to grasping the central theme of the text.

Such an establishment of the structural features of the Chinese language throughout Lesson 2A is in line with the "diversified approach" which sprang to the fore in the Chinese character-reformation movement in the 20th century and emphasises the part-whole relationships between different linguistic units and the usefulness of the linguistic context for acquiring new words in the language (Wu et al., 1999). It also concurs with the findings of a number of psycho-linguistic studies conducted in the late 20th century. For example, the studies by Chen et al., 1996 and Tseng et al., 1986, suggest that native learners tend to process Chinese characters in terms of various linguist symbols (components and radicals) arranged in certain structures at different levels of composition. Chan and Nunes (2001) note that young native learners are often aware of part-whole relationships between the symbols (parts) and the Chinese character (whole) in relation to its context, for example a word or a sentence, well before they develop sensitivity to the structural features of Chinese characters.

Lesson 2B. Lesson 2B consisted of several parts, each having a distinct focus and involving patterns of variation and invariance that thematized particular aspects of the text, one after the other. The teacher first gave an overview of what the text was about then, after eliciting the title of the text ("有禮貌的小客人 [jau5 lai5 maau6 dik1 siu2 haak3 jan4 / A Polite Little Guest]") from the students, the teacher raised two questions. The first question was "Why did the father tell his children to be polite?" A student gave the answer, "They were to become guests of a friend." The teacher accepted this answer and asked the second question: "What should not be done if one is to be polite?" A student volunteered the answer by reading out a word: "挑來挑去 [tiu1 loi4 tiu1 heoi3 / pick and choose]". The teacher thought that this answer was too brief and asked for elaboration. Another student, supplementing his classmate's answer, read out a sentence in the text, "不要在菜盤裏挑來挑去 [bat1 jiu3 zoi6 coi3 pun4 leoi5 tiu1 loi4 tiu1 heoi3 / Do not pick and choose food in the dish]"; and another student proposed another sentence, "別人談話時，不要隨便插嘴 [bit6 jan4 taam4 waa6 si4, bat1 jiu3 ceoi4 bin6 caap3 zeoi2 / When people are talking, do not interrupt as you like]." With these various examples of being polite, a pattern of variation and invariance was formed serving to help generalise what students ought not to do in order to be polite. This was the invariant theme in the discussion.

The lesson then moved on to the teaching of the forms of five characters ("呼 [fu1 / call]", "禮貌 [lai5 maau6 / polite])", "插 [caap3 / insert])" and "盤 [pun4 / tray]"). These characters, according to the teacher, were selected because they involve complicated stroke sequences and are most difficult for students to write. For each character, the teacher invited an individual student to write it on the board, after which the teacher invited comments from the class on the written forms. If the character was written incorrectly, the teacher would ask another student to come and write it again. The teacher did the same until each character was written correctly. Then, she made use of the correct and incorrect written forms on the board to highlight the critical features in the writing of the characters. Patterns of variation and invariance were thus observed between the proper and improper forms of a character, serving the function of contrast in helping students to distinguish what is and what is not critical in writing the target characters correctly.

The third part of the lesson centred on teaching the meanings of four words ("禮貌 [lai5 maau6 / polite]", "菜盤 [coi3 pun4 / dish]", "挑來挑去 [tiu1 loi4 tiu1 heoi3 / pick and choose]" and "東張西望 [dung1 zoeng1 sai1 mong6 / look around]). For each word, the teacher invited individual students to try to explain or enact its meaning. If the student's explanations of the word were considered insufficient or inappropriate, the teacher would ask another student to contribute, or she would elaborate on the student's answers in the context of daily life or in the context of the text. As an example, a student explained the meaning of "有禮貌 [jau5 lai5 maau6 / being polite]" as "要尊敬別人 [jiu3 zyun1 ging3 bit6 jan4 / to show respect to others]", which the teacher extended to include "要接受別人 [jiu3 zip3 sau6 bit6 jan4 / to accept others]." The teacher asked a student to come out and enact the meaning of "東張西望 [dung1 zoeng1 sai1 mong6 / look around]", then another student described it in spoken Cantonese (望嚟望去 [mong6 lai mong6 heoi3/ look around]. In this way, patterns of variation and invariance were opened up which focused on each chosen word with variations either between brief and elaborate descriptions or between different representations, spoken and enacted, that helped students to generalise the meaning of the word.

After the teaching of the meanings of some of the words, the lesson focused on teaching the pronunciation of ten words: "禮貌 [lai5 maau6 / polite]", "作客 [zok3 haak3 / be a guest]", "打招呼 [daa1 ziu1 fu1 / greet]", "挑來挑去 [tiu1 loi4 tiu1 heoi3 / pick and choose]", "談話 [taam4_waa6 / talk]", "東張西望 [dung1 zoeng1 sai1 mong6 / look around]", "隨便 [ceoi4 bin6 / as one likes]", "插嘴 [caap3 zeoi2 / interrupt]", "離開 [lei4_hoi1/ leave]" and "答應 [daap3 jing3 / promise]". The teacher asked groups of students to take turns at slowly reading out the words one by one. While one of the groups was reading, the teacher required the other groups to pay attention to their pronunciation. In one case, a group of students pronounced the word for "being polite" incorrectly. The teacher corrected them and had the group practise it until they pronounced the word perfectly. Thus, a pattern of variation and invariance in the pronunciation of "禮貌 [lai5 maau6 / polite]" occurred, contrasting a wrong pronunciation (by the group of students) with the right one (by the teacher and the students). In cases where all groups read the word properly, patterns of variation and invariance were again yielded, but this time functioned to help generalise the proper pronunciation of a particular word (constant) through the proper responses by different groups of students (varied).

In the last part of the lesson, the teacher introduced a group competition that required the students to look for three words ("作客 [zok3 haak3 / be a guest]", "禮貌 [lai5 maau6 / polite]" and "插嘴 [caap3 zeoi2 / interrupt]") in the text to match the formal definitions given by the teacher one at a time. Each group was given a blank card and they had to discuss amongst themselves what the right answer was and write it down on the card using a felt pen. Then, one member of each group came to the front to show their answers to the class. Different groups were invited by the teacher to pass judgment on whether or not the answers were correct. In the competition, all of the groups gave the correct answers. This time, variation was not found in the answers of different groups, but in the different expressions given for the same meaning of the words. For instance, a formal definition, "說話 做事恭敬虛心 [syut3 waa6 zou6 si6 gung1 ging3 heoi1 sam1 / to be humble and respectful while talking and working]" provided by the teacher was summarised by the students in the word "禮貌 [lai5 maau6 / polite]".

As reported above, Lesson 2B was mainly organised around highlighting the three word attributes of form, pronunciation and meaning. In teaching each attribute, the teacher formed a different list of words she considered difficult for her students to master with regard to that attribute. Although there were some overlaps in the words chosen (e.g., "禮貌 [lai5 maau6 / polite]" and "插嘴 [caap3 zeoi2 / interrupt]"), they were subordinate to the teaching of a particular attribute and were not related to other attributes when they appeared on the list to be taught. In other words, the structure of Lesson 2B was predominantly sequential, focusing on one aspect of the content at a time (see Figure 6.2 below). As an example, the form of the first character "插 [caap3 / insert]" of the word "插嘴 [caap3 zeoi2 / interrupt]" was first dealt with on its own; then, the pronunciation of this word "插嘴 [caap3 zeoi2 / interrupt]" was taught as one on the list of words to be taught; then, in the group competition the word "插嘴 [caap3 zeoi2 / interrupt]" was given a formal definition as "加入別人的談話 [gaa1 jap6 bit6 jan4 dik1 taam4 waa6 / to put in a word in others' conversation]". The explanation was independently arrived at and not cited in the context of the text.

Unlike Lesson 2A, where different attributes of words were related to each other in bringing out the part-whole relationships of the target words in different language contexts, the structure of Lesson 2B was sequential. Discrete patterns of variation and invariance focused on single word attributes. The words on the list for teaching a particular attribute were used to illustrate that attribute, and the variation which emerged from the lively student-student interactions served the function of generalisation, making it possible for the students to learn that there are three word attributes, namely form, meaning and pronunciation. At the beginning of the lesson, when the teacher and the students talked about the content of the text with a particular focus on what it takes to be a polite guest, the students might themselves have paid attention to the meaning of "有禮貌的客人 [jau5 lai5 maau6 dik1 siu2 haak3 jan4 / A Polite Little Guest] in terms of the various examples of behaviour taken from the text as illustrations.

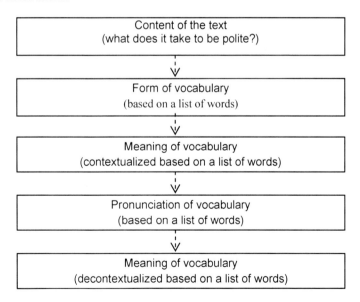

Figure 6.2. Different aspects being held in focus and structured in Lesson 2B.

A major difference between the two lessons concerns whether the specific words (as in Lesson 2A) or attributes of a list of words (as in Lesson 2B) were superordinate (invariant) as defined by the different ways in which the lessons were structured (see Table 6.1). Keeping the words super-ordinate (invariant), instead of attributes, could be expected to facilitate discernment of the hierarchical structure of the text, since the words form parts of the sentences, not the attributes.

The differences noted between the two lessons in terms of teaching foci and lesson structure resulted in different patterns of variation and invariance being enacted. This, in turn, seems to have offered different possibilities for students' learning. In the next section, the students' perspective is presented to show how they themselves perceived the lesson and how well they performed on content-related tasks.

Table 6.1. A comparison of the structures of Lesson 2A and 2B

Lesson 2A			Lesson 2B		
Word 1 →	*Word 2* →	*Word 3* →...	*Attribute 1* →	*Attribute 2* →	*Attribute 3* →...
attribute 1;	*attribute 1;*	*attribute 1;*	*word 1;*	*word 1;*	*word 1;*
attribute 2;	*attribute 2;*	*attribute 2;*	*word 2;*	*word 2;*	*word 2;*
attribute 3	*attribute 3*	*attribute 3*	*word 3;*	*word 3;*	*word 3;*
			...	...	...

STUDENT PERSPECTIVE: WHAT WAS PERCEIVED TO HAVE BEEN LEARNT IN THE LESSON AND THE LEARNING OUTCOMES

After each lesson, the students involved were invited to complete a diagnostic worksheet relating to the lesson. Thirty were collected from Class 2A and thirty-one from Class 2B. Individual interviews with the students were also conducted to probe their perception of the lesson. Twenty-eight students from Class 2A and thirty-one from Class 2B were interviewed for about fifteen to twenty minutes after the lesson. Both the diagnostic worksheet and the interviews contained two types of questions: the first being general questions designed to reveal how the students experienced and made sense of the lesson; the second set of questions being specific to what was taught in both lessons and were aimed at assessing how well the students learnt in the lesson.

Students' Perception of What was Taught or Learnt in the Lesson

Diagnostic worksheet: the general question. In the first part of the diagnostic worksheet, the students were required to answer two general questions: (1) "What was the most important thing taught in the lesson?" and (2) "What else did you learn in the lesson?" In answering these two questions, some students gave more than one response.

As shown in Table 6.2 below, the responses from both classes to the two general questions fell into two main categories. Some students reported that they had learnt about the text theme (the main theme and/or sub-themes of the text). Some claimed that they had learnt some language items (in general terms or with specific examples). However, remarkable differences were found between the two classes in terms of what the students saw as the most important thing taught versus other things covered in the lesson. About half of the students in Class 2A reported that the most important thing taught was the main theme and/or the sub-themes of the text, slightly more than half of them considering language items as other things learnt in the lesson. In comparison, a higher proportion of the students in Class 2B considered language items as the most important thing taught (22/39 chose language items and 10/39 the text theme) or as other things learnt in the lesson (20/36 chose language items and 7/36 the text theme).

Table 6.2. Students' responses to the general questions of the diagnostic worksheet

First part: General Questions	Q1. What was the most important thing taught in the lesson?		Q2. What else did you learn in the lesson?	
Class (n = total number of responses *)	2A (n=35)	2B (n=39)	2A (n=42)	2B (n=36)
1. Text theme	18	10	11	7
2. Language items	5	22	18	20
3. Irrelevant responses	12	7	13	9

* Some students put down more than one response.

Individual interviews: the general questions. In the first part of the interview, each student was asked to describe his or her general perception of the lesson. The questions included "How did you feel about the lesson?", "What did you learn in the lesson?" and "Suppose one of your classmates was absent on that day, what would you tell him or her about the lesson?" A similar pattern of responses to that revealed by the general questions of the diagnostic worksheet was apparent in this part of the interview data. While responses in both classes could be classified into bringing out the main theme and/or sub-themes and words of the text, the two classes differed in what they thought had been learnt or taught in the lesson.

As shown from Table 6.3, slightly more than half of the students in Class 2A thought they had learnt both vocabulary and the theme of the text, whereas most students in Class 2B considered that they had only learnt some word attributes in the lesson. The data also showed that students in both classes were able to give at least one specific word item they had learnt in the lesson, but only students from Class 2A mentioned the main theme and/or sub-themes of the text with reference to either the text or their daily life experiences.

Table 6.3. Students' responses in the first part of the interview

General questions: (1) What did you learn in the lesson? (2) Suppose one of your classmates was absent on that day, what would you tell him or her about the lesson?		
Responses \ Class (n=total number of students)	2A (n=28)	2B (n=31)
(a) Vocabulary and text theme were reported * with at least one specific word and/or subtheme being reported	15	0
(b) Vocabulary (with at least one word specified) or word attributes only	7	27
(c) Text theme and/or sub-themes only	6	3
(d) Did not respond	0	1

Learning Outcomes

Individual interviews. In the second part of the interview, each student was required to recognise, read and explain two words that had been taught in both lessons ("polite" and "interrupt"). The results are summarised in Table 6.4. It may be seen from the table that all students in the two classes were capable of recognising the two words from a given number of characters and able to read them out correctly. However, they were remarkably different in how they explained the meanings of the two words. In Class 2A, a noteworthy number of students explained the word "polite" by quoting the theme or the sub-themes of the text as examples (22/28). In comparison, the number of students in Class 2B giving a conceptual definition (15/31) was higher than the number explaining the word in terms of the main theme or sub-themes of the text (6/31). A similar pattern of results was observed in the students' explanation of the word "interrupt". In Class 2A, 16 of the 28 students explained the word in relation to what ought not to be done in order to be polite and 12 explained it in relation to behaviour depicted by the word. In contrast, many students in Class 2B provided a conceptual

Table 6.4. Students' responses in the second part of the interviews

Specific questions	Class 2A (n=28)	Class 2B (n=31)
Task I: Recognising words		
1. "polite"	28	31
2. "interrupt"	28	31
Task II: Reading out words		
1. "polite"	28	31
2. "interrupt"	28	31

Table 6.4. (Continued)

Task III: Explaining words		
1. "polite" by		
(a) quoting the sub-themes or the theme of the text	22	6
(b) quoting examples from daily life	3	7
(c) providing a context from daily life in which people should behave politely (e.g., when meeting the principal in school)	1	3
(d) providing a conceptual definition (e.g., "to respect others" or "to be nice to others")	1	15
2. "interrupt" by		
(a) relating the word to what ought not to be done in order to be polite	16	0
(b) describing the behaviour to which it refers	12	10
(c) providing a formal definition (e.g., "adding a word into others' conversation") which was also related to what ought not to be done in order to be polite	0	20
(d) providing a context in which the word could be used without explaining the word	0	1

definition with or without relating the word to what should not be done so as to be polite (20/31). The differences in the students' responses reflect how the two teachers interpreted the words in the lesson. While the teacher of Class 2A frequently made reference to the sentences (the sub-themes) and the theme of the text when teaching the words, the teacher of Class 2B explained the words in isolation with reference to their conceptual meaning.

Diagnostic worksheet: the specific question. In the second part of the diagnostic worksheet, the students were required to complete a text using appropriate words that had been taught in both lessons. The translated version of the text and a summary of the results are provided in Table 6.5. Class 2A were better at using the words that had been taught in both classes to complete the given text: all students correct in Class 2A and 9 out of 31 correct in Class 2B. The students in Class 2A also did better at writing the characters, the forms of which were focused on in both lessons ("insert" and "appearance"). Only one 2A student made a mistake in writing "insert", whereas 11 mistakes were made by the 2B students writing both words.

Table 6.5 Students' performances in the second part of the diagnostic worksheet

Second Part: Complete the following text with appropriate words / phrases you have learnt in the lesson.

Our teacher often tells us to **greet**[2] teachers and classmates when we meet them in school. In the classroom, when the teacher is talking with other classmates, do not **interrupt**[3] as you like; when the teacher talks to you, do not **look around.**[4] After school, we have to say goodbye to our teachers and classmates. Then, we can be counted as good students who are **polite.**[5]

Outcomes \ Class (n=total number of responses)	2A (n=30)	2B (n=31)
(a) Appropriate use of all words	30	9
(b) One to three blanks missing/ inappropriate	–	22

In order for students to be able to use the words learnt in the lesson to fill in the blanks in the given text, it was not enough for them simply to know how to write the forms of the words. They also had to understand the meanings of the words and be able to use them in an appropriate context. In other words, they had to be able to discern the form, meaning and the usage of the words. As mentioned in the beginning of this chapter, in the Chinese language, characters are monosyllabic. On the one hand, there are many homophones - different characters having the same pronunciation. For example, the characters "月 [moon]", "閱 [read]" and "越 [surpass]" all have the same pronunciation in Cantonese, "jyut6". On the other hand, there are many homographs - the same character carrying different meanings. The same character, when coupled with other characters will give rise to words of very different meanings. For example, when the character "插 [caap3 / insert]" is coupled with "嘴 [zeoi2 / mouth]", the word means to interrupt; when coupled with "秧 [joeng1 / seedlings]", the word means to transplant; and when coupled with "隊 [deoi6 / queue]", the word means to jump the queue. Therefore, it is important for students to understand that the form and the meaning of the characters are not independent of each other. They also must realise that knowledge about the context and the text are also essential for them to fully grasp and understand the meaning of a character and be able to use it properly. Lesson 2A was structured in such a way as to allow students to experience the form, meaning and usage of the words simultaneously.

In Class 2B, although the same words were taught to the students, each critical attribute of the words was taught in different parts of the lesson (e.g., the form of the character "插 [caap3 / insert]" and the meaning of the word "插嘴 [caap3 / interrupt]", which consists of the two characters "插 [caap3 / insert]" and "嘴 [zeoi2 / mouth]", were taught in separate sessions. As a result, with no explicit linkage established between the three attributes, the students might not be able to discern the relationship between the word and its two constituent parts - the character "插 [caap3 / insert]" forms a part of the word "插嘴 [caap3 zeoi2 / interrupt]". Instead, they may consider them as two unrelated entities - a character "插 [caap3 / insert]" and then a word "插嘴 [caap3 zeoi2 / interrupt]". This means that even if only three words were taught in the lesson, when three different attributes of each word were taught as unrelated entities, rather than presenting them as three critical attributes of those words, some students might think they had learnt nine unrelated entities. The large number of unrelated entities may then cause some students to be confused, so that some may not be able to cope with so many new entities in a short time. This may account for the fact that, although the teacher of Class 2B had spent time teaching her students how to write "插 [caa3 / insert]" and "貌 [maau6 / appearance]" correctly, many students still got them wrong in the worksheet.

DISCUSSION

Although the two lessons were based on the same text and focused on teaching more or less the same set of new words appearing in a text, they were remarkably different in the ways they were planned by the teacher and experienced by the students. The teacher of Class 2A aimed to introduce the theme of the text through teaching the words it contained. Thus, she organised her lesson in a hierarchical way in which the words were kept invariant throughout the whole lesson while their attributes and the context of usage varied. This contributed to patterns of variation and invariance that were enacted simultaneously and served the function of *fusion*, helping students to relate different aspects of the words. A very different pattern was observed in Lesson 2B, where the teacher aimed to teach the three attributes of the words identified from the text and therefore organised her lesson in a sequential manner, keeping each of the three word attributes invariant one at a time while varying the words that illustrated the attribute in question. By focusing on what was kept invariant, each pattern helped students discern each attribute by *generalisation*.

Post-lesson interviews revealed that what the students of the two classes reported as having learnt in the lesson corresponded to what was made possible for them to discern via the patterns of variation and invariance enacted and functioning in the lesson. The majority of the students in Class 2A believed that the lesson was chiefly about different aspects of the text, for instance the main theme and sub-themes, whereas a larger proportion of Class 2B thought that they had mainly learnt about reading and writing words in the text. The 2A students who were enabled to discern and perceived themselves as having learnt about the text outperformed their counterparts who focused on the learning of words on the written task that required them to make use of the words taught to complete a short passage. This seems odd in the sense that the students who did not perceive themselves as having learnt the words actually performed better than those who did. As evident in the study reported in Chapter 3 and in other studies (Pang & Marton, 2005), the learners who show better understanding of the objects of learning are often provided with an experience of the fusion or connection between aspects critical for their learning. This leads us to believe that the presence (as in Lesson 2A) or the absence (as in Lesson 2B) of experience leading to the fusion of the interrelationships among the attributes and linguistic contexts of the words contributed to a difference between the two classes in terms of their ability to use the words learnt in the lesson.

The findings of this study suggest that the differences in the students' learning probably originated from the structural differences between the hierarchical and sequential organisation of the two lessons. With such difference in the lesson structures, the objects of learning were enacted differently via different patterns of variation and invariance, i.e., what was in focus, what varied and what was kept invariant. These differences were driven by what the teachers believed to be critical to the learning of the target words. The patterns of variation and invariance created and how these patterns related to each other in the lesson seems to explain what actually happened between the teacher and the students in the interactions, and how these interactions contributed to the learning outcomes. Similar findings in terms of lesson structure and its relationship with student learning outcomes were also observed in the study reported in Chapter 8 and other studies (e.g., Chik, 2006).

The evidence would seem to imply that, in curriculum planning, thought should be given to what critical aspects of the object of learning to focus on, vary and keep invariant during lessons. Care should also be taken over the choice of instructional approach, examples, tasks and activities intended to maximise the opportunities for students to experience the patterns of variation and invariance in aspects critical for the learning. In other words, what the object of learning should be and how it is structured and perceived by students may be much more important for improving the quality of classroom learning and teaching than the way the classroom is organised and children are grouped, a view supported by Kilpatrick et al. (2001) in the context of teaching and learning mathematics.

Despite the fact that patterns of variation and invariance enacted in the two lessons were different in respect of the relationship between the words and their attributes presented, the truth is that the careful lesson planning by the two teachers paid off. What was taught and the experiences helping students learn were as the teachers had planned and forecast. The students learnt and in all probability would recall what they have been taught over a period of time. When asked to cite a successful instance which she found satisfactory, the teacher of Class 2A pointed out that her students were "at least able to use the words learnt in the lesson to complete the given text appropriately" in the diagnostic worksheet. The teacher of Class 2B thought that her class would require more practice in order to be able to complete the given text, but she was nevertheless satisfied with the students' performance in writing and explaining the words she chose from the text during the lesson.

What is clear is that there is no general rule setting out what should vary and what should remain invariant in lessons, unless specific features or aspects are specified, such as helping foreigners to master the tone of Cantonese in the study referred to earlier in this chapter. However, too much variation in a disorganised fashion will lead to confusion and a lack of clarity on the part of the student about what they are supposed to be learning in lessons. In helping the foreigners master the tones of Cantonese in the study, allowing the learners systematically to see similarities and differences between tones facilitated the learning. Planning is crucial and it takes a conscious effort by the teachers themselves or in collaboration with colleagues to find out what specific features or aspects or part-whole concepts are critical for students to learn a particular object of learning; and how these should be brought to the attention of students.

Subsequent to a two-year research project[6] from which this study took root and which aimed to identify and describe the characteristics of good language teaching per se, another three-year government funded study was developed. In this three-year study, we collaborated with local primary school teachers to design lessons to help students learn particular objects of learning by taking into their planning appropriate patterns of variation and invariance. The results demonstrate a remarkable improvement in the learning of both the teachers and students involved (Lo et al., 2005). Similar projects are currently being conducted in Hong Kong as well as in countries like Sweden, aimed at providing support for teachers to improve the quality of classroom teaching and learning. The aim is also to help teachers see a theoretical rationale for their pedagogy and how practice links with theory.

NOTES

[1] Since the main object of teaching for the two lessons was words, the original Chinese characters and their Cantonese pronunciations are also provided, where appropriate, to allow potential readers to arrive at an independent viewpoint, understanding and judgment in regard to the analysis of the word teaching and learning in the two lessons. The Cantonese pronunciations of the Chinese characters follows the website: http://arts.cuhk.edu.hk/Lexis/Canton/ designed by S. L. Wong.

[2] The word "打招呼 [daa1 ziu1 fu1 / greet]" is made up of three Chinese characters: "打 [daa1 / beat]", "招 [ziu1 / wave]" and "呼 [fu1 / call]".

[3] The word "插嘴 [caap3 zeoi2 / interrupt]" is made up of two Chinese characters: "插 [caap3 / insert]" and "嘴 [zeoi2 / mouth]".

[4] The word "東張西望 [dung1 zoeng1 / look around]" is made up of four Chinese characters: "東 [dung1 / east]", "張 [zoeng1 / open]", "西[sai1 / west]" and "望 [mong6 / watch]".

[5] The word "禮貌 [lai5 maau6 / polite]" is made up of two Chinese characters: "禮 [lai5 / polite]" and "貌 [maau6 / appearence]".

[6] This two year research project funded by the Standing Committee on Language Education and Research of the Hong Kong Government.

REFERENCES

Bowden, J., & Marton, F. (1998). *The university of learning.* London, UK: Kogan Page.

Chan, L., & Nunes, T. (2001). Explicit teaching and implicit learning of Chinese characters. In L. Tolchinsky (Ed.), *Developmental aspects in learning to write.* Dordrecht, The Netherlands: Kluwer Academic Publishers.

Chen, Y. P., Allport, D. A., & Marshall, J. C. (1996). What are the functional orthographic units in Chinese word recognition: the stroke or the stroke pattern? *Quarterly Journal of Experimental Psychology, 49A,* 1024–1043.

Chik, P. P. M. (2006). *Differences in learning as a function of differences between hierarchical and sequential organisation of the content taught.* Unpublished Ph.D. Thesis, The University of Hong Kong, HKSAR.

Kilpatrick, J., Swafford, J., & Findell, B. (Eds.). (2001). *Adding it up: Helping children learn mathematics.* Washington, DC: National Academy Press.

Lo, M. L., Pong, W. Y., & Chik, P. P. M. (Eds.). (2005). *For each and everyone: Catering for individual differences through Learning Studies.* HKSAR: The HKU Press.

Marton, F., & Booth, S. (1997). *Learning and awareness*. New Jersey, NJ: Lawrence Erlbaum.

Marton, F., & Morris, P. (Eds.). (2002). *What matters? Discovering critical conditions of classroom learning*. Kompendiet, Goteborg: Acta Universitatis Gothoburgensis.

Marton, F., Tsui, A. B. M., Chik, P. P. M., Ko, P. Y., Lo, M. L., Mok, I. A. C., et al. (2004). *Classroom discourse and the space of learning*. New Jersey, NJ: Lawrence Erlbaum.

Pang, M. F., & Marton, F. (2005). Learning theory as teaching resource: Another example of radical enhancement of students' understanding of economic aspects of the world around them. *Instructional Science, 33*(2), 159–191.

Tseng, O., Hung, D., Chen, S., Wu, J., & His, M. (1986). Processing Chinese logographs by Chinese brain-damaged patients. In H. Kao, G. v. Galen, & R. Hoosain (Eds.), *Graphonomics: Contemporary research in handwriting*. Amsterdam: Elsevier Science Publishers.

Wu, X., Li, W., & Anderson, R. C. (1999). Reading instruction in China. *Journal of curriculum studies, 31*(5), 571–586.

Pakey Pui Man Chik
Faculty of Education
The Chinese University of Hong Kong

Allen Leung
Department of Mathematics and Information Technology
The Hong Kong Institute of Education

Ference Marton
Department of Education
University of Gothenburg

SHEK KAM TSE, FERENCE MARTON, ELIZABETH KA YEE LOH
AND PAKEY PUI MAN CHIK

7. LEARNING TO READ AND WRITE BETTER

INTRODUCTION

The school curricula of most developing countries in the world include the objective of helping school leavers to attain standards of literacy that enable them to take their place in communities in which information flows in ever increasing number of technological forms, and where knowledge based economies seek to establish local and global dimensions. If a mandate like Hong Kong is to compete economically with trading counterparts, its school leavers need to be able to hold their own against students in neighbouring lands in their ability to adjust to societal and technological changes. To achieve these objectives, the reading and writing ability of students needs to extend beyond basic mechanical processes to the ability effectively to use and apply advanced literacy skills.

Being literate is considered an essential asset of individuals who are able to contribute to the political, socio-cultural and economic well-being of the community and nation (Campbell et al., 2001; Stierer, 2002). Although it is unreasonable to expect schools to equip students with every single skill used in society, they can be expected to ensure that students securely grasp rudimentary mechanical processes on the one hand, and the ability to comprehend everyday text on the other. Furthermore, if the very diverse literacy demands of an information laden society are not to overwhelm the school leaver, the interface between the classroom and society merits thought and imagination.

As the information networks within society increase in complexity and literacy requirements expand, more and more employers are complaining that employees fresh from school are unable to cope with the demands of the workplace. There are claims in the press of falling literacy standards in developed countries like the USA, Canada and the United Kingdom. There have also been suggestions that wider social, political and economic changes are predominating and that the aforementioned allegations of decline are not simply a matter of imperfectly learnt processes taught in the classroom (Stierer, 2002; Welch & Freebody, 2002). In many places, this has led to a growing concern among educators, policy makers and practitioners over the difficulties of teaching reading and writing that is pertinent to today's rapidly changing world. This is providing impetus for various initiatives and interventions to a literacy curriculum that aims to equip students with skills relevant to society's demands.

There has been rising concern over students' literacy standards in Hong Kong since the turn of the century and the publication of the results of comparative

F. Marton, S.K. Tse and W. M.Cheung (eds.), On the Learning of Chinese, 123–145.

international literacy attainment tests. In 2001, the International Association for the Evaluation of Educational Achievement (IEA) launched the first in a planned 5-year cycle of international trend studies in reading literacy: the Progress in International Reading Literacy Study (PIRLS 2001). The findings revealed that, among 35 participating countries or regions, fourth graders in western countries outperformed their counterparts in Asian regions, including Hong Kong.

Since 2000, the Hong Kong SAR Government has introduced a number of educational reforms from Grade 1 onwards that emphasise students' ability to "read to learn". In PIRLS 2006, Hong Kong ranked second among 45 participating countries or regions, only one point behind Russia. Although Hong Kong students performed very well in PIRLS 2006, it has been suggested that most are examination-oriented and lack the ability to learn independently. The Education Bureau of the Hong Kong SAR Government encourages teachers to help students to "learn how to learn" and to refine the skills of independent learning. The Education Bureau has also provided initiatives and supported research to tackle the problem.

This chapter is concerned with an initiative aimed at developing a one-year Chinese language curriculum in Secondary 1 classes as part of a government-funded research project in Hong Kong (2003–2004). The project involved collaboration between four parties: the Curriculum Development Institute of the EDB, local secondary schools, a Chinese literacy research team in the University of Hong Kong and Gothenburg University. This initiative had both theoretical and practical foundations. Based on the Theory of Variation (Marton & Booth, 1997; Marton & Morris, 2002; Marton et al., 2004), it set out to develop a one-year curriculum that would (a) combat the inadequacies of current practices and (b) incorporate procedures and methods to enhance students' reading comprehension and ability to express themselves in writing.

The writers first describe current practices in the development of the Chinese language curriculum and discuss its limitations in fostering students' literacy. They then report the development of a one-year curriculum project aimed at enhancing the Chinese literacy of S1 students in Hong Kong.

CURRENT REFORMS AND PRACTICES IN THE CHINESE LANGUAGE CURRICULUM

Chinese language education in Confucius-heritage communities like Hong Kong has in recent years undergone a major transformation. Rapid growth in the economy has brought wealth to people of modest means, whilst advances in science and technology in recent decades have made it possible for such individuals to obtain and exchange information and to communicate worldwide in real time. Such communication has been for both utilitarian purposes at work, and for personal purposes at home and in leisure time. Such developments have instilled in many school students a purpose for acquiring knowledge and skills in subject domains, as well as a meaningful reason for learning how to comprehend what is written and to express themselves clearly and correctly when writing. In response to such drives, the traditional emphasis on knowledge-transfer in Chinese language teaching and learning in the curriculum has given way to the development of skills of communication. This focus has alerted curriculum reformers in Mainland China, Macau, Taiwan, Singapore and Hong Kong to the need to reshape the literacy curriculum (Tse & Ng, 2004).

Although there is ample room for change and despite the shift in focus on the part of Chinese language curriculum reformers, current practices in Chinese language teaching in the classroom differ little from approaches employed traditionally in the past. Lessons focus on textbooks that contain collections of short texts or simplified versions of classical literature (Tse et al., 2007). In other words, the basic teaching/learning resource in Chinese language lessons remains for the most part the traditional textbook. The belief underpinning such practice is that the acquisition of Chinese language and literacy is a gradual process that involves the learner building up insight and knowledge chiefly by rote and imitation. Once learners are able to recall without thinking what characters, strings of characters and passages say and mean, they are able to move on to focusing on a range of texts that contain key examples of language usage, including the ways language is used, distinctive linguistic characteristics and patterns and the moral values and cultural elements described.

Traditionally, the learning of Chinese proceeds via memorization of prescribed texts from an early stage and, unavoidably, short passages feature prominently in literacy lessons. This rote learning is by tradition deemed imperative for learning how to read and write Chinese, for Chinese is very difficult to master due to discrepancies between its spoken and written forms (Zhang, 1993). The selection of texts that exemplify different language genres is central to the curriculum and to becoming Chinese language literate (Ni & Tse, 2006). Practice in the classroom is also heavily dictated by the widespread tradition of teachers using textbooks and teaching guides produced commercially by publishers.

However, there have been gradual changes in the contents of textbooks and accompanying teaching guides in recent years. These reflect responses by publishers to changes to the foci of lessons and modifications to the style and organisation of learning that have become "accepted" classroom practice in schools. Prior to the introduction of curriculum reforms in the closing years of the 20th century, almost every textbook contained passages that exemplified the objectives of individual lessons and teachers spent time dwelling on literary, linguistic and moral aspects of the content of each passage. The individual texts were often unrelated and their chief function was to provide opportunities for repetition of points of learning and the revisiting of common points of grammar, style and so on. However, with the introduction of curriculum reforms, particularly in terms of the themes and sequences of learning, passages are no longer discrete and independent of one another. Rather, they are often assembled in modules or clusters that share similar themes or language characteristics, for example the uses of language, rhetoric, styles of writing, cultural elements and so on. Thematic continuity and interest are in-built, offering opportunities for learners to practise and acquire the communicative channels of reading, writing, speaking and listening that are emphasised in syllabus reforms (Ho, 1997; Tse, 2004).

Besides the accompanying teaching guide, there are also various resources such as multi-media learning packages, workbooks and teaching/learning aids developed to support diversified teaching and learning of Chinese language in the classroom. In addition, reforms to the curriculum have provided Chinese language teachers with more flexibility to tailor the curriculum to individual classes. Thus, although the teaching of Chinese language in schools continues to utilise textbooks, there has been a move away from the content of passages in the textbook dictating lesson format and content. Instead, the stress is on developing students' language processes and skills, with progress measured in terms of the acquisition of verbal communication prowess rather than coverage of the syllabus. At the same time, teachers now make use of a range of resources in addition to the textbook to achieve their teaching aims and objectives.

The approach and methods encouraged by curriculum reforms do not, however, guarantee a revolution in the use of textbooks. Despite the fact that textbook passages are organised thematically, this does not mean that the learning of the Chinese language is conceptually more logical. The passages selected for particular themes are inevitably written by different authors who have different purposes for writing. They also have different writing styles and ways of expressing ideas. It is not always easy therefore for teachers to focus on the development of particular aspects of language development when passages have not been specifically written for this purpose. This calls for teachers to supplement passage content, the result being that lesson content is in danger of lacking cohesion making it difficult for students to perceive the focus of lessons.

Reforms to the curriculum impose on teachers patterns of teaching that are much more taxing than in the past. Whereas it was relatively simple to allow the textbook to constitute the core of lesson preparation, it is now much more demanding to plan lessons so that separate skills and language processes are targeted. In addition, blocks of lessons have to be considered, and space allowed for students to revisit aspects of learning that have not been mastered the first time round. It has also to be borne in mind that, despite efforts to assemble texts into meaningful units or modules that help or favour the development of students' Chinese language, they were never originally written for this end. Inevitably, the grouping of texts into units or modules is somewhat arbitrary. Emphasising commonalities between passages may overshadow distinctive values within each text. It may also overload students by not only having them to learn a great number of texts, but also having to grasp features they have in common.

Although passages have been clustered into units or modules in many textbooks, it is tempting for teachers to continue to perceive them as comparatively independent. If the curriculum reforms are to succeed, it is essential that teachers grasp the ideas underpinning the new approach. Without such endeavour, learning based on clusters designed to permit abstraction of common characteristics among texts may constitute an obstacle rather than a facilitator of students' learning. There is a danger that students will lose focus and fail to appreciate the characteristics of different writing styles such as narrative, descriptive, lyrical, argumentative and so on. They may also fail to identify characteristics that distinguished writers display, such as the use of metaphors, parallel constructions and so on. There is clearly scope for exploration of the logistics of short and long-term planning so that progress can be monitored and continuity of learning is fostered.

A NON-TRADITIONAL APPROACH TO DEVELOPING THE CHINESE LANGUAGE CURRICULUM

Aware of the deficiencies of existing practices in secondary schools aimed at helping Hong Kong students become literate in Chinese, a research project was implemented in the academic year 2003–2004. Its aim was to develop a one-year Chinese language curriculum for Secondary 1 (S1) students in Hong Kong. The design of the curriculum incorporated the Theory of Variation and aimed to provide a more focused experience for students to develop reading comprehension and the capability to express themselves in writing.

Theory of Variation

According to the Theory of Variation, learning does not occur in a vacuum. It is always directed to a particular object or phenomenon and relates to the learner's way of experiencing, and to what and how the learner experiences, particular objects or phenomena in the situation. This in turn contributes to certain capabilities being developed in the learner to respond to or handle the situation in question. These capabilities are referred to as the "object of learning" (Marton et al., 2004; Runesson & Marton, 2002). Each object of learning has two aspects: a general aspect (the indirect object of learning) which relates to the long-term goals of education (for example, the nurturing of certain generic skills), and a specific aspect (the direct object of learning) and the way in which learners are expected to become able to handle the content (the indirect object of learning).

To experience an object or a phenomenon in a certain way involves one in discerning the given situation in a particular structure (structural aspect of awareness) with a meaning attached to the structure (referential aspect of awareness) (Marton & Booth, 1997). Such a process of discernment presupposes an experienced variation by the learner (Bowden & Marton, 1998; Marton & Booth, 1997). This means that when people come to experience a phenomenon in the learning situation, they will not be able to pay attention to all aspects of the phenomenon (Miller, 1956). Rather, their attention will be drawn to varying aspects against a background of what remains invariant in the situation. For example, a deer in the bushes may not be noticed until it runs away and its movement catches the eye of the observer. Features or aspects that are focused on and discerned thus help to define how the learner experiences or understands the phenomenon. These are referred to as "critical features/aspects".

What is discerned depends on the patterns of variation and invariance perceived: in other words what varies and what remain invariant - as experienced by the learner. This process of discernment usually goes from the whole to the parts in two intimately related senses (Bowden & Marton, 1998; Marton & Booth, 1997). One, the part is discerned *from* the whole, and, two, the part is discerned *in relation to* the whole. The part discerned is separate from but at the same time relates to the whole. While attending to the whole, one is also aware of its parts, and while one attends to the parts, the context is not lost. Learning is not an incremental accumulation of parts. It is a progression from awareness of undifferentiated wholes to an awareness of the parts that make up the whole.

It has been shown that students' discernment in the classroom can be fostered by consciously building in pertinent patterns of variation and invariance into what students are supposed to learn (Ki, 2003; Lo et al., 2006a; Lo et al., 2006b; Lo et al., 2005; Pang, 2002; Tse et al., 2004; Tse et al. in press). It is also evident that patterns of variation and invariance afforded in a hierarchical way of lesson structuring are better associated with the discernment of part-whole relationships, whereas those afforded in a sequential way, the discernment of specific features/ aspects, have less impact (Chik, 2006; Tse et al., 2004).

Design of the Project

Although the Theory of Variation was an important source of inspiration for the project, it was more eclectic than most of the other projects reported in this book. The authors drew on several different theoretical resources when they set out to modify the existing curriculum in order to improve students' response to lessons, boost attainment in reading comprehension and the ability to communicate in writing. To help achieve this, particular attention was paid to two main features considered particularly critical for developing the curriculum.

Use of narrative passages and novels as key teaching materials.   Evidence from research into effective reading instruction is that the use of narrative passages and novels at the heart of the reading curriculum is very effective for improving students' comprehension of text, ability to understand story structures, writing ability and attitudes towards reading and literature in their first language (Feitelson et al., 1986; Norton & McNamara, 1987; Sadoski et al., 1996). Such effects apply particularly to underachievers (Freedle & Hale, 1979; Graesser & Riha, 1984; Graesser, 1981; Spiro & Taylor, 1987; Turner, 1993). Similar effects have been reported in students' learning of a second language when they are constructively engaged in voluntary reading (Krashen, 2004).

Compared with the short passages that one finds in textbooks (around 200 to 300 words in length), novels are much longer and richer in content. The writing style of the author is easier to sense as well as the techniques employed for developing and linking themes over long sections of text and chapters. It is much easier to sensitise developing readers to such features of written text with a novel than is the case when short and diverse passages in textbooks are used in lessons.

Several novels were used in the project, including *The Little Prince* (de Saint-Exupéry, 2001), *Romance of the Three Kingdoms* (Law, 2003), *The Eagle-Shooting Heroes* (Cha, 1987) and *The True Episodes of SARS* (Tse et al., 2003). The use of novels as the core reading material in lessons is rare in secondary schools in Hong Kong. As noted earlier, many teachers plan sequences of lessons around consecutive passages when teaching Chinese language. Novels are commonly used as extended reading material when students are encouraged to read books, either individually or in groups, during recesses or after-school hours.

Focusing on the teaching of reading processes and strategies. Leading students into discerning the writing used by accomplished Chinese writers sensitises within them ideas about how to read skilfully and how to use different reading strategies. Applying such strategies enhances general reading comprehension. People develop meaning in different ways. The knowledge and experience that people bring to reading equip them with an understanding of language, textual styles and the world. Transcending these processes, students develop reading processes and strategies that allow them to interpret text and adjust their reading approach (Campbell et al., 2001).

A key focus of the project was conscious attention to the teaching of reading processes and strategies using a hierarchy outlined by Campbell et al. (2001) in their account of the reading sub-processes suggested in the PIRLS framework. The processes included the ability to focus on and retrieve explicit information, to make straightforward inferences, to interpret and integrate ideas and information and to examine and evaluate passage content, language and textual elements (see Appendix A for brief descriptions of these reading processes). Guided and repeated use of the skills by students under supervision was intended to heighten their awareness of the sub-processes and to help students to call upon them automatically whenever the occasion demanded. Hopefully, students would also be practised in a variety of reading activities, including decoding, summarizing, understanding word clusters and paragraphs, making predictions, analyzing themes and identifying key words and sentences. The secure acquisition of all these processes by Chinese language students is strongly recommended (So et al., 1996; Tse, 2001).

The two critical features described above were not taught in isolation. Rather, they were interwoven spontaneously during the project. Regarding the specific content for learning (the direct object of learning), the chosen novels formed undifferentiated wholes within which students were to tease out the relationship between different parts of the novels used, including the story plot, the main characters, the language used, writing skills and methods used. Students were also alerted to how the author was integrating these aspects into the complete novel as a whole. More general aspects (the indirect object of learning) concerned students' mastery of reading processes and strategies in comprehending the novels.

In summary, using the Theory of Variation as a basis for shaping curriculum design, the project set about helping students to differentiate and appreciate various ways of presenting information and using literary techniques used by accomplished authors. This practice helped students to become skilled in using various techniques of reading to penetrate the surface meaning of text (see Figure 7.1). This is remarkably different from the textbook-based approach conventionally adopted by Chinese language teachers. With the help of deliberate instruction about how noted authors construct and shape text, students in the project were better placed to appreciate the printed word and extended text independently.

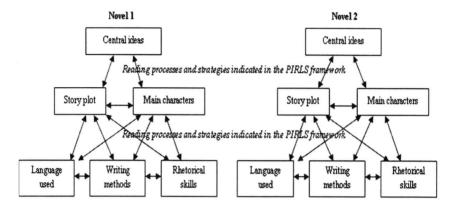

Figure 7.1. The hierarchical structure of the project curriculum.

In fairness, it would be misleading to suggest that conventional Chinese language teachers ignore the techniques authors use when writing books. However, attention to these aspects is usually emphasised late on in the sequence of lessons and with older students in much higher grades than Secondary 1.

The Use of Pattern of Variation and Invariance in Guiding Lesson Implementation

The success of any literacy instructional programme depends on whether the teacher is effective in adapting approaches and materials to suit the learners' needs (Heilman et al., 1998) and in realising the rationale of the curriculum design. To facilitate students' discernment of the part-whole relationships within the context of each novel and the uses of various reading processes and strategies in comprehending the chosen novels, patterns of variation and invariance were consciously developed to guide teachers' implementation of the project curriculum in the classroom. Using examples quoted from tactual practice, details of the project are presented.

a. Students were asked to read fiction and non-fiction reading material relating to the same novel. Through reading various kinds of materials, it was possible for students to discern how different writing strategies and presentation styles can be used to describe the same episodes in different types of texts. For example, *The True episodes on SARS* (Tse et al., 2003) is reportage recording the heroic circumstances of the doctors and nurses who sacrificed themselves in fighting SARS in Hong Kong in 2003. In studying this book, students were asked to read both fiction (the book) and non-fiction (newspapers) reading materials relating to the SARS incident. It was hoped that by having students read the two contrasting kinds of reading materials, they would be able to discern the difference between the two. They would see that different writing and presentation techniques can be used and become aware that different authors can have different points of view on the same issue and use different means to express their thinking.

b. Students were made to be aware that the same expression can denote different meanings and can be understood in different ways. For example, in reading a chapter about the merchant in *The Little Prince* (de Saint-Exupéry, 2001), some students thought that the merchant was very smart and that he knew how to manage his financial affairs. However, others thought that he was not very clever.

c. Students were made aware that the same phenomenon can be expressed in different ways. A typical example was that they saw how different rhetoric skills, including allusive, explicit, metaphor, divination and so on could be used to express the same opinion.

d. Understanding and expressing oneself in Chinese were practised within the context of different subjects (e.g., Geography, Physics, History) with the help of teachers of those subjects. It was hoped that such cross-curricular activities would help students recognize that reading processes and strategies used in Chinese language lessons can be transferred to the learning assignments in different subject areas.

e. The idea that one can learn the same thing in different ways, for example by rote learning or by secure understanding, was impressed upon students. This made students aware that the choice was theirs, and that they had a choice over the most appropriate way to learn relative to the learning objectives.

To enhance students' interest in reading, an on-line forum was established to encourage students from different schools to share their thinking and exchange opinions after reading the same novel in more or less the same period of time. On the website, students were also able to download information related to the selected novels. Teachers also made use of different reading instructional tasks, such as peer-group reading activities, instant dramas, role play and so on to bring out particular reading characteristics in the lesson (e.g., use of appropriate tones in drama). This is in line with literature on reading performance and its developmental trajectories that encourages differential use of reading instruction where the weight is on a specific reading component at a certain moment (Lerkkanen et al., 2004).

RESEARCH METHOD

Three Secondary schools were invited to take part in the project in the academic year of 2003–2004. It was not the authors' intention to have all the teachers work with ready-made teaching materials developed by the research team. Nor did the researchers wish to tamper with or replace the schools' original Chinese language curriculum. Therefore, the research team worked together with the teachers in a number of meetings to select an appropriate approach and to design teaching materials for the curriculum based on the conceptual framework referred to earlier. It was hoped that the curricula developed were able to best suit the needs of the students in each setting.

To validate the effectiveness of the reading curriculum for students' learning, a control group was set up in each of the participant schools. While teachers in the control group(s) followed the original curriculum and taught reading comprehension based on the set textbook, those in the experimental group(s) adopted the new reading curriculum and worked together in designing lessons and related materials, appropriating different patterns of variation and invariance in what students were expected to discern. Illustrations in the use of different patterns of variation and invariance will be provided in the next section when the authors focus on the classroom practices in the experimental groups.

Reading literacy tests were adopted from those used in the PIRLS study and administered to students in both the target and comparison groups before and after the implementation of the curriculum (in September, 2003 and January, 2004 respectively). At the end of the academic year, students were also given a language ability test that assessed their language ability in different dimensions. Classroom observation and video-taping of the experimental groups' lessons were also arranged throughout the academic year.

Since the curriculum was newly developed in the participant schools, training seminars were organised for the participant teachers. Various arrangements about the project were also explained to other teachers, students and parents of the schools to ensure ethical and consent issues were resolved before the implementation of the project.

THE PROJECT CURRICULUM FIELDWORK

Participants

To examine the effectiveness of the project curriculum, an experiment was conducted in three secondary schools involving 8 Chinese language teachers, 292 S1 students and their parents. Teachers and students were divided into two groups: an experimental group (151 students) which adopted the project curriculum and a control group (141 students) which used the school's usual curriculum based on the prescribed textbook. Introduction seminars were given to both groups of teachers, students and their parents about the rationale and arrangement of the project and to solicit consent. Teachers in the experimental group received training before they started the project curriculum in a series of training seminars and workshops. On-going support to resolve any difficulties that emerged during implementation was also provided for the teachers by the research team.

Instruments and Procedures

A reading literacy test developed for the PIRLS research and a specially cons-tructed writing test were given to the students to establish baseline ability and ensure equivalence between the groups. A one-way analysis of variance test found no statistically significant differences in attainment between the groups $(1, 259) = 2.05$, $p<0.153$, $MSE = 12.73$).

A standardized reading test was developed based on tests used in the PIRLS survey (Mullis, Kennedy, Martin, & Sainsbury, 2006) (see Appendix B for a sample of the original and translated copies of the test paper, and Table 7.1 for a description of the processes measured). Students were asked to answer questions relating to two types of text: literary and informational. The test was administered twice, before and after the experimental curriculum had been implemented. Students were allowed 40 minutes to answer questions on each passage with a ten minutes break between occasions of testing.

Table 7.1. Reading literacy test – reading purposes and processes

Processes of comprehension	Purposes of reading	
	Literary experience	Acquire & use information
Focus on and retrieve explicitly stated information	20%	20%
Make straightforward inference	30%	30%
Interpret and integrate ideas and information	30%	30%
Examine and evaluate content, language and textual elements	20%	20%

The students were also given a written test at the end of the academic year to assess their writing ability. The test consisted of two assignments, the first asking students to write a letter from a student to extend their regards to a form teacher who was unwell: the second letter had the same purpose but was written from the perspective of a parent (see Appendix C for a sample of the original and translated copies of the test paper). Students had 30 minutes to complete the paper.

Data Analysis

The students' scores were collated and the data of students who had taken both pre- and post- tests were subjected to a paired sample t-test to establish differences between the equivalent groups on each occasion of testing. A one-way analysis of variance was applied (ANOVA) to examine differences between the same group's performance before and after the period of the project.

RESULTS

Students' Attainment on Pre- and Post- Reading Literacy Tests

As mentioned above, only the scores of students who had taken both pre- and post-literacy tests were examined (experimental group n = 139; control group n = 145). The results showed increases in mean score between the pre- and post- tests for both groups, both statistically significant (2-tailed paired sample t-test, $p < 0.01$) (see Table 7.2).

Table 7.2. Pre- and post-test comparisons

Group	n	Mean score		Gain score (post - pre)	t-value
		Pre-test	Post-test		
Experimental group	139	54.14	72.98	18.84	9.77***
Control group	145	61.83	70.18	8.35	4.30***

Analysis of variance was applied to examine the relative differences in performance pre- and post-test for the control and experimental group. When the relative gain scores (post-test minus pre-test) were compared, it was found that the scores attained by the experimental group were statistically significantly larger than those of the control group (F (1, 282) = 14.674, p<0.001).

Language Ability Test (AAA)

A language ability test was administered at the end of the academic year. The test was divided into 3 parts: reading comprehension, language usage and writing. Students' language ability including decoding, identifying keywords, analyzing meaning of sentences, making inferences and prediction, finding out main themes of texts and writing topic sentences and summaries. It took 60 minutes to complete the test. The results revealed that the EG performed much better than the CG students. They obtained higher mean scores in all sections (see Table 7.3). There were statistically significant differences between EG and CG in "sum scores", "summary writing", "topic sentence writing", "composition 1" and "composition 2" (see Table 7.4).

Students' Performance on the Writing Test

One-way analysis of variance was applied to the control and experimental groups' writing assignment marks. The mean scores for the experimental group on assignment 1 were pre-A one way (on Question 1 = 20.60 and Question 2 = 19.18) on the two questions were consistently higher than those attained by the control group (on Question 1 = 16.54 and Question 2 = 14.86) suggesting that the differences in mean scores obtained by the two groups on the two questions in the test were statistically significant (Question 1: F (1, 287) = 31.00, p<0.001; Question 2: F (287) = 29.09, p<0.001).

Table 7.3. Overall performance of the students (N = 284)

Items		Experimental group		Control group	
	Full mark	Mean	S.D.	Mean	S.D.
Sum scores	100.00	61.42	12.89	54.99	17.21
Part 1					
Section A: Reading comprehension	17.00	12.73	2.29	12.04	2.81
Section B: Application of language	4.00	2.22	.80	2.06	.98

Table 7.3. (Continued)

Part 2: Use of language					
Section C: Summary	19.00	7.72	2.94	6.70	3.41
Section D: Writing of topic sentence	5.00	3.01	2.02	2.73	1.73
Part 3: Communicative writing					
Section E: Composition 1	30.00	20.60	5.16	16.54	6.83
Section E: Composition 2	30.00	19.18	5.39	14.86	7.34

Table 7.4. ANOVA analysis of overall performance of the students

Items	df	F
Sum scores	1, 287	29.59***
Part 1		
Section A: Reading comprehension	1, 287	.26
Section B: Application of language	1, 287	2.18
Part 2: Use of language		
Section C: Summary	1, 287	8.36**
Section D: Writing of topic sentence	1, 287	6.51*
Part 3: Communicative writing		
Section E: Composition 1	1, 287	31.00***
Section E: Composition 2	1, 287	29.09***

* $p < .05$; ** $p < .01$; *** $p < .001$

The Comparative Reading Performance of Students in the Control and Experimental Groups

Based on analysis of reading literacy tests, it was found that the EG had the lowest scores on the pre-test but made a great improvement and achieved very good post-test scores (see Table 7.2). The EG performed better than the CG on the Chinese language ability test, having remarkable performance on "communicative writing" and overall performance (see Table 7.3).

CONCLUSIONS

The results of this study of students' Chinese language in three secondary schools and with a single year group are encouraging. They offer evidence to suggest that modifications to existing practice merit serious consideration. Every attempt was made to avoid and suppress any "Hawthorne" effect and all of the students simply assumed that the curriculum they were experiencing was that faced by all students in the school. The website was available to all students. In fact, it was known prior to the experiment that all of the students taking part in the study were considered to be Chinese language low achievers.

The analyses show that although the matched groups of students commenced the study on a par, those who had studied Chinese presented in the form of book and novels had made greater gains than counterparts who had received the "usual" form of lesson and whose lessons had featured unrelated short passages. The students in the experimental group were able to make impressively large improvements on the two types of reading comprehension test, one on a transactional passage and the other on a passage of a more literary nature. At the same time, performance on the writing tasks involving adopting different roles was also found to be significantly better than their counterparts in the control group.

A key rationale for the existing curriculum is that the passages students study in lessons portray samples of exemplary Chinese for students to absorb and imitate. Over time, the essence of the style of writing of the known scholars whose writing had been presented will hopefully be assimilated and emerge as the student's own. It is suggested that similar examples of exemplary Chinese can be presented in the form of novels, and that the extended narrative attracts and engages students to such a degree that their learning of Chinese will be impressively enhanced. It is not suggested that the use of literary passages is ground-breaking in Chinese language curriculum development, since literary texts have for many years played a key role in Chinese language teaching and learning. This has been so since ancient times and such texts are to be found in most schools (Ni & Tse, 2006). The outcomes of the project suggest that schools should consider using alternative approaches to teaching and learning Chinese language and to relying on a single passage format.

It is also worth noting that there has been a long history for both the adaptation of the novel-based approach and the focus on teaching reading processes and strategies to developing reading literacy in the West. The use of The Theory of Variation in guiding both curriculum design and the implementation in the classroom, however, is far from untraditional in two senses. First, in recent decades researchers in different subject domains have been applying the theory in lesson intervention; yet, very few of them have attempted to make use of the theory as an essential feature of a year long curriculum framework, as was the case in the project reported here. Second, by adopting The Theory of Variation the project took an alternative perspective to the psychological learning perspective that has long been prevalent to establishing a systematic and coherent framework for both the design and implementation of reading literacy curricula. From a learning perspective, the result was nevertheless promising.

It ought not to be concluded that this one-year curriculum study offers a brand new or best way to enhance students' literacy. The project involved only three secondary schools and the student participants belonged to the same band of performance in Chinese language. Nevertheless, there is evidence to support an extension of the study to encompass a larger number of schools and with students of a wider range of ability. It must also be emphasised that the success of any curriculum depends on how effectively the teachers implement the goals of the curriculum, understand how students learn and meet their learning needs.

REFERENCES

Bonset, H., & Rijlaarsdam, G. (2004). Mother-tongue education (L1) in the learning-to-learn paradigm: Creative redevelopment of learning materials. *L1-Educational Studies in Language and Literature, 4*, 35–62.

Bowden, J., & Marton, F. (1998). *The university of learning*. London: Kogan Page.

Campbell, J. R., Kelly, D. L., Mullis, I. V. S., Martin, M. O., & Sainsbury, M. (2001). *Framework and specifications for PIRLS assessment 2001* (2nd ed.). Chestnut Hill, MA: PIRLS International Study Center, Lynch School of Education, Boston College.

Curriculum Development Council. (2004). *The curriculum guide of Chinese language education (Primary 1–6)*. Hong Kong: The Council.

Cha, L. (1987). *Shèdiāo yīngxióng chuán* [The eagle-shooting heroes]. Hong Kong: Ming Ho Publications Co. Ltd.

Chik, P. M. P. (2006). *Differences in learning as a function of differences between hierarchical and sequential organisation of the content taught*. Unpublished doctoral dissertation, The University of Hong Kong, Hong Kong.

Feitelson, D., Rita, B., & Goldstein, Z. (1986). Effects of listening to series stories on first graders' comprehension and use of language. *Research in the teaching of English, 20*, 339–355.

Freedle, R., & Hale, G. (Eds.). (1979). *Acquisition of new comprehension schemata for expository prose by transfer of a narrative schema*. Norwood, NJ: Ablex.

Graesser A., & Riha, J. R. (Eds.). (1984). *An application of multiple regression techniques to sentence reading times*. Hillsdale, NJ: Erlbaum.

Graesser, A. C. (1981). *Prose comprehension beyond the word*. New York: Springer-Verlag.

Heilman, A. W., Blair, T. R., & Rupley, W. H. (1998). *Principles and practices of teaching reading* (9th ed.). New Jersey, NJ: Prentice-Hall, Inc.

Ho, M. S. (1997). *Observations and reconstruction of the framework of the Chinese textbooks for target oriented curriculum*. Paper presented at the International Language in Education Conference, The University of Hong Kong, Hong Kong.

Ki, W. W., Lam, H. C., Chung, A. L. S., Tse, S. K., Ko, P. Y., Lau, E. C. C., et al. (2003). Structural awareness, variation theory and ICT support. *L1-Educational Studies in Language and Literature, 3*, 54–78.

Krashen, S. D. (2004). *The power of reading: Insights from the research* (2nd ed.). Portsmouth, NH: Heinemann/Libraries Unlimited.

Law, K. C. (2003). *Sānguó yǎnyì* [Romance of the three Kingdoms]. Hong Kong: Chung Hwa Book.

Lerkkanen, M.-K., Rasku-Puttonen, H., Annola, K., & Nurmi, J.-E. (2004). Reading performance and its developmental trajectories during the first and second grades. *Learning and Instruction, 14*, 111–130.

Lo, M. L., Chik, P., & Pang, M. F. (2006). Patterns of variation in teaching the colour of light to Primary 3 students. *Instructional Science, 34*, 1–19.

Lo, M. L., Hung, H. Y. H., & Chik, P. M. P. (2006). *Using patterns of variation to teach electro-chemical series in Hong Kong*. Paper presented at the 11th Biennial conference of European Association for Research on Learning and Instruction, Nicosia, Cyprus.

Lo, M. L., Pong, W. Y., & Chik, P. M. P. (Eds.). (2005). *For each and everyone: Catering for individual differences through learning studies*. Hong Kong: Hong Kong University Press.

Marton, F., & Booth, S. (1997). *Learning and awareness*. Mahwah, NJ: Erlbaum Associates.

Marton, F., & Morris, P. (Eds.). (2002). *What matters? Discovering critical conditions of classroom learning*. Kompendiet, Goteborg: Acta Universitatis Gothoburgensis.

Marton, F., Runesson, U., & Tsui, A. B. M. (2004). The space of learning. In F. Marton & A. B. M. Tsui (Eds.), *Classroom discourse and the space of learning* (pp. 3–40). New Jersey, NJ: Lawrence Erlbaum.

Marton, F., & Tsui, A. B. M. (Eds.). (2004). *Classroom discourse and the space of learning*. Mahwah, NJ: Lawrence Erlbaum Associatess

Miller, G. A. (1956). The magic number seven, plus or minus two. Some limits on our capacity to process information. *Psychological Review, 63*, 81–87.

Mullis, I. V. S., Kennedy, A. M., Martin, M. O., & Sainsbury, M. (2006). *PIRLS 2006 assessment framework and specifications* (2nd ed). Chestnut Hill: TIMSS & PIRLS International Study Center, Lynch School of Education, Boston College.

Norton, D. M., J. (1987). *An evaluation of the BISD/TAMU multiethnic reading program* (Research Report). College Station, TX: Texas A&M University.

Pang, M. F. (2002). *Making learning possible the use of variation in the teaching of school economics.* Unpublished doctoral dissertation, The University of Hong Kong, Hong Kong.

Runesson, U., & Marton, F. (2002). The object of learning and the space of variation. In F. Marton & P. Morris (Eds.), *What matters? Discovering critical conditions of classroom learning* (pp. 19–37). Kompendiet, Goteborg: Acta Universitatis Gothoburgensis.

Sadoski, M., Wilson, V., & Norton, D. (1996). The relative contributions of research-based composition activities to writing improvement in grades 1–8. *Research in the teaching of English, 31*(1), 120–150.

Saint-Exupéry, A. d. (2001). *Xiǎo wángzǐ* [The little prince; P. C. Ma, Trans.]. Hong Kong: Joint Publishing (H.K.) Co. Ltd.

So, Y. W., Yu, Y. Y., & Man, Y. L. (1996). *Zhōngwén yuèdú lǐjiě nénglì xùnliàn* [Training of Chinese reading comprehension abilities]. Hong Kong: Hong Kong Educational Research Centre, The Chinese University of Hong Kong.

Spiro, R. J. T., & Taylor, B. M. (Eds.). (1987). *On investigating children's transition from narrative to expository discourse: The multidimensional nature of psychological text classification.* Gukksdake, NJ: Erlbaum.

Stierer, B. (Ed.). (2002). *Simply doing their job? The politics of reading standards and "read books".* London, UK: Routledge-Falmer.

Tierney, R. J., & Readence J. E. (2000). *Reading strategies and practices: A compendium* (5th ed.). Boston: Allyn and Bacon.

Tse, S. K. (2001). *Handbook of independent learning project (teachers' guide).* Hong Kong: Faculty of Education, The University of Hong Kong.

Tse, S. K. (2004). The characteristics of the new Chinese language in Hong Kong. In S. K. Tse & W. Y. Ng (Eds.), *Zhōngguó nèidì, Gǎng, ào, Tái, Xīnjiāpō: Zhōngguó yǔwén xīn kèchéng yánjiū jí xiàobĕn jiàoxué yōuxiù ànlì* (pp. 92–119) [Chinese language curriculum and good practice in three countries and two regions]. Guangzhou, China: Guangdong Higher Educational Press.

Tse, S. K., Lam, J. W. I., Lam, R. Y. H., Loh, E. K. Y., & Westwood, P. (2007). Pedagogical correlates of reading comprehension in English and Chinese. *L1-Educational Studies in Language and Literature, 7*(2), 71–91.

Tse, S. K., Loh, E. K. Y., Marton, F., Law, H, C., Lee, P. M., & Leung, S. K. (2004). Developing good independent learning abilities: reading. In S. K. Tse & W. Y. Ng (Eds.), *Zhōngguó nèidì, Gǎng, ào, Tái, Xīnjiāpō: Zhōngguó yǔwén xīn kèchéng yánjiū jí xiàobĕn jiàoxué yōuxiù ànlì* (pp. 280–296) [Chinese language curriculum and good practice in three countries and two regions]. Guangzhou, China, Guangdong Higher Educational Press.

Tse, S. K., Marton, F., Ki, W. W., & Loh, E. K. Y. (2007). An integrative perceptual approach to teach Chinese characters. *Instructional Science, 35*(5), 375–406.

Tse, S. K., Shum, M. S. K., & Ki, W. W. (2003). *Fēidiǎn qíng* [The true episodes of SARS]. Hong Kong: Faculty of Education, The University of Hong Kong.

Turner, T. (1993). *Improving reading comprehension achievement of sixth, seventh, and eighth grade underachievers.* Uppsala: Nova University.

Tse, S. K., & Wu, W. Y. (Eds.). (2004). *Chinese language curriculum and good practice in three countries and two regions.* Guangzhou: Guangdong Higher Educational Press.

Welch, A. R., & Freebody, P. (Eds.). (2002). *Explanations of the current internationally "literacy crisis".* London, UK: Routledge-Falmer.

Ni, W. J., & Tse, S. K. (Eds.). (2006). *Xīnbiān yǔwén kèchéng yǔ jiàoxué lùn* [A new theory for the language curriculum and teaching]. Shanghai: East China Normal University Press.

Zhang, Z. G. (1998). Need a bridging science urgently. In B H. Wang (Ed.), *Collection of articles written by Zhang Zhi Gong: Out of the collection.* Beijing: Language Publication.

Shek Kam Tse and Elizabeth Ka Yee Loh
Faculty of Education
The University of Hong Kong

Ference Marton
Department of Education
Gothenburg University

Pakey Pui Man Chik
Faculty of Education
The Chinese University of Hong Kong

AUTHORS' NOTES

The authors thank the Education Bureau of Hong Kong SAR Government for its support. The authors would particularly like to acknowledge Professor Terry Dolan for his input to this article. Thanks also to the students, teachers and school principals in the three secondary schools in Hong Kong for their participation in the project.

APPENDIX A

Brief description of the reading processes

The four types of reading processes adopted from the PIRLS survey:

Level 1: Focus and retrieve explicitly stated information

Students are required to locate and understand explicitly stated information in the text. The following reading tasks may exemplify this type of reading processing:
- Searching for information that relate to specific reading purpose
- Looking for key concepts or ideas
- Identifying meanings of words or phrases
- Finding out keywords, topic sentences or main idea

Level 2: Make straightforward inferences

Students are required to construct meaning from the text which does not explicitly stated by making inferences about ideas or information. Reading tasks include:
- Finding out the causal relationship of events
- Concluding the main idea from two to three pieces of information
- Identifying key message made in the text
- Describing the relationship between two characters

Level 3: Interpret and integrate ideas and information

Students are required to focus on the meanings of the text beyond the phrase or sentence level, by drawing on their understanding of the world. Reading tasks such as:
- Finding out the entire message or theme of a text
- Suggesting an alternative ending of the story
- Comparing text information
- Inferring the mood of the character
- Interpreting text information with the real-world experience

Level 4: Examine and evaluate content, language, and textual elements

Students are required to shift their focus from constructing meaning to critically examining and evaluating the text. Reading tasks including:
- Evaluating the probability that the events described in the text could be happened in the real world
- Judging the tone or mood of the text
- Explaining how the author created an unexpected ending
- Determining an author's viewpoint made in the text
- Describing how the choice of vocabularies used by the author affect meanings of the text

APPENDIX B

Sample of the original and translated copies of the test paper which has been used in the PIRLS Study

Original English version

The Upside-Down Mice

Once upon a time there lived an old man of 87 whose name was Labon. All his life he had been a quiet and peaceful person. He was very poor and very happy.

When Labon discovered that he had mice in his house, it did not bother him much at first. But the mice multiplied. They began to bother him. They kept on multiplying and finally there came a time when even he could stand it no longer.

"This is too much," he said. "This really is going a bit too far." He hobbled out of the house down the road to a shop where he bought some mousetraps, a piece of cheese and some glue.

When he got home, he put the glue on the underneath of the mousetraps and stuck them to the ceiling. Then he baited them carefully with pieces of cheese and set them to go off.

That night when the mice came out of their holes and saw the mousetraps on the ceiling, they thought it was a tremendous joke. They walked around on the floor, nudging each other and pointing up with their front paws and roaring with laughter. After all, it was pretty silly, mousetraps on the ceiling.

When Labon came down the next morning and saw that there were no mice caught in the traps, he smiled but said nothing.

He took a chair and put glue on the bottom of its legs and stuck it upside-down to the ceiling, near the mousetraps. He did the same with the table, the television set and the lamp. He took everything that was on the floor and stuck it upside-down on the ceiling. He even put a little carpet up there.

The next night when the mice came out of their holes they were still joking and laughing about what they had seen the night before. But now, when they looked up at the ceiling, they stopped laughing very suddenly.

"Good gracious me!" cried one. "Look up there! There's the floor!"

"Heavens above!" shouted another. "We must be standing on the ceiling!"

"I'm beginning to feel a little giddy," said another.

"All the blood's going to my head," said another.

"This is terrible!" said a very senior mouse with long whiskers. "This is really terrible! We must do something about it at once!"

"I shall faint if I have to stand on my head any longer!" shouted a young mouse.

"Me too!"

"I can't stand it!"

"Save us! Do something somebody, quick!"

They were getting hysterical now. "I know what we'll do," said the very senior mouse. "We'll all stand on our heads, then we'll be the right way up."

Obediently, they all stood on their heads, and after a long time, one by one they fainted from a rush of blood to their brains.

When Labon came down the next morning the floor was littered with mice. Quickly he gathered them up and popped them all in a basket.

So the thing to remember is this: whenever the world seems to be terribly upside-down, make sure you keep your feet firmly on the ground.

1. Where did Labon put the mousetraps? (Reading Level 1: Focus and retrieve explicitly stated information)
   A. in a basket
   B. near the mouse holes
   C. under the chairs
   D. on the ceiling (Correct answer)

2. Why did Labon want to get rid of the mice? (Reading Level 2: Make straight-forward inferences)
   A. He had always hated mice.
   B. There were too many of them. (Correct answer)
   C. They laughed too loudly.
   D. They ate all his cheese.

3. Why did Labon smile when he saw there were no mice in the traps? (Reading Level 3: Interpret and integrate ideas and information)
   Marking scheme: These responses provide an appropriate interpretation of Labon's reaction within the context of the whole story.

   Examples of correct answers:
   A. He had a plan to fool the mice and get rid of them.
   B. Because he had other things in mind for the mice.

4. How does the story show you what the mice thought was happening? (Reading Level 4: Examine and evaluate content, language, and textual elements)
   A. by telling you what Labon thought of the mice
   B. by describing where the mice lived
   C. by telling you what the mice said to one another
   D. by describing what the mice were like

Chinese translation

《倒立的老鼠》

　　從前有一位八十七歲的老人叫<u>羅伯</u>，一生過□和平安靜的生活，他雖然貧窮但很快樂。

　　當他發現家裏有老鼠的時候，初時他並未感到十分困擾，但當那些老鼠開始倍數繁殖的時候，他便開始感到困擾。牠們不斷繁殖，最後羅伯再不能忍受。

　　「太過份了！」羅伯說，「實在太過份了！」。於是，他一拐一拐地走出屋外到路上的商店，買了一些老鼠夾、漿糊和芝士。

回家後，他把漿糊塗在老鼠夾的底部，然後黏到天花板上，再小心地放上芝士作餌，希望能趕走老鼠。

那天晚上，老鼠離開洞穴，看見天花板上的老鼠夾，覺得這簡直是天大的笑話。牠們在地上走來走去、你碰我、我碰你，並用前爪指□天花板捧腹大笑。他們心想，把老鼠夾放在天花板上實在太愚蠢了。

第二天早上，羅伯下樓，看見老鼠夾上沒有抓到老鼠，他微微一笑，沒有作聲。

他拿起椅子，在椅腳的底部塗上漿糊，把椅子倒懸在天花板上老鼠夾的旁邊，並把桌子、電視機和電燈都倒懸在天花板上，他甚至連小地毯也放到天花板上。

第二天晚上，老鼠離開洞穴的時候，仍把昨晚發生的事拿來開玩笑。可是，當牠們抬頭望向天花板時，笑聲突然停下。

「天啊！」其中一隻老鼠大喊，「看看上面！那裏才是地面！」

「天呀！」另一隻老鼠嚷□，「我們一定是站在天花板上了！」

「我開始感到頭暈眼花。」另一隻老鼠說。

「我身上的血全都湧到頭上去了。」又有另一隻老鼠說。

「太可怕了！」一隻長□鬍子的年長老鼠說，「這實在太可怕了！我們得立即想想辦法。」

「如果繼續倒立，我會暈倒的！」一隻年幼的老鼠大叫。

「我也是啊！」

「我不能再忍受了！」

「快!想想辦法，救救我們吧！」

老鼠開始變得恐慌了。「我知道我們該怎辦，」最年長的老鼠說道，「我們該倒立，那才是正確的方向。」

所有老鼠都聽從年長老鼠的說法，全都倒立起來。過了一段時間之後，老鼠都因為腦衝血而一一暈倒過來。

第二天早上，羅伯發現地上滿是老鼠，他迅速地拾起牠們，然後統統丟到垃圾籃裏。

這個故事教訓我們，當看見這個世界似乎是極度倒亂時，記得確定自己是腳踏實地。

1. 羅伯把老鼠夾放在哪裏？（閱讀過程一：集中及找回明確陳述的資料及意念）

    A. 籃內

    B. 老鼠洞附近

    C. 椅子下

    D. 天花板上（正確答案）

2. 為甚麼羅伯要擺脫那些老鼠？（閱讀過程二：直接推斷）

    A. 他一直都憎恨老鼠

    B. 因爲有太多老鼠（正確答案）

    C. 老鼠的笑聲太吵耳

    D. 老鼠把他的芝士全都吃光

3. 爲甚麼羅伯看到老鼠夾上沒有老鼠時，會微微一笑？（閱讀過程三：解釋及融入意見及文章資料）

    這些答案恰當解釋了羅伯（在整個故事內容中）的反應。

    例句：

    他計劃戲弄老鼠和擺脫牠們。

    因爲他心裏想着關於老鼠的其他事。

4. 這故事透過甚麼方式把老鼠的想法表達出來？（閱讀過程四：仔細閱讀並評估內容、語言和文章的要素）

    A. 透過羅伯對老鼠的看法

    B. 透過描述老鼠生活的地方

    C. 透過老鼠之間的對話（正確答案）

    D. 透過描述老鼠的樣貌

Appendix C

Sample of the original and translated copies of the test paper

English translation

Miss Lam, the class teacher of F1A is sick. Please write two letters to her with different identities, and sending your regards. Each letter should write about 100 words.

Letter 1: Please use an identity as a F1A student to write a letter to Miss Lam, and send your regards to her;

Letter 2: Please use an identity as the parent of a F1A student to write a letter to Miss Lam, and send your regards to her.

Original Chinese version

中一級甲班的班主任 — 林老師病倒了，請你扮演以下不同的角色寫信問候林老師，並表達你對林老師的關懷。試寫兩篇文章，每篇約寫一百字。

第一篇：請用中一級甲班學生的身份問候林老師，以表達你對林老師的關懷；

第二篇：請用某學生家長的身份問候林老師，以表達你對林老師的關懷。

WAI MING CHEUNG, FERENCE MARTON AND SHEK KAM TSE

8. SOARING ACROSS THE SKY LIKE A HEAVENLY HORSE

Enhancing Creativity in Chinse Writing

INTRODUCTION

In accordance with international trends in recent years, the urgent need to enhance Hong Kong students' creativity was repeatedly emphasized in connection with the 2001 curriculum reform. In the study reported in this chapter, we set out to do exactly this: we tried to enhance Hong Kong students' creativity. In order to do that you must start by reflecting on the question "What is creativity?" First, when you have a reasonably clear idea of what it is that you want the learners to develop, that you can reflect on the second question "How can creativity be advanced?" When you have a tentative answer to that question, an expectation, a conjecture, you might reflect on a third question, namely "How can we find out to what extent we are capable of advancing creativity?" The first two questions we are going to deal with below in this introductory section. The answer to the third question is reported later. After that, we will draw some conclusions from what has been said.

WHAT IS CREATIVITY?

All scholars of creativity seem to agree that creativity has to do with opening up, providing space for the individual to move around freely, producing something useful and novel, something like what is expressed by the Chinese expression "soaring across the sky like a heavenly horse".

In one of the curriculum reform documents, creativity was defined as 'the ability to generate original ideas and solve problems appropriate to the contexts' (Curriculum Development Institute, 2001). In the earliest book-length treatise in Chinese on literary creation complied in the sixth century, the Book of Literacy Design (Wenxin diaolong), Liu Xie (465–522) characterized: "the powers of imagination" in a way which we easily associate with the modern concept of "creativity":

> Literary thinking emphatically is magical, beyond analysis. Silent, lost in thought, you mentally move back a thousand years; and with a mere twitch in your face you direct your gaze to objects ten thousand miles away, The tinkle of pearls and jade pieces is heard and vanishes as you versify; the majesty of winds and clouds is spread out and then swept away when you do bat an unexpected eyelid. Such are the powers of the imagination (translated by Wong, Lo & Tam, 1999).

F. Marton, S.K. Tse and W. M.Cheung (eds.), On the Learning of Chinese, 147–162.

Creativity is a complex phenomenon involving the operation of multiple influences as we move from initial generation of an idea to the delivery of an innovative new product (Mumford & Gustafson, 1988).

Cognitive models of composition prevailed in the 1980's and 1990's, in which writing was seen as a problem solving process (Bereiter & Scardamalia, 1987; Flower and Hayes, 1984; Hayes and Flower, 1980). Sharples (1999) argued that writers operate as problem solvers, creative thinkers and designers, while Graves (1983) emphasized the importance of choice in writing. Creativity can be seen as the ability that helps a person generate ideas in the planning process. Without adequate creative capacity, limited ideas can be generated, which in turn significantly limits the planning process. As a result, the writing process cannot be completed or can be completed with only very limited ideas.

Creativity does not exist in a vacuum; when a person is creative, there is always something that he/she does creatively (Guildford, 1950; Csikszentmihalyi, 1988, 1990, 1996, 1999; Starko, 2005). Creativity is best understood as domain specific (Baer, 1996; Csikszentmihalyi, 1988, 1999; Feldman, 1994). Conceptualizing creativity as domain specific highlights the importance of subject matter knowledge (Feldman & Benjamin, 2006).

This chapter and the study reported in it originate from two points of departure. First, we do not consider creativity as a general human characteristic. We do not assume that some people are creative while others are not. We consider creativity as a way of doing something. We are not looking at creativity as something general. We look at creativity as a certain way of handling, for example, writing. We are interested in locating creativity in a domain. In this case, it is located in the domain of Chinese writing. How can we enhance creativity in Chinese writing? The second point of departure is to open up a space in a certain dimension which is strategically chosen in relation to the domain in which creativity is located.

HOW CAN CREATIVITY BE ENHANCED?

In this study we look at creativity from a pedagogical point of view and try to enhance creativity in Chinese writing by applying the Theory of Variation (Marton & Tsui, 2004; Runesson & Marton, 2002) within the framework of an arrangement called "Learning Study" (Holmqvist, Gustavsson & Wernberg, in press; Marton & Booth, 1997; Lo, Marton, Pang & Pong, 2004; Marton, 2006; Marton & Pang, 2006). Reid and Petocz (2004) mentioned that it is necessary to consider the domain in which the students and teachers are collaborating, and to set up specific classroom situations where ideas about creativity in that discipline are actively discussed and articulated, and then provide opportunities for students to be creative, to demonstrate creativity, and to critique creative processes and outcomes.

In this study we look at creativity in terms of ways of writing in Chinese, focusing on creativity in the context of the Chinese language classroom and on to what extent creativity in Chinese writing can be enhanced through the systematic use of variation and invariance.

THE STUDY

Carrying it out

Arrangement. This study is a quasi experimental attempt to enhance students' creativity in Chinese writing through the development of learning studies (refer to Chapter 2 for the description of the Learning Study). The Learning Study aims at developing the capability that the students are expected to acquire during a limited sequence of lessons, which we refer to as the "object of learning". The Learning Study focuses on the distinction between an intended object of learning (what the teachers are striving for), an enacted object of learning (what happens during the lesson and what it is possible to learn), and the lived object of learning (what the students actually learn). We examine the effectiveness of the Learning Study in enhancing students' creative writing skills. For the whole year, there were ten composition topics to be used for training Primary 3 students. Of these ten topics, we chose four to be used for developing the students' capability of writing the narratives creatively.

The target group participated in four learning studies during the whole year, all of which were based on the theoretical framework of variation, to help teachers plan and structure the lessons. The theory was supposed to guide the teachers in deciding what aspects to focus on, what aspects to vary simultaneously, and what aspects to keep invariant; it was supposed to help the teachers to consciously design patterns of variation to bring about the desired learning outcomes (Lo, Pong & Chik, 2006). The variation in the teachers' ways of understanding and dealing with particular objects of learning in creative writing was reflected when they and the researcher shared their ideas in collaborative lesson preparation meetings, when they taught their research lessons and when they took part in post-lesson conferences.

The comparison group followed the traditional approach to teaching Chinese writing, in which there was no collaborative lesson preparation or post-lesson conferencing among teachers. One of the teachers in the comparison group worked out the outline of the composition, and all teachers used this same outline. During the lessons, teachers provided the students with the outline and some vocabulary as the writing instruction. Then the students were given time to write their composition during the lessons. The comparison group served as a reference to reveal the effect of the instructional design based on the Theory of Variation.

Teachers. Eight Chinese teachers participated in the study after having given their informed consent. All teachers taught primary three in two aided primary schools located in the same district. Four teachers who taught primary three in the morning session school participated in the target group. They were females with ages ranging from 24 to 50 and teaching experience ranging from 2 to 24 years. They were trained in conducting learning studies and in facilitating creative writing of the student participants of the target group. Each member had equal status in the group and contributed her own expertise.

Another four teachers, who taught primary three in the afternoon session school formed the comparison group. They were females with ages ranging from 25 to 51 and teaching experience ranging from 3 to 25 years. They did not participate in any Learning Study, but taught Chinese Language to their students using the traditional approach to teaching writing currently practiced in mainstream schools.

Students. Two hundred and seventy-seven primary students were recruited from eight classes in two government aided primary schools after individual informed consent was obtained. Four P.3 classes belonged to the morning session school, and another four P.3 classes belonged to the afternoon session school. The P.3 Chinese Language teachers of the morning session and the four classes they taught were the target group, and the P.3 Chinese Language teachers of the school of the afternoon session and the four classes they taught were the comparison group. The target group used four learning studies to enhance creativity, while the comparison group followed a traditional approach to teaching writing as described above. The target group consisted of 137 students (65 boys and 72 girls), while the comparison group consisted of 141 students (68 boys and 73 girls). All the students were in the age range of 8–9 years old. Statistical tests showed that the difference in age and sex between the two groups was not significant.

Outcome Measures

The Chinese creative writing test. Students in both the target and the comparison group were asked to do the Chinese Creative Writing Test, which required them to write a story using the topic of "Today". The compositions of both groups were collected at the beginning of the academic year (pre-test), during the term break (mid-test), and towards the end of the academic year (post-test). The compositions were scored according to the number of idea units; the degree of diversity in time, space, person, character, characteristics of the story; and elements of original writing in story structure, novel qualities, emotional tone, individuality of response, and style of story as set out in the Chinese Creative Writing Scale (CCWS; Cheung, Tse, & Tsang, 2001). The 13-item scale was expanded and modified from Guildford (1967), Torrance (1965a) and the Carlson' Originality Scale (Carlson, 1965) to assess the indicators of the potentials of creativity in terms of fluency, flexibility and originality in compositions of primary school students in Hong Kong. Its content validity was endorsed by a small expert panel. Results show that the scale has excellent inter-rater reliability (.90 to .98), and moderate to good internal consistency. Exploratory factor analysis shows that the three factors (flexibility, originality, and fluency) accounted for 59.1% of the variability, which is consistent with the design of the scale.

The Williams scale (Williams, 1993). Another outcome measure was the Williams Scale, which is a teacher rating scale for children's divergent thinking and feelings related to creativity. It is an observational checklist consisting of eight creativity factors: fluency, flexibility, originality, elaboration, curiosity, imagination, complexity, and risk-taking. The scale yields a weighted raw score from the 48 multiple-choice items, and has good test re-test reliability (0.60) tested in a sample of 256 students from grade 3 to 12. It was also found to be valid with its results having significant correlation with ratings by students (0.59) and parents (0.67).

The Four Learning Studies

Four participating teachers of the target group worked together to determine the intended object of learning (i.e. what the students were supposed to learn). During the collaborative lesson planning, the teachers discussed the capability of writing narratives that the students were supposed to develop. The teachers were concerned with which creative writing strategies the students should use and hoped that the students could generate and share different options. Each Learning Study had a particular object of learning and a unique characteristic of the study that aimed at enhancing creativity. The object of the first Learning Study was to increase the students' awareness of causal sequence in real-life stories. The object of the second Learning Study was to enhance the students' capability to find solutions to problems in imaginary tales. The object of the third Learning Study was to enhance the students' capability to order events in a relatively long temporal sequence in real-life stories. The object of the fourth Learning Study was to develop the students' capability to depict characters in imaginative tales and develop their sensitivity to the relationship between characters and events.

Other than the experimental intervention, teaching conditions in the two groups (target and comparison groups) did not differ systematically. For instance, they used the same textbook and the teachers of these two schools used the same topics for students' composition throughout the academic year.

RESULTS

What Happened in the Four Learning Studies?

Target group. In the first Learning Study, the creative writing strategy "picture writing" (Lin, 1998) was used, where a set of six pictures was invariant. The students were asked to find the sequence between given components and compare the different ways of constructing the sequence. Comparing the differences of the sequencing among groups and becoming aware of the pattern of contrast variation (Marton, Runesson, & Tsui, 2004), helped each group of students to become more aware of its own sequence. In the second Learning Study, the creative writing strategy of "problem solving" (Mumford & Norris, 1999) was employed. The problem was kept invariant, and the students were invited to work out the solution by themselves and to compare the solutions with each other. In this way they were supposed become aware of their own way of solving the problem, through contrast variation.

"Creative drama" (Anarella, 1999) in this study provided space for the students to find a more promising resolution to the problem by building on the unsuccessful and successful attempts simultaneously using the pattern of fusion variation (Marton, Runesson, & Tsui, 2004). In the third Learning Study, the creative writing strategy of "image recall" (Jampole, Mathews & Konopak, 1994; Soh, 2000; Lee, 1992) was used. In this case, it meant that the students participated in a relatively long temporal sequence of events, a school cleaning day, which was a shared experience for all of them. They were then invited to write their own accounts of the day and to compare their different versions of what had happened, with a particular focus on their use of time indicators in a chronological order, such as "in times of the morning assembly", "8 o'clock" and "10 o'clock"; and connectives such as "first", "then" and "finally". The pattern of contrast variation helped students discern the different aspects of time sequencing. In the fourth Learning Study, the creative writing strategy of "story from boxes" (Peat, 2001) was employed to let the students choose characters and invent the course of events. The story schema of having problems and solutions were kept constant. The teachers hoped that comparing the strengths, weaknesses and personality of animals in the story in order to solve the problems would contribute to developing the students' capability to depict characters in imaginative tales. The pattern of contrast variation was supposed to help the students to develop their sensitivity to the relationship between characters and events. The lessons were full of different kinds of variation that opened up space for the students to develop the plots.

Comparison group.   Both the target and the comparison group used the same topic in their writing lessons, but without making comparisons between the students' differing solutions and accounts. Students in the comparison group were asked to identify the four elements (i.e., time, place, characters and event) from the topic. The teachers asked the students to find out the sequencing of events or correct solution of the problem and did not compare the differences of the sequencing and possible solutions among groups. The development of the story plots was very limited without the capacity for alternative solutions. Then teachers provided vocabularies and outline of the story on the blackboard to help the students write.

What were the Effects of the Four Learning Studies?

The creative writing abilities of students.   The total scores of the student participants in the target group for the mid-test and post-test of the Chinese Creative Writing Scale were significantly higher than those of the comparison group as shown in Figure 8.1.

The Williams Scale.   The total scores of the student participants in the target group for the Williams Scale for the mid-test and post-test were significantly higher than their scores for pre-test as shown in Figure 8.2.

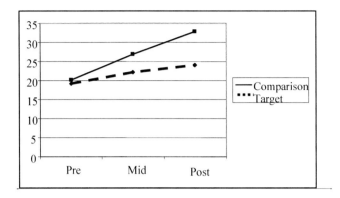

Figure 8.1. Total scores of the Chinese creative writing scale for the target and comparison group participants.

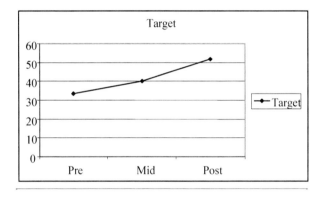

Figure 8.2. Total scores of the Williams scale for the target group participant.

SOME MORE RESULTS

The results were very much in accordance with what we expected and hoped for: the target group outperformed the comparison group as far as the development of creativity in Chinese writing during the year was concerned. Undoubtedly, we were very happy with the outcome, and we will comment on it later, but there was another, serendipitous finding which we would like to focus on now. We found that in spite of the agreement between teachers in the target group as far as the lesson plans in the learning studies were concerned, there were important differences in how the lessons were taught. In other words, the enacted object of learning differed between classes in the target group even though they had the same intended object of learning with the same lesson plan. Among the four classes of the target group, we noticed that differences in the enacted objects of learning were most remarkable between Class 3A and 3D. In the following paragraphs evaluating Learning Study 4, we focus on comparing what actually happened in the classrooms and highlighting the differences between these two classes in order to understand the underlying reasons for the unexpected differences.

Comparing Class 3A & 3D

The creative writing abilities of students. The total scores of the student participants in Class 3A for the mid-test and post-test of the Chinese Creative Writing Scale were significantly higher than those of Class 3D as shown in Figure 8.3. The group x time interaction effect for each of the sub-scales and total score was analyzed by a repeated measure ANOVA and presented as the F statistics. The overall effect was significant in all sub-scores and the total score: fluency ($F = 6.85$, $df = (2,60)$, $p = 0.002$); flexibility ($F = 3.30$, $df = (2,60)$, $p = 0.044$); originality ($F = 13.08$, $df = (2,60)$, $p = 0.000$); and the total score ($F = 7.99$, $df = (2,60)$, $p = 0.001$).

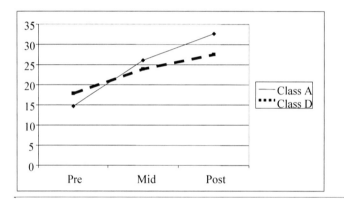

Figure 8.3. Total scores of the Chinese creative writing scale of class A and class D participants.

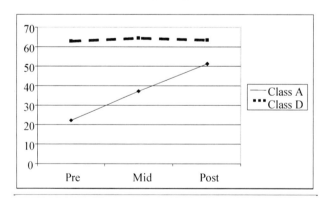

Figure 8.4. Total scores of the Williams scale of class A and class D participants.

Scores of the Williams scale. The total score of the student participants in the two classes for the Williams Scale for the pre-test, mid-test, and post-test is shown in Figure 8.4. The overall group x time effect was significant in all sub-scales and the total score. This implies that the scores of Class 3A increased significantly with time, while Class 3D did not, although the pre-test scores of Class 3D were significantly higher than those of Class 3A. This might have been due to chance. The pre-test difference had already been statistically adjusted when we performed further analyses.

Comparing the Teaching in Learning Study 4

The intended object of learning was to contribute to developing the students' capability to depict characters in imaginative tales and to developing their sensitivity to the relationships between characters and events. However, there were differences in the way in which the two lessons were conducted.

The teachers wanted to develop the students' capability to develop a plot by discerning and solving different problems of the imaginative story. The students also needed to develop the animal characters by discerning the animal characters' talents, ability and personification with regard to how they responded to the goal of the story. In Class 3D, students were asked to select an animal and describe one characteristic related to that animal, or to act out one characteristic of the animal for their classmates to guess. In the guessing game, the students usually imitated the animal's appearance and action. However, the teacher did not encourage the students to think of more aspects of the characteristics of the animal characters. Thus, there was not much variation in the different aspects/dimensions of the same animal. The teacher then deliberately chose two animals, the lion and the mouse, to be the main characters to develop the story plot.

The space of variation constituted here was rather limited, and it was therefore difficult for them to discern the most critical feature. We noted from Class 3D that students only thought of one or two aspects of the animal characters when the goal of the story was not discerned simultaneously with the characterization of animal characters. The students were able to discern the personality of the lion as fierce and the mouse as having two long teeth and fond of stealing things. The teacher only brought out the problem of the story, that the mouse woke up the sleeping lion, after students had discerned the characteristics of the lion and mouse. When the problem of the story was separated from the characterization of animal characters, there were fewer attempts to solve the problem.

The teacher tried to structure the lesson into three parts and organized them in a sequential structure (see Figure 8.5). This structure failed to help students discern the close connection between the first and the second problem in a part-whole relationship. In Part 1, teachers emphasized the elements of "setting" such as where the story happened. She chose two characters (a lion and a mouse) for the story. We could see that without variations, students were not able to discern the characteristics of the animals from different aspects like talents, weaknesses and personality. We learnt from the lesson that students only mentioned one or two characteristics

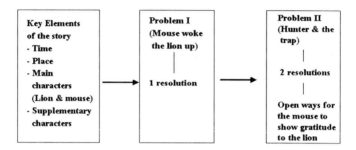

Figure 8.5. The Sequential structure of lesson 3D in learning study 4.

of the lion and the mouse. When the teacher fixed the main characters of the lion and the mouse, there was not much space left for contrast variation. There were not many attempts to solve the two problems in the story when the characterization of animals was too simple. The teacher only provided space in the last part of the story, where students could think of how the lion showed gratitude to the mouse.

In Class 3A, the teacher invited students to develop their story by opening six boxes which consisted of the story elements: when, who, where, what happens, what's the response of the characters, what happens next, and what's the solution. Each box of the story elements had lots of pictures inside for the students to develop more variations in each of the story elements. For example, students of different groups were invited to choose different animal characters in the "Who" box. Students took out the pictures of a rabbit, a kangaroo, a monkey, a mouse, an elephant, a lion, a whale, and an eagle from the story box. Teachers asked students to characterize the animals with reference to the talents and personality and the students did so, indeed. There was group discussion among nine groups of students on solving the same problem—who should be the king? Each group of students was allowed to choose from one of the three combinations:
- eagle, lion, and whale
- elephant and mouse
- rabbit, monkey, and kangaroo

When the characteristics of the animals were brought into focal awareness by using the creative writing strategy of crashing elements[1], students tried to compare and contrast the different dimensions of two to three animals such as appearance, talents, personality, special features and even weaknesses simultaneously to resolve the conflict. In this way, students were more able to discern the characteristics of the animal characters with regard to how they responded to the goal of the story. Through patterns of contrast variation (Marton, Runesson & Tsui, 2004), students compared which animal character had more strengths than the other. Students experienced more aspects of their characterization during contrast variation. In this way, they discerned more characteristics of the animals. For example, students working on combination 1 were able to discern the talents of a lion, an eagle and a whale, identifying the three of them as being very fast and strong. When they attempted to solve the problem of choosing the king, they tried to compare the difference between these three animals and reported that:

> The eagle was supported by the squirrels, etc. The lion was supported by the carnivores. The whale was supported by animals living in the sea. A monkey suggested that they would have a race to see who was the fastest to reach the foothill.

They kept on discerning other characteristics (e.g., the lion ran very fast, the eagle flew very fast and the whale swam very fast). The lived object of learning from the story also served as the tool for further exploration of the development into a more complex story. The content of the story of different groups varied. The eagle, the elephant and the kangaroo were chosen to be the potential king in combination 1, 2 and three respectively. Comparing and contrasting the lived object of learning of the first problem enabled students to discern the characteristics of the animals and relate these characteristics to the new plots of the story. When there were resolutions concerning combination 1, 2 and three which consisted of different animal characters, the teacher gave another problem to the students. A small animal was found hurt, and students had to discuss the ways in which the wounded animal could be saved by the eagle, the elephant and the kangaroo in turn. Students were asked to focus on the discussion of who could really help the wounded animal. The students once again tried to compare the talents of the eagle, the elephant and the kangaroo and in attempting to solve this problem, discerned other characteristics of the animals.

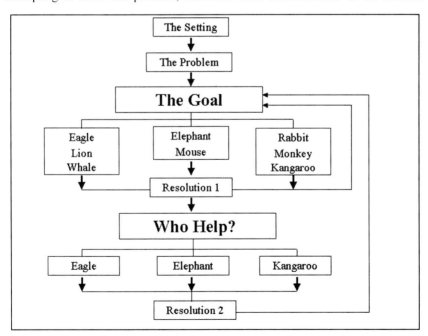

Figure 8.6. The part-whole relationship of lesson 3A in learning study 4.

The kangaroo could offer a better solution as she would like to be a nurse and could use the pouch to take care of the wounded animal. Finally, the kangaroo was chosen to be the king. In this way, the students saw that resolution of the first and second story was part of the whole story related to the goal of the story, and that they were intertwined very closely. Figure 8.6 shows how the lesson was structured with the part-whole relationship of constructing the story.

Therefore, we understood from these two teachers' classroom practice that more variations would lead to more complex development of plots.

Discussion of the Comparison between the Two Classes

This discussion is only about the serendipitous finding, and the overall conclusions will follow. Because of lack of space, we have only made a comparison between the two classes with respect to one lesson. However the picture is similar as far as the differences in structure are concerned across all 4 learning studies, and those differences are described in Cheung (2005).

The use of problem solving to enhance creativity in Chinese writing in the learning studies gave the students options in a certain aspect and allowed them to compare each other's options. Such differences were described in terms of those aspects that the teacher varied, and those aspects that the teacher kept invariant. In Learning Study 4, the creative writing strategy of "story from boxes" (Peat, 2001) was employed to let them choose characters and invent the course of events. The story schema of having problems and solutions were kept constant. By comparing the strengths, weaknesses and personality of animals in the story to solve the problems, the teachers developed the students' capability to depict characters in imaginative tales. The dimensions of the aspects that varied formed the space of learning which made learning possible. It is impossible to grasp anything without having experienced an alternate option (Marton, 2006). Without a contrast, what students can do is to learn only the "whole", often by rote. Unfortunately, this does not prepare them for handling novel problems in a powerful way in the future. The traditional writing lesson involves simply providing an outline to students that they follow to write a composition. This explains why students find it difficult to write compositions without an outline. Teachers find the compositions repeating one another if students are asked to use the same outline. The reason is that they often write by rote without expressing their own opinion. One way of enhancing creativity in Chinese writing as shown by this research is to embed difference in what varies and what is invariant. Students of Class 3A were free to develop the characters by comparing the talents of animals to solve two strategically chosen problems in imaginative tales. The characterization of animal characters was in students' focal awareness. This can be compared with what Stokes (2006) says about the workings of the minds of famous creative artists. From Picasso to Stravinsky, Kundera and Chanel to Frank Lloyd Wright, it is not boundary-less creative freedom that inspires new ideas, but self-imposed, well-considered constraints. She uses the example of Monet, who forced himself to repeatedly paint the way light broke on, between, and around his subjects, contrasting color instead of light and dark, and softening edges in the process. He simultaneously promoted specific new ways like contrasting close-valued colors and flat patterns with soft-edged shapes. They were strategically chosen to realize his new goal criterion. His constraints catapulted the art world from representational to impressionist art.

More powerful ways of understanding amount to a simultaneous awareness of those features that are critical to achieving certain aims (Chik & Lo, 2004). Teacher of Class 3A focused on letting students experience a high degree of simultaneity. By discerning animal characters and problems simultaneously, the students in Class 3A developed qualitatively different ways of arriving at a solution. When learning to deal with novel situations, people have to learn to take different features into consideration simultaneously (Marton, 2006).

This study reported dramatic differences in the outcome of learning in the two classes in enhancing creativity in Chinese writing. These differences were linked to specific differences as to how the object of learning was handled, structured, and presented in the two classes in terms of variation and invariance. These differences were to a significant extent associated with the teachers' awareness of the role of variation and invariance for learning as demonstrated in their lesson plans and in the way they conducted the lessons (Lo, Marton, Pang & Pong, 2004; Marton & Pang, 2006; Pang & Marton, 2003; Pang, 2003). The differences in the results of the two scales also corresponded to differences in the "structuring" of the content of the lessons. The teacher of Class 3A structured the lessons in a hierarchical manner, whereas the teacher of Class 3D structured the lessons in a sequential manner. This explains the fact that the creativity scores of Class 3A were higher than those of Class 3D. The difference may be attributed to the differential effects of hierarchical versus sequential structuring of the content of teaching on creativity in Chinese writing. Chik (2006; chapter 2) reported that the same kind of structural differences led to differences in the learning outcomes of students in learning Chinese words. Säljö (1982) also reported that the students who understand the text in the hierarchical way have more organized and meaningful understanding, and are better able to grasp the main idea of the text than the students who understand the text in a sequential way.

CONCLUSION

In this chapter we have illustrated how creativity in Chinese writing can possibly be enhanced in the classroom. Creativity is seldom seen from the pedagogical point of view. Teachers' original perception of enhancing creativity is to give more freedom and space to students in writing (Cheung, Tse & Tsang, 2001; Cheung, 2005). However, four participating teachers learned from the Learning Study that this space is not unlimited; it is a freedom within well-defined boundaries. A particular space is created, but certain frames are given at the same time. It is consistent with the Theory of Variation that the presence of a particular pattern of variation and invariance is a necessary condition for learning to discern a particular object of learning. The enhancement of creativity in Chinese writing in the study was to a significant extent associated with the teachers' awareness of the role of variation and invariance for learning as demonstrated in their method of conducting the lessons. Our contribution to the enhancement of creativity is the idea to strategically choose what is given and what varies freely. The object of learning in each Learning Study was very carefully chosen to develop students' capability to write creatively. By doing so, we were able to develop creativity in relation to a particular aspect of writing Chinese. The divergent points of view among the students of the target group are like "a heavenly horse soaring across the sky". This echoes Stokes (2006), who redefines creativity as creating constraints paradoxically to enhance imaginative thinking. She argues that creativity is not boundary-less creative freedom that inspires new ideas, but has self-imposed and well-considered constraints. Learning Study facilitated and illuminated teachers' awareness of teaching Chinese writing creatively. Teachers in the target group found that being involved in collaborative lesson planning meetings, peer lesson observations and post-lesson conferences helped them facilitate creativity in classroom by the use of the Theory of Variation as a pedagogical tool and sustaining a focus on the object of learning. Learning Study appears to be a powerful way to help teachers become competent in teaching creativity in Chinese writing. The pedagogical change which was not only found in the four learning studies; teachers used creative writing strategies and the Theory of Variation throughout the academic year. What they learnt from the Learning Study was transferred to their everyday teaching. Such differences were related to the effects on teachers but, due to lack of space, we are not going to report them here. Other studies (Holmqvist, 2006; Wernberg, 2005) have reported similar effects of learning studies on teachers. In the next chapter, the authors are going to share how pre-service teacher after the creative teaching training was able to open up novel dimensions of variation for their students to handle novel tasks in creative ways. In this way, both the space of learning and teaching is widened.

NOTES

[1] Crashing elements is a creative writing strategy to enhance students' story writing (Raimo, 1981). A plot is provided by a group of student, a character is provided by another group, and a setting is provided by a third group. The students then come together to find relationships among these elements and to fashion a story, by completing the details and adding more characters. Different groups have many alternatives and variations.

REFERENCES

Aljughaiman, A., & Nowrer-Reynolds, E. (2005). Teachers' conceptions of creativity and creative students. *Journal of Creative Behavior, 39*(1), 17–34.

Anarella, L. A. (1999). *Using creative drama in the writing process.* ERIC database.

Baer, J. M. (1996). The effects of task-specific divergent-thinking training. *Journal of Creative Behavior, 30,* 183–187.

Bereiter, C., & Scardamalis, M. (1987). *The psychology of written composition.* New Jersey, NJ: Lawrence Erlbaum Associates.

Cheung, W. M., (2005). *Describing and enhancing creativity in Chinese writing.* Unpublished PhD thesis. Hong Kong: The University of Hong Kong.

Cheung, W. M., Tse, S. K., & Tsang, W. H. (2001). Development and validation of the Chinese creative writing scale for primary schools students in Hong Kong. *Journal of Creative Behavior, 35*(2), 1–12.

Cheung, W. M., Tse, S. K., & Tsang, H. W. H. (2003a). Creative writing practice in primary schools: A case study in Hong Kong. *Korean Journal of Thinking & Problem Solving, 10*(2), 55–66.

Cheung, W. M., Tse, S. K., & Tsang, W. H. (2003b). Teaching creative writing skills to primary school children in Hong Kong: Discordance between the views and practice of language teachers. *Journal of Creative Behavior, 37*(2), 77–98.

Chik, P. P. M. (2006). *Differences in learning as a function of differences between hierarchical and sequential organisation of the content taught*. Unpublished PhD thesis. Hong Kong: the University of Hong Kong.

Chik, P. P. M., & Lo, M. L. (2004). Simultaneity and the enacted object of learning. In F. Marton, A. B. M. Tsui with P. Chik, P. Y. Ko, M. L. Lo, I. Mok, et al. (Eds.), *Classroom discourse and the space of learning* (pp. 89–110). New Jersey, NJ: Lawrence Erlbaum.

Carlson, R. K. (1965). An originality story scale. *The Elementary School Journal, 65*(7), 366–374.

Csikszentmihalyi, M. (1988). Society, culture, and person: A systems view of creativity. In R. J. Sternberg (Ed.), *Handbook of creativity* (pp. 325–339). Cambridge, England: Cambridge University Press.

Csikszentmihalyi, M. (1990). The domain of creativity. In M. A. Runco & R. S. Albert (Eds.), *Theories of creativity* (pp. 190–212). Newbury Park, CA: Sage.

Csikszentmihalyi, M. (1996). *Creativity: Flow and the psychology of discovery and invention*. New York: Harper Collins.

Csikszentmihalyi, M. (1999). Implications of a systems perspective for the study of creativity. In R. J. Sternberg (Ed.), *Handbook of creativity* (pp. 313–324). Cambridge, England: Cambridge University Press.

Curriculum Development Council. (2001). *Learning to learn: Life-long learning and whole-person development*. Hong Kong: Curriculum Development Council.

Feldman, D. H. (1994). *Beyond universals in cognitive development*. Norwood, NJ: Ablex.

Feldman, D. H., & Benjamin, A. C. (2006). Creativity and education: an American retrospective. *Cambridge Journal of Education, 36*(3), 319–366.

Flower, L., & Hayes, J. R. (1984). Images, plans and prose: The representation of meaning in writing. *Written Composition, 1*(1), 120–126.

Fryer, M., & Collings, J. A. (1991). British teachers' views of creativity. *Journal of Creative Behavior, 25*(1), 75–81.

Graves, D. (1983). *Writing: Teachers and Children at Work*. London & Portsmouth, New Hampshire: Heinemann.

Guilford, J. P. (1950). Creativity. *American Psychologist, 5*, 444–445.

Hayes, J. R., & Flower, L. S. (1980). The cognition of discovery: defining a rhetorical problem. *College Composition and Communication, 31*, 21–31.

Holmqvist, M. (Ed.). (2006). *Lärande i skolan. Learning study som skolutvecklingsmodell*. [Learning at school. Learning Study as a teacher in-service training]. Lund: Studentlitteratur.

Holmqvist, M., Gustavsson, L., & Wernberg, A. (2008). Variation theory: An organizing principle to guide design research in education. In A. Kelly (Ed.), *Handbook of design research in education*. Mahwah, NJ: Lawrence Erlbaum Associates, Inc.

Jampole, E., Konopak, B. C., Readence, J. E., & Mosher, E. B. (1991). Using mental imagery to enhance gifted elementary students' creative writing. *Reading Psychology, 12*, 183–197.

Jampole, E., Mathews, F. N., & Konopak, B. C. (1994). Academically gifted students' use of imagery for creative writing. *Journal of Creative Behavior, 28*, 1–15.

Lee, H. C. (1992). *The evaluation of the effectiveness of creative writing strategies*. Unpublished Master's thesis. Hong Kong: the University of Hong Kong.

Lo, M. L., Marton, F., Pang, M. F., & Pong, W. Y. (2004). Towards a pedagogy of learning. In F. Marton, A. B. M. Tsui, P. Chik, P. Y. Ko, M. L. Lo, I. Mok et al. (Eds.), *Classroom discourse and the space of learning* (pp. 189–226). New Jersey, NJ: Lawrence Erlbaum.

Lo, M. L., Pong, W. Y., & Chik, P. P. M. (2006). *For each and everyone: Catering for individual differences through learning studies*. Hong Kong: Hong Kong University Press.

Marton, F. (2006). Sameness and difference in transfer. *Journal of the Learning Sciences, 15*(4), 499–535.

Marton, F., & Booth, S. (1997). *Learning and awareness*. Mahwah, NJ: Lawrence Erlbaum Associates, Publishers.

Marton, F., & Pang, M. F. (2006). On some necessary conditions of learning. *Journal of the Learning Sciences, 15*(2), 193–220.

Marton, F., Runesson, U., & Tsui, A. B. M. (2004). The space of learning. In F. Marton, A. B. M. Tsui, P. Chik, P. Y. Ko, M. L. Lo, I. Mok et al. (Eds.), *Classroom discourse and the space of learning* (pp. 3–42). New Jersey, NJ: Lawrence Erlbaum.

Marton, F., Tsui, A. B. M., Chik, P. M., Ko, P. Y., Lo, M. L., Mok I. A. C., et al. (2004). *Classroom discourse and the space of learning.* Mahwah, NJ: Lawrence Erlbaum.

Marton, F., Asplund-Carlsson, M., & Halasz, L. (1992). Differences in understanding and the use of reflective variation in reading. *British Journal of Educational Psychology, 62*, 1–16.

Mumford, M. D., & Gustafson, S. B. (1988). Creativity syndrome: Integration, application and innovation. *Psychological Bulletin, 103*, 27–43.

Pang, M. F., & Marton, F. (2003). Beyond "lesson study" – Comparing two ways of facilitating the grasp of economic concepts. *Instructional Science, 31*(3), 175–194.

Pang, M. F. (2003). Two faces of variation – On continuity in the phenomenographic movement. *Scandinavian Journal of Educational Research, 47*(2), 145–156.

Raimo, A. (1981). Three to get started: Story writing as a collaborative effort. *Journal of Creative Behavior, 15*(3), 205–208.

Reid, A., & Petocz, P. (2004). Learning domains and the process of creativity. *The Australian Educational Researcher, 31*(2), 45–62.

Runesson, U., & Marton, F. (2002). The object of learning and the space of variation. In F. Marton & P. Morris (Eds.), *What matters? Discovering critical conditions of classroom learning,* (pp. 19–37). Goteborg: Acta Universititatis Gothoburgensis.

Säljö, R. (1982). *Learning and understanding: A study of differences in constructing meaning from a text.* Goteborg, Sweden: Acta Universitatis Gothoburgensis.

Schacter, J., Thum, Y. M., & Zifkin, D. (2006). How much does creative teaching enhance elementary school students' achievement? *Journal of Creative Behavior, 40*(1), 47–52.

Sharples, M. (1999). *How we write – Writing as creative design.* London, UK: Routledge.

Soh, K. C. (2000). Indexing creativity fostering teacher behavior: A preliminary validation study. *Journal of Creative Behavior, 34*(2), 118–134.

Starko, A. J. (2005). *Creativity in the classroom: schools of curious delight.* Mahwah, NJ: Lawrence Erlbaum Associates.

Stokes, P. D. (2006). *Creativity from constraints: The psychology of breakthrough.* New York: Springer.

Wernberg, A. (2005). *Learning from ones' practice: Teachers' growth during in-service training in the classroom.* Paper presented in the 11th Biennial Conference, Nicosia, Cyprus.

Williams, F. (1993). *Creativity assessment packet.* Austin, TX: Pro-Ed.

Wong, S. K., Lo, C. H. A., & Lam, K. T. (1999). *The book of literary design (Wenxie diaolong)* (L. Xie, Ed.) (pp. 465–522). Hong Kong: Hong Kong University Press.

Wai Ming Cheung and Shek Kam Tse
Faculty of Education
The University of Hong Kong

Ference Marton
Department of Education
University of Gothenburg

9. ENHANCING CREATIVITY IN CHINESE TEACHING

THE THEORY OF VARIATION AND CREATIVE TEACHING

The study on which this Chapter is based was not inspired by the Theory of Variation. We are using the theory post hoc, i e it is brought in after the study had been completed. We are using it to analyse a lesson aimed at enhancing creativity in the students' ways of dealing with a particular task. We want to demonstrate that, looking at the pattern of variation and invariance constituted in the interaction between teacher and students and between students, might help us to understand how the creativity in the students' ways of dealing with the task given might have been enhanced.

We also distinguish between the teacher's and the students' creativity. In this chapter we are dealing with the latter. We want to argue that enhancing the creativity in the students' ways of dealing with certain tasks does not necessarily depend on the creativity in the teachers' way of going about it.

As was shown in the previous Chapter, bringing systematically about particular patterns of variation and invariance might open up for completely novel ways of handling the tasks by the students.

According to the Theory of Variation, learning takes place whenever one actively responds to differences in the world around. Learning may occur when one recognises that observed experiences are at variance with previous understandings and beliefs, and when one actively seeks to rationalise or accommodate the differences. Through this process, individuals at different levels of understanding may arrive at different answers to the same question or different explanations or understanding of the same phenomenon. From this perspective, the process of learning is a creative process and the Theory of Variation and creative teaching are not too far apart. Creative teaching has its own characteristics and associated routes to learning, including the ability to generate in the learner fluency of ideas, flexibility in approach, originality of thought and strategies, openness to change, curiosity and tolerance of ambiguity (Cropley, 2001; Lee, 2007). The fostering of these abilities and attributes in students is a major objective of creative teaching. For teaching to be successful in the creative sense, teachers need to be aware of critical features in the learning environment, and steps need to be taken to present environmental input in such a way that the student takes the initiative to challenge pre-existing views and beliefs.

In recent years, many teaching programmes have been implemented in schools around the world with the main emphasis on creative thinking and teaching strategies. Activities such as brainstorming and role play are seen as routes to leading learners into discovering for themselves insights into the world around them, and into ways of approaching and learning new information and routines. In the real classroom and teaching environment, however, many teachers feel they have so much content to cover that they cannot spare the time for the "penny to drop" for each and every student. Their response is to engineer lessons and lesson content so that the task of discerning critical features of specific objects of learning is facilitated for the child. However, since critical features of different objects of learning vary, a strategy that is effective in one lesson might not achieve the same outcome in another lesson or with a different class. At the same time, if students see through the teacher's strategy, many will take the short-cut and simply learn to give the answers the teacher is looking for, whether or not any lasting learning has taken place.

Chapter Eight reports a study comparing the learning outcome of four Chinese writing classes. The author demonstrates convincingly that, even though the strategies and intended learning outcome of the classes studied were the same, the outcome varied significantly across the classes. She also showed that, through the systematic manipulation of variation and invariance, teachers can successfully help students to achieve better learning outcomes. Cheung's study is a reminder of the importance of arranging content so that creative thinking is likely to occur and of the importance of ensuring that students are genuinely involved in their own learning.

This chapter reports how creative teaching featured in a Chinese reading lesson taught by a student teacher who had participated in workshops on creative teaching. The theoretical framework of the Theory of Variation was employed post hoc to help discern key characteristics in the student teacher's teaching and the conduct of the lesson in an effort to analyse how learning occurred, and the pertinence of key teaching strategies and classroom activities for effective learning by students.

CREATIVE TEACHING IN CHINESE LANGUAGE TEACHING

The Curriculum Framework of Hong Kong stresses three important components: Key Learning Areas, Generic Skills and Values and Attitudes. Chinese Language education is a Key Learning Area and creativity[1] is one of nine generic skills explicitly identified in the Framework. Key Learning Areas provide the context for the development of generic skills, and generic skills are to be developed through learning and teaching in the context of different subject disciplines. As noted earlier, Chinese Language education and creativity are inter-related processes and, in principle, creative teaching in Chinese Language teaching is supposed to integrate two components: (a) helping students grasp content knowledge and developing Chinese language competence, whilst (b) fostering students' creative learning prowess. To achieve this objective, teachers charged with implementing creative teaching in Chinese Language lessons should have a thorough understanding of both areas so that they can help students acquire a critical outlook and develop creativity in their Chinese language.

Six workshops, each lasting 3 hours, on adopting the Holistic Approach[2] were organised to train student teachers to implement creative teaching. According to the Holistic Approach, teacher training about creative teaching should integrate domain relevant training, teaching relevant training and creativity relevant training. Such training seeks to develop in student teachers knowledge, ability and personal qualities necessary for implementing effective creative teaching. In the workshops, emphasis was put on how to apply different creative thinking strategies, including synectics, free association, brainstorming, mind maps, role play, creative problem solving, SCAMPER and creative questioning techniques in the context of Chinese Language teaching of writing, reading, listening and speaking.

A large number of authentic teaching examples and language teaching activities were employed to demonstrate the critical features of creative teaching, and techniques for using creative thinking strategies in Chinese Language lessons. The student teachers were asked to modify their usual way of thinking and to focus on discerning as many different aspects of phenomena as they could. To encourage them to adopt a wider perspective, they were invited to participate in activities not only as teachers, but also as primary school students. The latter was intended to help them experience the joy, the difficulties and excitement of creative teaching. This would hopefully help them to reflect on their own teaching and appreciate how various teachers' strategies impact on learning.

It was reported by her tutors that student teacher Ching Yee[3] had previously experimented with different creative teaching strategies in her teacher training, not always at a satisfactory level. After attending the training workshops, she was able more successfully to integrate creative thinking strategies into her Chinese Language teaching. The framework of the Theory of Variation has been applied post hoc in the section that follows to illustrate how its use throws light on the mechanisms of successful creative teaching of Chinese Language.

LESSON ANALYSIS: HOW TO USE A DICTIONARY

Background to the Lesson

The lesson analysed below was a Primary 6 reading lesson involving a passage on how to use a dictionary. The lessons analysed were the third and fourth lessons in the curriculum unit and followed two lessons in which the content and writing skills used in the text had been explained. In the lesson reported, Ching Yee's plan was to elaborate on the above points and to guide students into using what they had learnt in the first two lessons. The core activity of the lesson was a 'product design' activity in which the students were asked to design a super dictionary for the 21st century, and introduce it to their classmates.

Intended Object of Learning

According to Ching Yee's teaching plan, following the lesson students should be able:
– to identify and appreciate the expository writing skills used in the article;
– to think creatively and design a dictionary that would be both useful and novel;
– to present their products clearly and answer questions raised by classmates.

Enacted Object of Learning

Objectives of the lesson. The student teacher had two main objectives: (i) to develop students' expository writing ability using methods learnt previously, and (ii) to apply their creativity in designing a useful and novel product.

According to the Theory of Variation, teachers wishing to help students learn need first to identify the salient features of the object of learning then bring these to students' attention for discernment. Expository teaching ability consists of knowing how to explain the nature, appearance, characteristics, structure and functions of phenomena using appropriate expository methods (Tse & Shum, 2000). In light of primary students' lack of refinement in the skills of expository writing, the key objective in the lesson studied was to help them develop an ability to explain matters logically so that the readers/audience would be able to discern the main characteristics of the product. Since few primary students are able always to identify main points accurately, their powers of explanation are often unclear. As few primary students at the age in question have a clear sense of audience, they also tend to see things from their own point of view[4] and are unable to realize that other people might think differently and might not understand what they have said. In view of this, Ching Yee designed a worksheet incorporating the creative thinking strategy SCAMPER[5] to guide students into examining different aspects of the product at the same time in an orderly way. Role-play was also used to lead students into appreciating views that had not occurred to them previously.

Various definitions of creativity emphasise the notions of fluency, originality, insightfulness and elaboration (Guilford, 1988; Torrance, 1988). Fluency is the ability to produce large numbers of ideas and various types of ideas from different perspectives. Originality refers to the ability to come up with unusual ideas that others have not thought of, while elaboration refers to modifying or adding ideas on reflection to improve a product. Most experts seem to agree that creative products should be novel, useful and appropriate (Mayer, 1999). In these circumstances, the task of guiding students into designing a dictionary which would be both novel and useful was demanding. Some students were bound by traditional concepts and failed to display any creativity in their thinking and ideas. In contrast, others were quite unrestrained and their ideas were quite impractical and impossible to put into practice. In fact, they were as unable to create a useful product as the first group. To deal with these problems, Ching Yee organized activities to help students settle on the focus of the learning, and to produce realistic proposals by the end of the lesson. Details of these activities are presented in the following sections.

Organization of the lesson. According to the lesson plan, the lesson was divided into 3 stages: introduction, development and conclusion. However, according to observation of the proceedings, the second stage could also be sub-divided into lecturing, group discussion, reporting, question and answer and peer review evaluation. Therefore the organization of the lesson was changed to the format presented below. In fact, Ching Yee taught according to her plan but with structural modifications. In the eyes of the lesson observers, the modifications were well thought out and helped to achieve good learning outcomes.

	Stage	Mode of teaching & learning		Content
1	Introduction	Questioning		Retrieving prior knowledge: point out the weakness of traditional dictionary
2		Questioning		Stimulating creativity: stimulate students to look at objects from a new angle
3	Development	Product Design	Group discussion	Stimulating creativity: generating new ideas to design a super dictionary
4			Verbal report/Presentation	Applying knowledge: using expository skills learnt to introduce and promote their agreed product
5			Question & Answer	Elaborating ideas: responses to classmates' questions
6	Evaluation		Peer review	Evaluation: evaluating the product and the performance of students
7	Conclusion	Lecturing		Conclusion

Space of learning. According to Marton et al. (2004), noticing variation enables learners to experience features that are critical for a particular learning task, as well as for the development of key capabilities. In other words, these features are experienced as dimensions of variation. In the lesson in question, creative thinking strategies were incorporated into the teaching and learning processes to create variations that enabled students to experience critical features relating to the development of expository ability and creativity. The following section describes how Ching Yee employed different teaching and thinking strategies to yield space for learning.

Variation 1
As shown in the above table, Ching Yee started the lesson by questioning, asking students to answer questions about text content. This helped her to gauge their knowledge as the bases for learning activities that followed. She also questioned the children in ways that led them to see the weaknesses of traditional dictionaries. Changing the point of view brought up new ideas.[6] The first two sets of questions raised by Ching Yee in the first two episodes thus opened another space of learning for the students: a key variation opportunity in the lesson.

Variation 1

Questioning	Invariance	Variation
	Content (usage and function of dictionary)	Point of view (advantages, weakness)

Variation 2
After students' thinking was stimulated by the questions, Ching Yee changed the mode of teaching to a more student-oriented activity, that of designing a super dictionary for the 21st century. The activity was a follow up of the first two episodes. After reminding students of the weaknesses of traditional dictionaries, she asked students to design a dictionary that was better than the traditional dictionary. Product design is a commonly used creative teaching activity, and using it in this lesson was appropriate as it offered opportunities for students to produce creative ideas. When designing the new dictionary, students had to use knowledge from the text alongside ideas of their own. In the process, students learning went from apprehension to comprehension to evaluation, then to the creation of a new product.

In order to guide students into explaining logically and clearly, Ching Yee reminded them to consider one-by-one the functions, characteristics and uses of the dictionary. She also provided a worksheet that incorporated SCAMPER, a commonly-used divergent thinking strategy, to help students see how variations might be made to different aspects of the dictionary, for example updating old materials with newer materials, changing the size of the dictionary, modifying the design, adding more functions and so on. SCAMPER helped students to note different aspects of the product and possible variations. By considering the various effect of possible changes, students were able to develop their ideas step by step and discover novel ideas they had not thought of before. To help students to break away from commonly held ideas about dictionaries, Ching Yee emphasized that the dictionary they were to design was a dictionary for the future. This freed students' imagination and more and more ideas were stimulated as the students listened to different ideas during the group discussion. After the discussion, all groups produced lots of new ideas. The following table shows the second set of variations created in this episode.

Variation 2

Product Design	Invariance	Variation
	Usage and Function of dictionary	Different characteristics of the dictionary

Variation 3
In episode 4, Ching Yee asked students to introduce their groups' product to the whole class, and to play the role of designers and salesmen. They had to explain their design, then promote their product like a salesman. As noted above, a critical aspect of training expository techniques is the ability to present information clearly and logically. Presentation in this episode provided the opportunity to evaluate whether students had acquired these abilities, whilst the role play strengthened the sense of audience for the students. They were aware that they need to consider the customer's understanding and responses. At the same time, selling an imaginative product to their customer stimulated them into showing their creativity and seeing

how to improve their product. Challenging the taken-for-granted nature of experiences possessed by students is a very powerful way to create variations. In this episode, the teaching of expository ability and developing students' creativity were combined: the third variation in this lesson.

Variation 3

Promoting their product	Invariance	Variation
	Object of presentation (product)	Multiple Role (customer, designer, salesman)

Variation 4

The 4th episode was a 'question and answer' session, where the object of presentation was still the dictionary they had designed whilst the mode of communication changed. This was an interactive and multi-direction communication process. Students from every group were able to raise questions freely and even challenge designers and salesmen. The latter then had to clarify points that were unclear and respond to challenges from other groups. This helped train students' sharpness and flexibility of mind and their ability to respond to unexpected situations. Through the challenges and questions raised by other groups, students were able to spot weaknesses in their design and points that were unclear in their presentation. Changing the mode of communication opened a larger space of learning for the students.

Variation 4

Q & A	Invariance	Variation
	Object of presentation	Different responses of the consumers

Variation 5

Finally, an evaluation form was handed to all students, who were asked to nominate the best design and best salesman. This final episode was part of the learning process, but also a form of assessment. In the first six episodes, students focused on one aspect in each episode only, whereas in the final episode Ching Yee asked them to evaluate the learning outcome more comprehensively. Various criteria were provided by the teacher, including the design of the dictionary, its novelty and usefulness, its practicality and feasibility. Also assessed were the quality of the verbal presentation, presentation and answering skills, body language and voice.

Students had to consider all aspects of the product in the final episode, helping them to gain a comprehensive view of what they had learnt in this lesson.

Variation 5

Evaluation	Invariance	Variation
	Presentation	Aspects of presentation

As shown from the above analysis, the lesson centred on a product design. Different creative thinking strategies were introduced at different stages of teaching to create variations that helped students discern different aspects of the object of learning. At the beginning of the lesson, Ching Yee guided students to reverse what they had learnt in the previous lesson. In stead of pointing out the advantages of traditional dictionary, students had to brainstorm the weaknesses of traditional dictionary. The contrast of the advantages with the weaknesses helped students to develop a new understanding to the nature and function of dictionary. Based on the new understanding, Ching Yee then introduced the Future Product Design activity that incorporated the strategy SCAMPER. While the Future Product Design activity provided a context for students to express their creativity and apply expository skills that they had learnt, SCAMPER guided students to look at different aspects of the product separately and demonstrate how flexibility brings creativity. As the above activities were designed tofacilitate students' creativity and expository ability separately. Ching Yee then fused them together via the role-play and peer evaluation activity. The Theory of Variation holds that seeing a certain class of phenomena in terms of a set of aspects that are separated but simultaneously experienced provides a more effective basis for productive action than separating aspects first then fusing them together. In this respect, the arrangements in the above activities were well organized, they complimented each other and opened up dimensions of learning for students to experience variations. During the process, the teacher played the role of a facilitator. She structured the lesson carefully to moderate and facilitate students' learning outcome.

Lived Object of Learning/Student's Learning

The students designed new products in the lesson, including a solar-powered, environment-friendly electronic dictionary, a super slim multi-function dictionary, a multi-lingual voice control card-shaped dictionary and a bi-literacy and tri-lingual waterproof dictionary. In terms of creativity, all groups demonstrated creativity to a certain degree. Fluency of thinking was evident in the large number of ideas gene-rated in the classroom discussion, many of these being produced out of using strategies like reverse thinking, considering other uses and approaching the task flexibly.

Two experienced creative thinking teachers who witnessed the lesson thought the ideas generated were very novel and highly original. They were also impressed by the way the ideas were refined and integrated to produce a new type of dictionary that was an improvement on the traditional dictionary, evidence of elaboration. In terms of teaching students to present ideas logically and clearly, the lesson was clearly successful. Students were able to use appropriately the method of classific-ation learnt from the prescribed text in their presentations. Some lacked fluency of expression and some even missed out main points but with the help of the teacher they were all eventually able to finish the task.

Although the lesson was quite successful and achieved the objectives set, whenever lessons are planned that offer students the chance to pay attention to whatever they like in the lesson, students' foci might centre on unintended criteria, negatively impacting on the lesson and learning outcome. This happened in Ching Yee's lesson and a detailed look at what happened might cast light on the teaching and learning that may occur in even the best planned lesson. The following excerpt shows Ching Yee's classroom instruction.

T: Firstly, you can think about the features of this new dictionary, e.g. colour, shape and materials. Just now, some classmates said the traditional book-type dictionary is too heavy, inconvenient and boring. So, can you invent one which is not like this? It is up to you to think about it. Secondly, the function. A current trend is to combine different functions in one product. So, you can think about whether besides presenting the meanings of words, a dictionary may have other functions. The following is a must. It is method. Since you said you do not like the current method of finding a word, then you might have a better way to do it. What is the procedure? Write it down. OK. After you finish, you have to promote your dictionary so you will have to think about its selling points.

Ching Yee highlighted four main points (features, function, method and selling point) in her instructions and reminded students to include them in their design. The instructions to the four groups in class were pretty much identical, but the outcomes differed. The following table shows features included in the students' presentation.

	Group 1	Group 2	Group 3	Group 4
Features:				
Colour	✓	✗	✓	✓
Shape	✓	✗	✓	✗
Material	✓	✓	✗	✗
Function	✓	✓	✗	✗
Method	✓	✓	✓	✓
Selling point	✓	✓	✓	✓

Although the overall performance of the class was considered to be quite good by the observers (except for Group 4), the above table demonstrates that the characteristics students actually focused on in the lesson were to an extent different. Some groups included all the items mentioned in Ching Yee's instructions, whilst some omitted some aspects. In fact, the groups that attended to more aspects were more successful. Among the four groups, Group 1 was rated the best by peers, the teacher and the observers. The following is an excerpt of their presentation and responses in the question and answer session.

S1: The **main feature** of my dictionary is its colour. It is sky blue, is made of recycled paper and is environment-friendly. About the function, it is an electronic dictionary. The procedure (to look up a word) is very simple: no need to find the word by sorting out the radical. It is also a luminous watch game station.

T: Luminous game. Quiet! Otherwise you can't hear what they said.

S1:   The **method** to look up a word is very simple: you can just write the word on the monitor, then the word, the meaning, and the page number will appear. If you want to know more, you can turn to the relevant page to get a detailed explanation.

T: Meaning of the word?

S1:   A **special feature** is solar energy. (Other pupil: your special feature?) Yes, a special feature of this dictionary, no need to use electricity, so you save energy.

The emboldened words are features mentioned in Ching Yee's introduction. As shown in the first excerpt, she guided students to consider different aspects of the product. However, she was very careful not to restrain students' thinking and left a lot of space for students to manifest their creativity. With the help of the "SCAMPER" worksheet, she facilitated students' divergent thinking by pointing out directions for designing without providing substantial content in her introduction ("invent one which is not like this", "can a dictionary have other functions?"). That is why Group 1 was able to use the space created by the teacher to look at the design from different perspectives and bring more ideas to their design. Besides items mentioned in Ching Yee's introduction, they brought out new elements such as the energy supply (solar energy, energy saving device) and price reduction in their presentation. This made their design more comprehensive, appealing and novel than was the case with the other groups.

Another point worthy of note in the lesson is the quality of interaction between the students. Ching Yee had arranged a lot of activities to provide opportunities for students to interact in the lesson. Through the group discussion and question and answer session, students were able to discover their own blind spots, things that they had taken for granted or information they knew nothing about previously. This helped them to improve their thinking and achieve a better learning outcome. The case of Group 1 is a good example of how classroom interactions can improve learning. The representative of Group 1 was challenged by classmates in the question and answer session, the following excerpt from the dialogue between them illustrating the interaction.

S2:   What will happen if there is no sunlight?

S1:   It can store energy. If you put the dictionary under the sun for two minutes, then it can store enough energy for two hours. It uses recycled paper...

S2:   How can you use recycled paper if it uses solar energy?

S1:   Calm down! calm down! Only the first page (the monitor) uses solar energy. You can write on it, then the word will appear.

The Group 1 representative answered questions from other groups without hesitation. For a primary pupil, his presentation was clear and thoughtful, especially when he was challenged by a classmate. As mentioned above, primary students often lack a sense of audience and are weak in turning creative ideas into a useful product. The question and answer session provided a real audience for them, helping them to discover their own weaknesses and things that they had not previously thought about. In the above example, using a solar powered dictionary was a good idea. However, not all students had considered its usage in indoor situations, and they failed to explain how to use it in these circumstances in their presentation. On receiving the question from his classmate, the speaker improvised immediately and, as apparent in the video, was not upset or embarrassed by the challenge. On the contrary, he smiled with appreciation and answered confidently. The comment of his classmate helped him to see what he had not previously thought about and helped him refine his product. In Chapter Eight, the author pointed out that the lived object of learning can serve as a tool for further exploration and development, this episode illustrating her point.

However, the performance of some groups in the question and answer session produced a quite different result. The following is an example from Group 4.

S3: It is so thick! You want it to fill the whole school bag? No need to bring books? And the characters are so small. It will make me short-sighted.

S4: It can (put into the school bag). The school bag is big enough.

The pupil in this group failed to give a proper response to his classmate's first question and ignored the second one completely. He refused to accept the other's comment and insisted that the school bag was big enough. This kind of attitude was also noted in other groups.

S5: I want to know, what is the difference between this dictionary and an ordinary dictionary? You have to check the radical, and you need to write it down. It is so complicated.

S6: It won't be very complicated.

His classmate was obviously not satisfied with his answer, but when he wanted to follow it up, the other pupil simply replied that ordinary dictionaries are also very complicated and it takes a lot of time to find words.

Looking at the responses of the groups, the representative for Group 1 responded positively to questions by offering new ideas. He brought in new functions and elaborated on the design. The representatives of other groups tended only to defend their own design, their negative responses to others' opinions preventing them from seeing things from a different perspective and blocking new ideas. The lesson here is that fostering of open and accepting attitudes is essential both for the training of language ability and promotion of creative thinking.

The above examples illustrate the importance of constructive classroom interactions in Chinese language learning and teaching. However, the effect on teaching may vary for several reasons. Firstly, real interaction is a dialogue of minds, not just a dialogue of voices [7]. The exchange of ideas in the activity should provide variations to help students discover different perspectives of the object of learning and enrich their understanding. Secondly, students' attitudes play an important role.

If students are reluctant to admit their own weakness and unwilling to change, the space for learning is likely to be restricted. Finally, the ability to transform the result of the process into creative ideas is crucial. Variation allows learners to experience features that are critical for learning but it is up to the learner to apply or transform their observations into new ideas that allow creative thinking to occur.

CREATING VARIATION TO STIMULATE CREATIVITY

In the lesson discussed in this chapter, the arrangement of activities and the opportunities for teaching and learning strategies to be deployed in the lesson were vital for the success of the lesson. Without these, the creation of variations that help students experience different kinds of learning experiences and use language in different situations would have been absent. Creative learning would almost certainly have been stifled. In the event, a large number of creative language utterances had been produced by the end of the lesson.

As it happened, Ching Yee used a number of strategies to highlight the kinds of variations that offer opportunities for learning. She used guided questioning to switch the angle of observation and thinking, such switching of direction leading students to go beyond the content of the text and to open up new dimensions. She also provided an activity that forced students to depart from their established points of view, especially by asking them to design a super dictionary of the future and promote it in the role of a salesman. The task assigned was in fact in large part related to the content of the prescribed text. However, the task and its context was entirely created by the teacher. She ensured that the students would have to express their ideas in terms of designing a new product, a context that would stimulate new directions of thinking. She also put the students into a world very different from that of their ordinary life, forcing them to discard their regular thoughts and opinions and to think of new ideas. The students were very interested in the task and had lots of chances to express themselves creatively.

In terms of using creative thinking strategies to expand the scope of thinking, SCAMPER was incorporated into the worksheet to guide students to explore different possibilities to design a new dictionary. It stimulated students' imagination and helped them to think logically. The positive effect of the worksheet was obvious in the students' presentations, especially in its ability to create opportunities for students to exchange ideas. The planned activities allowed students to exchange ideas and challenge one another in a controlled manner. The activities and strategies were orchestrated efficiently and harmoniously, and different episodes in the lesson were interrelated and progressed in a logical manner. Every episode worked in concert with the other episodes, the level of learning transformed from the acquiring of knowledge was then applied for a genuine purpose. Training of language ability was integrated seamlessly with creative thinking and this facilitated both students' language ability and creative insights.

Creative teaching is not guaranteed simply by providing creative teaching activities and the stimulation of creative thinking strategies. Nor do brainstorming and role play in lessons on their own constitute the central thrust of creative teaching. It is only when activities and strategies are arranged in a way that creates a space of learning to help learners experience variation and thereby produce fruitful creative language outcomes that the momentum of enduring learning will accelerate.

NOTES

[1] It included "ability to produce original ideas, and adapt according to circumstances is one of the main aim of education." (Curriculum Development Council, p. 22, 2001)

[2] According to Cropley, creativity arises from an interaction among different components, namely general knowledge and a thinking base; a specific knowledge base and area-specific skills; divergent thinking and acting; focusing and task commitment; motivation and motives and openness and tolerance of ambiguity. (Cropley, 2001)

[3] Pseudo name, full-time pre-service student teacher studying post-graduate diploma in education.

[4] They regard explaining according to the prescribed format as a full expression.

[5] A very commonly-used divergent thinking skill originated by Osborn and modified by many others. The S in SCAMPER stands for substitute, C for combine, A for adapt, M can stand for magnify or minify, P stands for put to other uses, and finally, R stands for rearrange or reverse (Eberle, 1982).

[6] Reverse brainstorming is a strategy intended to open up fresh perspectives and allow participants to view the original problem from a new point of view.

[7] Robin Alexander argued that the essence of dialogue is not so much its observable dynamics. Dialogue in education should be a meeting of minds and exchange of ideas (Alexander, 2006).

REFERENCES

Alexander, R. (2006). *Education as dialogue. Moral and pedagogical choices for a runaway world.* Hong Kong: Hong Kong Institute of Education.

Amabile, T. (1996). *Creativity in context.* Oxford, UK: Westview Press.

Cropley, A., & Urban, K. K. (2000). Programs and strategies for nurturing creativity. In K. A. Heller et al. (Eds.), *International handbook of giftedness and talent* (2nd ed, pp. 481–494).

Cropley, A. (2001). *Creativity in education and learning: A guide for teachers and educators.* London, UK: Cogan Page Ltd.

Curriculum Development Council. (2001). *Learning to learn: Life-long learning and whole-person development.* Hong Kong: Curriculum Development Council.

Fellaheen, J. F., & Refiner, D. J. (1976). Design and evaluation of a workshop on creativity and problem-solving for teachers. *Journal of Creative Behavior, 10*(1), 12–14.

Guilford, J. P. (1988). Some changes in the Structure-of-Intellect model. *Educational and Psychological Measurement, 48,* 1–6.

Lee, H. C. (1998). *Teaching of creative writing.* Hong Kong: Hong Kong Institute of Education.

Lee, H. C. (2007). *Creativity in Chinese language teaching: A study of the development of student teacher's concepts of creativity and their ability to implement creative teaching.* Unpublished doctoral dissertation, University of Hong Kong.

Marton, F., & Tsui, A. (2004). *Classroom discourse and the space of learning.* New Jersey, NJ: Lawrence Erlbaum Associates, Publishers.

Marton, F., Runesson, U., & Tsui, A. (2004). The space of learning. In F. Marton & A. Tsui (Eds.), *Classroom discourse and the space of learning.* New Jersey, NJ: Lawrence Erlbaum Associates, Publishers.

Mayer, R. E. (1999). Fifty years of creativity research. In R. J. Sternberg (Ed.), The handbook of creativity. Cambridge, UK: Cambridge University Press.

Torrance, E. P. (1988). The nature of creativity as manifest in its testing. In R. J. Sternberg (Ed.), *The nature creativity* (pp. 43–75). New York, UK: Cambridge University Press.

Tse, S. K. (2002). *Comprehensive and effective teaching and learning of Chinese characters.* Hong Kong: Greenfield Enterprise Ltd.

How Chung Lee
Department of Chinese
The Hong Kong Institute of Education

Ference Marton
Department of Education
University of Gothenburg

Shek Kam Tse
Faculty of Education
The University of Hong Kong

FERENCE MARTON

EPILOGUE

This chapter summarizes some of the main points emanating from the studies presented in the previous chapters. All of the studies build on or relate to the Theory of Variation, which holds that drawing learners' attention to patterns of variation and invariance in learning material, environmental input and concepts helps to secure quality, enduring learning. Such an approach applies to many of the forms of learning students encounter in schools and is very pertinent to the acquisition of Chinese literacy. The units of Chinese language to be learnt in school include sounds, words, phrases, sentences and text: phonetics and phonology dealing with sounds, lexicology dealing with words, and morphology dealing with word forms. Lexicology and syntax are concerned with phrases; syntax is concerned with the sequencing of sentences and text to communicate meaning; and semantics is concerned with the presentation of units of languages so that they are meaningful to others.

When teaching language, teachers deal with units of language of various kinds, many of which are units within larger units. There may be important differences between units on the same level; between units on different levels and in the conventions accepted by people who speak the same language. Since similarities and differences in various units of language are crucially important in language learning, variation and invariance is focused on in terms of relationships between the experience of units of language at different levels.

Experiencing Differences

As pointed out in Chapter 2 and exemplified in subsequent chapters, the theory underlying the various studies of how Chinese is learnt assumes that the learners experience differences in that which is learned (the object of learning) and that these differences are central to understanding how learning does or does not take place. It is widely taken for granted, for instance, that the relationship between the sign, for example the word "red", and the signified, for example the colour red, is basic to learning a language. But in order to grasp the meaning of "red", there must be more than one colour otherwise colour would not be noticed at all. The basic unit is thus the relationship between the experience of different things signified (e.g. colours) and the experience of different signs (e.g. colour words). Likewise, it is not the relationship between the word "woman" and women that is meaningful, but the relationship between the difference between the words "woman" and "man" on the one hand, and the difference between women and men on the other. According to this line of reasoning, a main function of words is to differentiate one "thing" or concept from another. The meaning of a word originates from the meaning of the difference between that to which the word refers and that to which other words refer. The experience of that which differs springs from the experience of the difference between them. Since the difference cannot be experienced without experiencing that which differs, the experience of difference and the experience of that which differs thus mutually constitute each other and are necessarily simultaneous.

Chapter 3 presents an example where hearing different words with the same tone but with different sounds is a less effective way of enabling a non-tonal language speaker to identify the tone than hearing different words with the same sound, but with different tones: in other words awareness of a particular tone occurs through the simultaneous experience of the difference between different tones. The concept of tone is super-ordinate to the specific tones and here what is super-ordinate is simultaneous with elements that are sub-ordinate. Realisation of this accounts for why students grasp more securely the different functions, semantic or phonetic, of the components of Chinese characters due to their position when the same component appears in two characters in different positions, having different functions, compared to two different components appearing in two different characters in the same position and having the same function.

This comparison is illustrated in Chapter 4. Actually, the function of the components is meaningful only if there is more than one function. In fact, "function" can only be defined through variation and the concept of function is super-ordinate to specific functions, such as the semantic and the phonetic functions. The specific functions simply lack grasp of the true meaning outside the super-ordinate concept. It is argued that the awareness of specific functions is simultaneous with differentiations within the super-ordinate concept. This line of reasoning follows de Saussure's (1983) semiotic thesis that, in addition to the real world context in which language is used and to which it refers, linguistic units also have another context: they belong to systems of linguistic units and the meaning of each unit derives from awareness of the differences between the unit and other units that could have been used instead. For instance, the meaning of "three" derives from how it differs from the meaning of other numbers, and the meaning of "dog" is brought home by how this animal's attributes differ from the those that characterise other animals. I maintain that it is vital for learners to perceive and grasp these differences, differences which are super-ordinate to the things that differ. This is the first kind of relationship between units of language at different levels, dealt with here.

Whole-Part Relationships

Language is invariably used in a context and thus "lived language" is always part of a whole: the entire situation in which it is used. This is one of the senses in which one finds a whole-part relationship as far as units of language are concerned. As the whole can be considered as a unit on a higher level than its parts, one has to deal with a relationship between the experience of units of language on different levels. Taking the concept "furniture" as an example, "tables" and "chairs" are sub-ordinate classes of the super-ordinate "furniture". However, "furniture" may itself be a subordinate since there are different kinds of household goods. Realisation of such insights comes slowly to the young learner, and it is hardly surprising that Chan and Nunes (2001) found that children notice differences between drawings and characters before they notice differences in the internal structure of the characters and between different characters.

One can thus identify relationships between experiences of units of language on different levels of more than one kind. In the previous section the relationship between the experience of differences between linguistic units and the experience of the linguistic units themselves, was dealt with. In the case discussed in this section, the whole is a linguistic unit itself, for example a character or a section of text, and the parts are sub-ordinate linguistic units within the whole. The latter includes components within characters, characters within words, words within sentences and so on.

In the study reported in Chapter 5, the relationships between parts of characters and between whole characters and their parts are explored to highlight relationships between characters. The first and second kinds of relationships between the experience of units of language on different levels are brought together and their grasp facilitates the learning of Chinese characters. In Chapter 6, a teacher is helping students to learn words by dealing with them (a) in the simultaneous context of the sentences in which they appear and (b) with the sentences in the simultaneous context of the entire text of which they are parts. This way of going from wholes to parts was associated with strikingly better results than when the words, sentences and whole text were dealt with separately and in linear order.

In the attempt to boost students reading comprehension reported in Chapter 7, use was made of two kinds of relations between experiences of units of language on different levels. The meanings of different genres were derived from reading texts about the same subject matter presented in different genres. The students were exposed to different meanings of the same expression and thus gained insight into the fact that their own understanding of the expression was just one among other possible interpretations. The students became aware of the differences between different ways of expressing the same message and so forth. This is an instance where experiencing the higher order unit of language (the difference) and the lower order units (the things that differ) occurred simultaneously, i e the case discussed in the previous section. In the same study, the whole-parts relationship between the experience of a linguistic unit and its parts was utilised, i e the case discussed in this section. The most obvious example of this was using entire books, instead of many unrelated short texts, as the reading material. Each book thus offered a whole, within which parts on different levels could be discerned and identified.

Increasing Differentiation in Spontaneous Language Learning

The first kind of relationship between super-ordinate and sub-ordinate units of language discussed above concerned the simultaneity of the experience of differences between attributes and the experience of these attributes. The higher order unit (the difference) and the lower order units (those which differ) appear at the same time. The third kind of relationship between super- and sub-ordinate units of language concerns the relationship between an entity and its attributes. In this case the entity can be seen as a whole and the attributes as its parts (although not parts in the same sense as in the previous section), but the experiences of the two do not have to be simultaneous. The learner discovers the entity in question as an undifferentiated whole, and subsequently discovers more and more of its attributes (corresponding to different ways in which it differs from other entities).

This kind of relationship is not dealt with in depth in the studies reported in this book, but is frequently found in children's spontaneous learning of the language. It may seem as if the child picks up more and more words, puts them together to form longer and longer sentences, then as parts of a story and so on: going from parts to wholes. In actual fact, the meaning of single words, is much less differentiated when used by the infants in their first words vocabulary. A single word like "mummy" may have varying and complex meanings when used in early utterances. It may refer to "I am hungry", "I need some food" or "I have fallen and hurt myself. I've got pain. Please do something so it stops hurting!" The correct use of the word is usually acquired later as a label for a parent and to distinguish one parent from the other. In other words, awareness of the name of a particular person usually originates from and is simultaneous with the discovery of the correlated difference between persons and between their names.

The sequence "from higher order units to lower order units" and "from more holistic to more specific features" is perhaps more obvious when the development of reading and writing is examined. Tolchinsky (2003) shows how the child's acquisition of written language may follow a path from wholes to parts where the formal learning of letters and letter-sound correspondence is preceded by the discovery of more holistic features. Tolchinsky maintains that there are graphic entities which correspond to what is uttered, and that these differ from each other just as words differ from each other even though the differences are actually correlated. In Chapter 5, reference is made to Chan and Nunes' (2001) study in which it is shown that, before children differentiate the internal structure of characters, they notice more holistic features of the Chinese language in its written form. In fact, they learn to differentiate between drawings and characters; they notice that every character corresponds to a single syllable in speech; that in texts there are different characters following each other from the left to the right or from the top to the bottom, each character occupying an imaginary square.

Going from the discernment of more holistic features of phenomena experienced to the discernment of more specific features is the third kind of relationship between the experience of super- and sub-ordinate units of language I am using here in summarising the content of the book.

Using Language Creatively

In the preceding pages I have suggested that the child's experience and use of units of language at higher levels of abstraction often occur either simultaneously or precede experience of lower units of language I would argue that this applies in particular to the mastery of written Chinese. In the various Chapters there seems to be cumulative evidence for the thesis that going from wholes to parts and helping the students experience units of language on different levels simultaneously is a powerfully effective pedagogical approach. Two of the three kinds of relationship between the experience of units of language on different levels have been dealt with in this book: (1) the relationship between the experience of differences between language units and the experience of linguistic units that differ, and (2) the whole being a linguistic unit and the parts being linguistic units of lower order within the whole.

In the studies reported in chapters in this book, either a teacher or researchers have engineered for the child access to varying instances or strengths of patterns of variation and invariance in order to help students discern critical features of various objects of learning. Chapter 8 and Chapter 9 are concerned with helping students handle novel tasks in creative ways. The students are set the tasks of discerning that which varies against the background of what is invariant: they are then invited to bring variation into spotting new dimensions of variation and not taking situations for granted. This is intended to help students to "widen the space of learning" (Marton et al., 2004) and to go beyond constraints that limit further exploration of variation.

REFERENCES

Chan, L., & Nunes, T. (2001). Explicit teaching and implicit learning of Chinese characters. In L. Tolchinsky (Ed.), *Developmental aspects in learning to write* (pp. 33–53). Dordrecht, The Netherlands: Kluwer Academic Publishers.

Marton, F., Runesson, U., & Tsui, B. M. (2004). The space of learning. In F. Marton & B. M. Tsui (Eds.), *Classroom discourse and the space of learning.* New Jersey, NJ: Lawrence Erlbaum Associates, Inc.

Saussure, F. de (1983). *Course in general linguistics.* London, UK: F. Duckworth.

Tolchinsky, L. (2003). Childhood conceptions of literacy. In T. Nunes & P. Bryant (Eds.), *Handbook of children's literacy.* Dordrecht, The Netherlands: Kluwer Academic Publishers.

Tolchinsky, L. (2003). *The cradle of culture and what children know about writing and numbers before being Taught.* New Jersey, NJ: Lawrence Erlbaum Associates, Inc., Publishers.

Ference Marton
Deparment of Education
University of Gothenburg

NOTES ON CONTRIBUTORS

Wai Ming Cheung is an Assistant Professor at the Faculty of Education, the University of Hong Kong. Her research interests include creativity, Phenomenography, learning study, teacher professional development, Chinese writing skill, reading literacy, word acquisition, gifted education, and bilingual education.

Pakey Pui Man Chik is a Postdoctoral Fellow at the Faculty of Education, the Chinese University of Hong Kong. She is interested in studying literacy development, Phenomenography and Theory of Variation, classroom teaching and learning, teacher professional development, lesson and learning study.

Wing Wah Ki is an Associate Professor at the Faculty of Education, the University of Hong Kong. He has been the Deputy Director of Chinese as Medium of Instruction Teacher Support Center, and the Center for Information Technology in School and Teacher Education Center, at the Faculty of Education, the University of Hong Kong. His fields of interest include mathematics and computer education, learning technologies, and the use of information technology in Chinese language education.

Ho Cheong Lam is an Assistant Professor at the Department of Early Childhood Education, the Hong Kong Institute of Education. His primary research interests involve learning of Chinese characters, the Theory of Variation, teaching and learning with technology, and software design for learning.

How Chung Lee is the Deputy Head of the Department of Chinese at the Hong Kong Institute of Education. His main research interests focus on creative teaching and learning, reading literacy education, writing education, teacher professional development, and Chinese language education.

Allen Leung is an Assistant Professor at the Department of Mathematics and Information Technology, the Hong Kong Institute of Education and an Honorary Assistant Professor at the Faculty of Education, the University of Hong Kong. His main research interests include learning and teaching of mathematics in information and communication technology (in particular dynamic geometry) environments, the Theory of Variation in teaching and learning, lesson and learning study, and language and mathematics.

Elizabeth Ka Yee Loh is an Assistant Professor of the Centre for the Advancement of Chinese Language Education and Research (CACLER), Faculty of Education at the University of Hong Kong. Her research interests include new methods in teaching Chinese characters, writing and reading, assessment of Chinese characters, writing and reading, teaching strategies to help children with special education needs learn Chinese language, and teaching and learning of Chinese language as a second language.

Ference Marton is Professor Emeritus at the Department of Education, the University of Gothenburg, who also serves as Advisory Professor at the Hong Kong Institute of Education and as Honorary Professor at the Faculty of Education, the University of Hong Kong. His main research interests include learning, Phenomenography, and the Theory of Variation.

Ming Fai Pang is an Associate Professor of Education at the Faculty of Education, the University of Hong Kong. His main research interests focus on sciences of learning and instruction, in particular on the use of Phenomenography, variation theory of learning and learning study to improve learning at different levels (i.e. primary/secondary schools, higher education, teacher education and work-place), in different areas (such as Liberal Arts Education, Economics, Mathematics, Science, English Language, Chinese Language, Geography, Professional Learning and Vocational Learning) and in different learning environments (such as on-line collaborative learning, whole-class teaching, collaborative inquiry and independent enquiry study/project).

Shek Kam Tse is a Professor of Chinese Language Education at the Faculty of Education, and the Director of the Center for Advancement of Chinese Language Learning and Research, at the University of Hong Kong. His research interests include students' reading literacy performance in national and international large-scale assessments, the process involved in writing Chinese, development of multi-media computer-learning packages related to Chinese language, child language development, and new methods in teaching Chinese language.

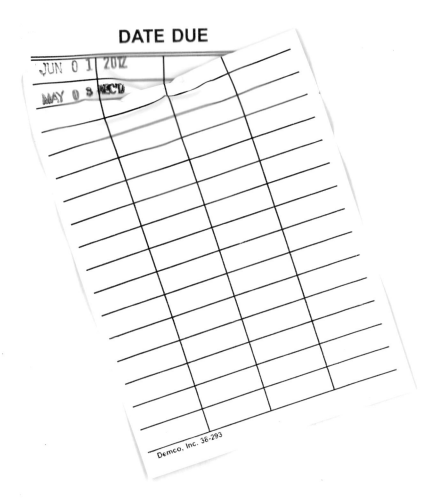

DATE DUE

JUN 0 1 2012

MAY 0 3 RCD

Demco, Inc. 36-293

9 789460 912672